SEVENTH EDITION

Sensible LISTENING

THE KEY TO RESPONSIVE INTERACTION

PAUL J. KAUFMANN

Iowa State University

Kendall Hunt
publishing company

Cover image and Chapter 6 illustrations provided by Henry Kaufmann

Kendall Hunt
publishing company

www.kendallhunt.com
Send all inquiries to:
4050 Westmark Drive
Dubuque, IA 52004-1840

Printed in the United States of America

Contents

Preface

Background

In the early 1980s Iowa State University was encouraging faculty to participate in "Seminar 80," a program to generate student interest in new topics. So I decided to put a listening seminar together. I knew there were excellent materials available, but before zeroing-in on what materials to use, I had some goal clarifying to do.

For years, I've been telling my students and clients that developing a goal is the very first step in preparing a presentation.

"How do we develop a goal?" I'm asked.

"By knowing what you want your audience to take with them when they leave," I tell them.

"So our goal is know what we want for them."

"Exactly."

Well, when writing this text, I practiced what I'd been preaching, and after researching and discussing, here's the goal I came up with for that first listening course, and it is, of course, the goal for this book.

The Goal for *Sensible Listening:* I want the readers to be able to listen and interact responsively in face-to-face communication settings.

There are eight levels of understanding that build this goal: level 1) there is no communication without listening; level 2) listening affects relationships, time, and resources; level 3) listening includes all senses; level 4) listening is hard work; level 5) listening to ourselves can improve how we listen to others; level 6) personality plays a substantial role in listening; level 7) managing stress can sharpen listening; and, level 8) different types of listening have different rules.

By the way, that first seminar in the 80s attracted about ten students, and today it has grown to serve about two hundred students per semester, and has expanded into numerous workshops for a variety of organizations. From a handful of scrawled notes and Xerox copies, this seventh edition of *Sensible Listening* has evolved while staying focused on that fundamental goal.

Description

Overall Structure

Sensible Listening: The Key to Responsive Interaction is a proven, practical guide for effective listening. The title suggests the main goal, which is to help the reader move toward responsive interaction that is thoughtful, dynamic, and accurate. The word "sensible" implies two ways to reach this goal: first, by listening logically and reasonably—making sense—and second, by bringing all five senses into the listening process.

Sensible Listening is divided into two parts in a"theory-practice" format. Part One—A Background for Sensible Listening—explores the major theories and parameters of listening; Part Two—Practicing Sensible Listening—simulates the actual activity. This structure is loosely analogous to learning to fly. Part One parallels pilot ground school where the forces, rules, and theories are examined, and Part Two discusses the practical application of these skills to flying.

The Chapters

Before previewing the text's organization, I have a suggestion that might help you get into this whole listening business a little easier—start by reading the last chapter, Chapter 16, Listening Improvement. This summary chapter touches the major topics, and gives a general overview of what's covered in each of the chapters.

The eight chapters in Part One (Theory/Background) cover: 1) the significance of listening in organizations, 2) the role of listening in the communication process, 3) listening with all senses, 4) listening and media, 5) listening to the forces behind the words and gestures, 6) listening to ourselves, 7) listening and personality, and 8) listening and stress.

Part Two (Practice)—Chapters 9 through 16—prepares the readers for five listening roles: 9) listening to comprehend and detect, 10) listening to help, 11) listening to decide, 12) listening to purchase, and 13) listening to appreciate; Chapter 14 examines how listening affects partnerships, and Chapter 15 focuses on cross-cultural listening. The last chapter, 16, summarizes major listening principles and provides a checklist to analyze and prepare for a variety of listening situations.

Awareness Exercises

At the end of each chapter are Awareness Exercises.

These written assignments are designed to increase involvement and identity with chapter topics by helping you understand how listening principles are at the center of your every-day interactions. In addition to generating involvement with the aspects of listening, your responses to these exercises are excellent discussion starters and are useful for evaluating your grasp of the chapter content. They are used in professional training sessions and seminars to help focus on specific aspects of listening.

I've worked with this text since the early 1980s and along the way have often discussed it with families, students, trainers, and colleagues who have used it in a variety of settings. The consensus is that it is a solid, unique, effective tool for understanding and improving listening. I hope it proves worthwhile for you and am always eager to visit about it.

Paul Kaufmann
kaufmann@iastate.edu

Acknowledgments

My Wife, Linda
Andrea, Andrew, Arlo, Aya, Brenda, Brynn, Carter,
Drew, Dylan, Gina, Greyson, Hal, Hallyanna,
Hattie, Jalen, James, Jeremy, Johnny, Kiley, Kristin,
Leyton, Lily, Niko, Noah, Oriana, Paul Christopher,
Paul Kenneth, Sarah, Shawna, Tristan
Al Paul, Warren Gore, Connie Ringlee
John D. Kaufmann, Bert Miller

Part One

A Background for Sensible Listening

Chapter One

Listening in the Organization

The goal of this chapter is to explain the significance of listening as it functions in all organizations. The skills of writing and speaking have been studied for thousands of years; listening, however, has only been examined as an important part of our communication process within the last fifty years. It has only been in the last three decades that entire texts have been devoted to listening. Today, more than 433,000,000 sites come up on Google when a search for "listening" is run.

Active listening—*defined as attending with all of our senses to gain meaning*—is central to all human communication. No matter what role we take—parent, spouse, friend, manager, lawyer, clergy, physician, teacher, salesperson, technician—we will be listening at least 50 percent of the time.

Families are the first organizations that give us models for listening behavior, and the quality of listening behavior has lasting effects on family relationships. Parents and guardians who consciously focus on improving their listening with family members—spouses, partners, kids, relatives—will increase the probability of developing meaningful, productive, and enduring connections.

Families are being pulled apart by exploding amounts of electronic gadgetry, the early availability adult-like relationships, and available drugs. Of course, distractions have always been around to erode family cohesion, but as family members get together less frequently, the quality of their together-time needs a boost. One big boost comes with attentive, responsive listening.

Parents often wonder why their children will not talk to them and what they can do to improve their relationships with their kids. The comment they frequently make to express their bewilderment at a non-communicative relationship is: "But I gave them everything!" Yet what this often means is: "I bought them everything money could buy . . ." And the one thing that cannot be bought is time. For parents, time alone with their children means a chance to listen to their needs and concerns, and respond.[1]

The following text message expresses a teen's screaming, bristling anger about her mom's not listening.[2]

They Never Listen—my parents never listen

i swear that i'm gonna duct tape my mother's <u>mouth</u> if she doesn't start listening to what i say. She always gives me crap for not listening to her, but really its the other way around. I get into trouble from her aLL The time because she never actually listens to EXACTLY what i say. she'll pretend she's listening and only catch a FEW of the details like . . . if i said i was going to wear a red and pink dress with black butterflies on it she

CALVIN AND HOBBES © 1988 Watterson. Reprinted with permission of UNIVERSAL UCLICK. All rights reserved.

would only catch that i was going to wear a dress. her listening to me saying what i'm gonna wear isn't realli important cuz i have a much better fashion sense then her anyways but when its important stuff she NEVER listens !! am i just being a *BLEEP* and its normal for parents to do this or is she just being rude? do ne of you guyz get that?

The solution to this girl's swelling anger is no mystery, is it? One simple program that could improve this situation is The 15+Make Time to Listen . . . Take Time to Talk campaign which is

. . . based on the premise that parents who talk with their children about what is happening in their lives are better able to guide their children toward more positive, skill-enhancing activities and friendships. The campaign provides practical guidance for parents and caregivers on how to strengthen their relationship with their children by spending at least 15 minutes of daily, undivided time with them and focusing on them.[3]

As with families, business effectiveness also rises and falls with the quality of listening. According to one report, 60 percent of employee time in North American businesses is spent listening.[4] Executives are reported to spend 63 percent of their time listening.[5]

In addition, people at all organizational levels express concern about the importance of listening in carrying out their daily responsibilities. A production manager of a large corporation realized that his entire job was centered in listening:

I listen to the words, the feelings, the needs of my people; I listen to the current climate. Are workers content? Are new innovations making certain areas of production insecure? Is there dissatisfaction? I listen to the machines. I listen to the flow of the whole operation. My office door is open, and so are all my senses, so I can listen to find the meaning of all the information coming at me.[6]

Managers and executives are increasingly aware that success depends on listening. One highly regarded business leader sums up the importance of listening within his organization:

I only wish I could find an institute that teaches people how to listen. After all, a good manager needs to listen at least as much as s/he needs to talk. Too many people fail to realize that real communication goes in both directions.

You have to be able to listen well if you're going to motivate the people who work for you. Right there, that's the difference between a mediocre company and a great company. The most fulfilling thing for me as a manager is to watch someone the system has labeled as just average or mediocre really come to his own, all because someone has listened to his problems and helped him solve them.[7]

Peters and Waterman's book *In Search of Excellence,* a classic analysis of successful business cultures, arrives at a simple yet significant conclusion: "The excellent companies are better listeners."[8]

Listening is important for success in family, business, and professional settings. Parents, spouses, corporate leaders, and other professionals study listening because it significantly affects relationships with people, time, and other resources.

Listening's Relationship to People

Psychologists emphasize the importance of listening to develop and maintain successful relationships. Carl Rogers, the highly regarded and widely read founder of Rogerian psychology, developed a specialized form of attending to people called *empathic listening,* which instructs the listener

> to see the expressed idea and attitude from the other person's point of view; to sense how it feels to him; to achieve his frame of reference in regard to the idea he is talking about.[9]

Further evidence of the importance of listening in building and maintaining relationships comes from counselors who listen to people's everyday problems. As one counselor stated:

> My profession is to listen and to allow my clients to solve their own problems. So many of their problems have to do with spouses, relatives, bosses, teachers, co-workers, and friends. The single biggest problem that keeps repeating itself over and over is that people don't listen to each other. If I were to start a school of human problem solving, the basic course would be in communicating: with listening at its core.[10]

The part listening plays in relationships is difficult to measure, since many human variables are involved. However, one study clearly demonstrates that active listening builds relationships, and passive listening weakens them.[11]

In this investigation, participants were interviewed in a one-to-one setting about their future plans. The participants were not aware that active or nonactive listening was being examined as an aspect of relationship development. They were simply asked general questions by the interviewer, and were given time to respond at length. Moreover, the interviews were not instructive—the interviewers just wanted informal information. The interviewer did little talking, but listened either actively or nonactively to the responses. Each interview, then, involved two people: an interviewer, who listened actively or nonactively, and an interviewee, who did most of the talking.

Active listeners were interviewers who were trained to be relaxed, have appropriate eye contact with the interviewee, and respond verbally to the message being sent by the interviewee. Most of us know people who listen this way. These people are attentive and comfortable when listening to us; they are interested in what we have to say, and they look at us as they respond verbally ("uh-huh") and nonverbally (nodding, smiling), letting us know that they are "with us" as we talk with them.

Nonactive listeners were interviewers who were trained to exhibit tension, establish minimal eye contact, and offer no verbal responses to the interviewee. Again, we have probably met people who are nonactive listeners. They seem in a hurry to end the visit, a bit tense and uncomfortable. They might look out the window or at objects in the room and give little verbal and nonverbal feedback. In fact, we wonder how much they are "with" the conversation at all.

After an eight-to-ten-minute interview session, the interviewees (who did most of the talking) completed a written form to evaluate these active or nonactive listening interviewers using a scale of descriptive adjective pairs. For example, the interviewees were asked, "How much do you think this interviewer feels the following toward you?" and they could respond on a scale that went from "not at all positive" to "very positive"; "not at all understanding" to "very understanding," and so on.

As the table of adjective pairs in Figure 1.1 shows, active listeners were rated at the favorable end of the adjective scales, and the interviewees expressed a desire to return for another interview with the active listeners. The interviewees who received nonactive listening put their interviewers at the low end of the scales, and they did not want to return for another visit.

••• **Figure 1.1** The Effect of Active and Nonactive Listening on Relationships

Adjectives that interviewees used to describe:

Active Listening Interviewers*	Nonactive Listening Interviewers**
positive	negative
understanding	not understanding
skillful	clumsy
competent	incompetent
decisive	indecisive
conscientious	indifferent
industrious	lazy
secure	insecure
concerned	unconcerned
stable	hostile
friendly	unfriendly
helpful	indifferent

*Interviewees said they wanted to return for another interview.
**Interviewees said they did not want to return for another interview.

It is no surprise that active listening strengthens relationships, and this study quantitatively confirms that fact. So now we have clear evidence that family members, friends, customers, vendors, co-workers, and managers can all be drawn into better relationships through active listening. There are many real-life examples of relation building gained through active listening.

The founder of Adventureland, Jack Krantz, brought family and business together through active listening. He began planning his amusement park, hotel, and campground dream in the early 1970s, and today his dream attracts 550,000 people a year and is acknowledged as one of the most successful family-owned parks in the country.

Krantz listened actively and built warm, lasting relationships. "His affinity for children and family not only drove the vision that became Adventureland Park and Resort in Altoona [Iowa], it insured that his legacy will live on without him." These relationships are so solid that many of the family members remain actively involved in the operation. Krantz believed in people and listened to them. In an interview, he summed his view: "The success of a company like this is the people who work with it—the staff. If you see a turtle on top of a fence, he didn't get there by himself." At Jack's death, his son, Adventureland's president, said, "My dad, to me, was larger than life."[12]

The late Sam Walton, the driving force behind Wal-Mart and Sam's Club, is one of the biggest success stories in America. Wal-Mart and Sam's Club expanded to the point that Sam Walton became one of the richest men in America. The culture that Walton brought to his business included listening and caring about his employees and his customers. He referred to his employees as associates, and most important of all, he listened to them. He would go into his stores, talk with and listen to the clerks and stockers, and see for himself what needed to be changed or improved.

Executive offices at Wal-Mart were virtually empty. Managers spent their time walking the floors with employees. Employees at all levels got involved and worked together to contribute to Wal-Mart's success. Walton emphasized the empty headquarters rule: "The key is to get into the store and listen."[13]

In a similar vein, Lee Iacocca, who spearheaded the development of Ford's *Mustang*, also emphasized that active listening promotes involvement and improves relationships. He writes:

> In corporate life, you have to encourage all your people to make a contribution to the common good and to come up with better ways of doing things. You don't have to accept every single suggestion, but if you don't get back to the guy and say, "Hey, that idea was terrific," and pat him on the back, he'll never give you another one. That kind of communication lets people know they really count.[14]

Successful, productive relationships grow from knowing and analyzing people, and listening is the key to this "people analysis." We analyze our relationships with family members, friends, peers, administrators, supervisors, clients, consumers, competitors, and investors. We listen to their attitudes and values to determine their concern, confusion, or enthusiasm for particular projects and ideas, and from this information, we can better adapt to their needs.

Listening within the organization is a basic step in improving relationships and implementing or improving programs. We listen so we can respond appropriately. We may take a few seconds to listen to the situation and analyze it, or we may need weeks or months of listening to develop an effective and acceptable plan. For example, simply listening at a family meal or a coffee break can elicit valuable information. Or, listening might extend over a longer period of time. One manufacturing organization spent three years in interviews with foremen and workers before implementing a new production strategy.[15]

These years of listening and analyzing were crucial in providing valuable information for the implementation of the new strategy. Additionally, since the employees knew they were being listened to and were included in the change process, their ownership of the plan helped the efficiency of the production changeover.

Inside and outside any organization—whether family or business—active listening builds and strengthens relationships and is at the center of any successful organization. Through people analysis, procedures can be implemented and needs met. *Time*, the second crucial resource, is also affected by active listening.

Listening's Relationship to Time

Active listening saves time—certainly a highly valued commodity. In some professions, listening must occur in the shortest amount of time possible. Time is literally a matter of life and death in the case of the nurse answering the telephone at an emergency ward, since this professional must listen to symptoms, addresses, and directions calmly and accurately. A listening error in this demanding time frame could result in a significant loss of time and ultimately the loss of a life.

On a less dramatic scale, recall situations where nonactive listening has cost time and a certain amount of frustration: directions that were misunderstood, or items that were forgotten. These lapses in listening, although not life or death incidents, cost time and make our daily functioning less efficient.

On the job, seemingly short listening lapses can result in substantial lost time. A corporation with 3,000 employees who each lose just ten minutes in a given day because of nonactive listening has lost five hundred hours of productive time!

Time is saved by associates who are sensible, active listeners. We meet with them, and we listen to each other. Appropriate questions are asked, and we paraphrase or repeat each other's ideas to be sure we understand. Because of effective listening, our time is used productively, and few time-wasting problems will result from misunderstanding.

In the relationship-building study just discussed, accuracy of specific information or the time taken to communicate it were not issues. What was at issue, however, was whether style of listening (active, nonactive) affected the strength of the relationship between the interviewer and the interviewee. In the following experiment, active and nonactive listening are isolated to observe their effect on message *accuracy* and the amount of *time* taken to complete the message.

Communicologists[16] have studied the effects of listening on the accuracy of verbal messages and the amount of time taken to communicate the message.[17] They were curious to find out which listening behaviors would achieve accurate understanding of a message in the least amount of time. The listening behaviors centered on feedback and active and nonactive listening. In the active listening part of the study, the senders carefully listened to feedback in the form of comments and questions, and were as responsive as possible. In the nonactive part, the senders were unresponsive to feedback and did not welcome comments or questions—they communicated almost as if the room were empty. Basically, the active part encouraged full feedback; the nonactive part ignored feedback.

To gauge the effect of these listening behaviors, the experimenters developed a task in which someone described a drawing of five rectangles arranged in a specific pattern. Throughout the description, the describer would listen either actively or nonactively to the participants. The goal in both parts of the experiment was to communicate the rectangle configuration so that the subjects could draw all five accurately in size and in relationship with each other.[18]

In the nonactive listening part of the study, the sender described the rectangles as well as possible but would not respond to questions or comments. The receivers were discouraged from commenting or questioning while they attempted to draw the shapes as they were described by the sender. When the exercise was finished, the receivers were instructed to write their feelings about this nonactive listening situation.

In the active listening part of the study, the sender again described a series of rectangles in a specific pattern, and the receivers were encouraged to question and comment. In addition, the sender welcomed feedback and addressed it appropriately. That is, the sender listened and took time to respond to receiver concerns, which usually focused on the size and position of the shapes they were drawing. As in the nonlistening part of the study, the participants in this part of the study were asked to write their feelings about this active listening exchange.

This study found that senders who did not listen to feedback were not well understood, and few receivers completed their drawings accurately; however, the task was completed quickly. So, with passive listening, accuracy was poor, but the time spent was short. Not surprisingly, participants recorded feelings of anger, frustration, and low morale, because they knew they had failed at the task and felt the sender did not care about their performance.

When the sender describing the rectangle patterns was listening actively—responding to feedback from the receivers—message accuracy significantly increased: most of the drawings were correct. The task, however, took three to four times longer than the nonlistening part. So the price for higher accuracy was time. The receivers reported that they felt comfortable and confident, and morale was high, because they believed the sender cared about them and the accuracy of their performance.

This study demonstrates that messages are accurately received if the sender listens actively and responds to feedback. However, listening and responding to feedback takes time, so *initially*, increasing accuracy through active listening takes more time. Importantly, as the active listener repeated the directions to different groups, the accuracy of communication remained high, and *the amount of time taken to give the directions became progressively shorter each time the directions were given.* However, even when repeating directions to different groups, the nonactive listener never achieved high accuracy with the receivers.[19]

What happened in this study? Why did active listening heighten the accuracy of the message and ultimately save time? The answer is that with repeated communication experiences with different groups, the sender who actively listens is able to anticipate questions or comments that came up in previous experiences. Consequently, with experience, questions can be addressed without being asked, and the explanation time is shortened. In addition, the actively listening sender develops a common vocabulary for giving directions, and therefore uses examples and illustrations that have been useful with previous groups (see Figure 1.2).

What this important study found is that active listeners approach communicating with their eyes and ears open. They are willing to take the time to listen and respond to feedback, knowing that this will result in an accurate and satisfying exchange that will become more time-efficient with experience.

Nonactive listeners close themselves off to new information and remain inefficient communicators. If they value saving time more than communicating accurately, then in their minds they have been successful. We have all known listeners who are unresponsive to feedback. They might be the teacher who for thirty years lectured from the same notes, seldom responding,

• • • Figure 1.2

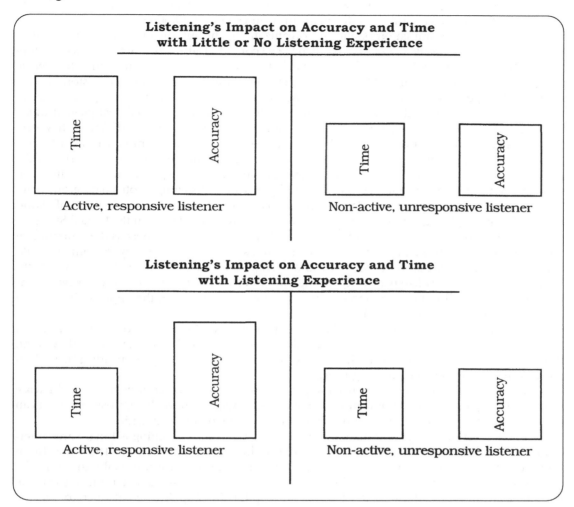

seldom changing his/her approach. Or the manager who takes the attitude, "We've always done it this way," ignoring other possibilities or approaches. Sure, their lectures or instructions are finished quickly, but often the accuracy of communication is questionable.

Farsighted, successful organizations value active listening and encourage feedback at all levels. They will take the time to listen actively and build a culture that values listening, because timely and accurate communication will result. Moreover, experience has taught these organizations that when feedback and active listening are ignored, frustration, wasted time, and improperly completed projects increase. The final topic that will be discussed in this chapter is listening's relationship to other resources.

Listening's Relationship to Other Resources

Organizations need productive people, good use of time, and adequate resources—money, inventory, and equipment—to operate effectively. In a newspaper article titled "Poor Listening Is Big Problem for Business" an executive officer writes:

> Poor listening is one of the most significant problems facing business today. Business relies on its communications system, and when it breaks down, mistakes can be very costly. Corporations pay for their mistakes in lower profits, while consumers pay in higher prices.[20]

American Airlines saved olives (and money) by listening to a flight attendant who noticed that the olives on passengers' salads were not being eaten. Not a single passenger complained when they stopped serving olives, and American Airlines saved $40,000.[21]

In its landmark examination of effective organizations, the authors of *In Search of Excellence* describe a store in Norwalk, Connecticut, called Stew Leonard's Dairy, which was founded in 1969 with seven employees. At the time of their research, this store carried 750 items, while the average store carried 16,000 items. Leonard's store grossed $1.5 million per week; the average store grossed $200,000 in a good week. Leonard's store grossed $80 million per year; the average store, $10.5 million per year. Compared to the average grocery store, his store was small, yet yielded much higher profits. Clearly, the operators of this little store were doing something different: they were actively listening to customers' needs and as a result earning substantially more customer loyalty.

Stew Leonard attributed this success to listening: "I went around to the customers' side of the table; I keep an ear to the ground and keep listening to customers. I keep listening and doing what they say." Since the time he adopted the philosophy of actively listening, profits have grown, and in 2004 his is the world's largest dairy store and is recorded in the Guinness Book of World Records for having "the greatest sales per unit area of any single food store in the United States."[22]

Leonard carried out his philosophy of actively listening to his customers as they shopped in the store, and, in addition, he arranged special meetings. Every other Saturday, customers would volunteer to meet in the store conference room to share their views of procedures and products. Stew and his associates listened to them and, whenever possible, put customers' suggestions into practice. In addition to these face-to-face meetings, customers had the opportunity to use a suggestion box to give written feedback.

Clearly, Stew Leonard believes that customer relations are the number one priority; he and his associates listen to the customers for needed information and give them what they want. Regarding revenue, this active listening helped Stew Leonard's Dairy gross nearly $70 million more than the average comparable grocery store.[23]

The examples show that active listening can grow family unity, and, in business, increase profits and help expand an organization. Nonactive listening can have the opposite effect; it can splinter families, erase profit and diminish the effectiveness of an organization.

Sadly, the list of human and material loss from irresponsible listening is long. Three interesting case studies are the oil tanker *Exxon Valdez* running aground in Alaska in 1989, the Union Carbide plant explosion in India in 1984, and the Bay of Pigs invasion in Cuba in 1961. The captain of the *Exxon Valdez* did not listen to his crew or to the sea and terrain; instead, he remained in his cabin, allowing the first officer to pilot the ship. The plant operators at the Union Carbide plant in India did not listen to employees' warnings of explosive potential, and the group of U.S. experts planning the Bay of Pigs invasion in Cuba, did not listen to the facts and figures involved. Listening failure was a substantial cause of these three human disasters. The interested reader can research these events—abundant information is available. Four additional disasters that occurred as the result of faulty listening are described here in more detail.

The first describes listening errors between a flight crew and air traffic control. The second and third highlight listening problems between engineers and administrators involved in the *Challenger* and *Columbia* space shuttle projects, and the fourth is the result of driver distraction. All four ended in a monumental loss of resources.

Example: The Crash of Two Boeing 747s

On March 27, 1977, KLM flight 4805, a Boeing 747 carrying 248 passengers, began its take-off on runway 1-2. At the same time Pan Am Flight 1736, another 747 with 335 passengers aboard, came out of the fog and mist at the end of the same runway. The resulting crash was one of the worst in aviation history: 576 people lost their lives; two multimillion-dollar 747s were destroyed, and damages reaching into the hundreds of millions of dollars were incurred, all because of faulty listening. This is the sequence that led to the crash of two airplanes that never became airborne.

The air traffic control tower told the Pan Am 747 to taxi to the third ramp—ramp C-3—but perhaps the Pan Am crew understood "first" instead of "third." The taped control tower voice reiterated: "The third, sir. One, two, three—the third, third, third." The instruction was then confirmed by the co-pilot. The Pan Am 747 taxied to ramp C-3, but the crew found a problem turning into that exit so they continued taxiing to ramp C-4, perhaps thinking they were to go to the third free exit.

The control tower told KLM to taxi to runway 1-2's holding position. KLM did, and replied, "We are now at take-off."

Meanwhile, Pan Am was taxiing on the same active runway toward the KLM 747 to reach exit C-4. At that time KLM requested clearance to take off, and the control tower answered, "Okay, stand by for take-off. I will call you." Apparently the KLM crew thought they had been given clearance to take off, because the KLM 747 began accelerating.

As they were moving toward exit C-4, Pan Am told KLM, "We'll report when we're clear [off the runway]," but this message apparently did not warn KLM that Pan Am was still on the runway. "We'll report when we're clear," were the last words before the impact. By the time the pilots realized that they were on a collision course, the KLM plane was going too fast to avoid the taxiing Pan Am ship.

The investigation of the tragedy acknowledged that the cause of the accident was faulty listening and interpretation on the part of the KLM captain, a man with 39,000 hours of flying time.[24]

Example: *Challenger* Explosion

On January 28, 1986, the *Challenger*, a United States space shuttle, exploded thirteen seconds after launch. Six astronauts and the first teacher to attempt a space flight were killed. Roger Boisjoly, a shuttle engineer, describes how the events that led to the tragedy were a mix of technical and listening flaws.

According to Boisjoly, the joint seals that caused the explosion had shown problems early in 1985. His team found that colder-than-normal temperatures allowed hot gases to flow freely into the joint and burn the O-ring seal: "At this time, we knew we had a serious problem, but officials said the information was 'too sensitive to tell anyone.'"

Boisjoly was outraged by this response, especially after he found a joint seal totally destroyed after a January 1985 flight. He was so concerned that the next month, he and a co-worker presented a report detailing a solution to the joint seal problem. However, the committee that could have solved the problem did not act because, in Boisjoly's words, "No one would listen to the material that we presented!"

In a formal memo dated July 31, 1985, Boisjoly wrote: "If we do not take immediate action . . . we will lose a flight and possibly a launch pad." No response was made to this memo.

On January 27th, the eve of the *Challenger* flight, Boisjoly had his final chance to stop the flight. At an emergency meeting, he and his partner, Artie Thompson, presented a report with graphed data to emphasize the importance of redesigning the joint before another flight.

But the failure to listen continued. According to Boisjoly, "The officials were guilty of one of the most unethical decisions in history because they misconstrued and even ignored our findings in order to keep the shuttle on schedule." One official told them their data were "inconclusive." Again Boisjoly and Thompson warned against launching at low temperatures and showed the committee members photographs of destroyed joints from the January 1985 flight. They would not listen.

Since no one had listened to his concerns and taken corrective action, Boisjoly's fears mounted: "I vowed not to watch the space shuttle launch that next morning." However, at the urging of a colleague, he did watch, and after a successful launch remarked, "We have just dodged a bullet." Thirteen seconds later, the shuttle exploded.

Twenty-four hours afterward, Marshall Space Flight Center knew from pictures of the launch that the joint seals had caused the disaster. Boisjoly targeted faulty listening as the problem: "We were led down blind alley after blind alley and were told cold temperatures had nothing to do with it, when indeed this was exactly the cause."

During the Presidential Commission hearings, Boisjoly and Thompson told of the information they presented the night before the explosion, and how it was not listened to by the decision makers.[25]

Example: *Columbia* Disaster

On Saturday, February 1, 2003, the space shuttle *Columbia* tore into pieces on reentry into the atmosphere—the first shuttle to be lost when landing. All seven astronauts died. *Columbia*, the oldest space shuttle in the fleet (first launched into Earth orbit in 1981) had been on a sixteen-day mission performing experiments.[26]

Persons responsible for the space program were informed of safety problems, but chose not to listen. In fact, six scientists were fired from the Aerospace Safety Advisory Panel in March 2001 after repeatedly complaining about problems in NASA's handling of the shuttle program.

About two months prior to *Columbia*'s demise, the Bush administration refused to listen to warnings from Don Nelson, a retired NASA engineer who communicated with the White House on several occasions trying persuade them to stop all space shuttle launches. In one letter, he said immediate action was needed "to prevent another catastrophic shuttle accident." Nelson referred to a number of malfunctions—hydrogen leaks, dented fuel lines, wiring problems, and computer failures.

The director of the Office of Science and Technology and President G. W. Bush's chief science adviser, John Marburger, discussed Nelson's concerns with NASA officials. He then communicated to the retired engineer, praising NASA's safety practices and concluding, "Based on these discussions, I do not think that it is appropriate for the President to issue a moratorium on Space Shuttle launches at this time."

After a report of a propellant leak on the shuttle, Nelson made one last attempt, writing to the White House December 21:

> I assume that you are aware that there has never been a launch vehicle that has not had multiple catastrophic failures. I assume you have informed the president that the request for a moratorium has been denied and his administration is accepting the responsibility for the fate of the space shuttle crews.
>
> Nelson received no reply.[27]

Example: Text Death

The Boeing Crash, the *Challenger* explosion, and the *Columbia* disaster are classic, vivid examples of listening errors, but they may seem to have happened long ago and far away. There are, however, listening disasters right now, right next to us, whenever we drive with a cell phone. Here's one about Aaron Deveau, 18, who knew his state law—Massachusetts—prohibits texting while driving. He had been warned, "Don't text while driving," but didn't listen, or if he heard the words, he didn't act on them.[28]

> Deveau's car crossed the center line of a street in Haverhill, Massachusetts and hit a car driven by Donald Bowley, 55 who was with his girlfriend, Luz Roman. Both were seriously injured—the investigating Detective noted they were "almost folded into the floorboards." Bowley died of severe head trauma the next month. Ms. Roman, suffered from her physical injuries and additionally, ". . . loss of sleeping, loss of my boyfriend. So many losses, I can't tell you how many."
>
> The case went to trial.

The central issue of the trial was texting. The prosecution's job was to build a case to prove that Deveau had been informed that texting was dangerous and illegal—that it went beyond ordinary negligence or "momentary distraction." In other words, if Mr. Deveau knew texting while driving was dangerous but did it anyway, his behavior would be categorized as "gross negligent operation."[29]

Predictably, the prosecution set-out to prove the cause of the wreck was texting. The defense argued the crash was the result of a momentary distraction and, Deveau held that he wasn't texting at the time of the wreck. However, there was evidence that he had erased some texts and lied about his texting, attempting to shift the blame on fatigue: "I was tired. I was distracted. When I looked away for one quick second, I came too close to her and I was trying to hit my brakes," he said in a taped police interview.

The judgment came down that Deveau knew texting was dangerous, and he was found guilty of vehicular homicide, texting while driving, and negligent operation of a motor vehicle. He was sentenced to a year in jail and lost his driver's license for fifteen years.[30]

Summary

Listening, defined as attending with all of our senses to gain meaning, is central to the success of any organization. Successful leaders spend a substantial amount of time listening, and they study and practice active listening to optimize the productivity of three most important organizational assets: people, time, and resources.

People are central to any organization, and they are most productive when their ideas and concerns can be expressed in an accepting, active listening environment. Effective listening in any organization, whether family, social, or corporate, establishes strong, satisfying relationships and encourages people to be a part of the team. Moreover, actively listening to people outside the organization allows adaptation to new ideas, programs, and markets.

Time, the second resource, is optimized by active listening. An alert organization will encourage active listening and feedback, which will initially take extra time to complete projects. Ultimately, however, active listening will result in saving time and increasing accurate communication.

Active listening increases the potential to build and maintain necessary resources. Resources might include finances, inventory, or facilities, and whether the organization is a family or business, active listening will help provide needed resources to assure successful functioning. Large and small organizations realize that active listening increases productive activity and, consequently, unity, revenue and resources. Nonactive listening lowers cohesion, profit margins, and resources.

Notes

1. Claire Matze, *The Power of Active Listening in Family Relationships*, http://www.babyzone.com/toddler_preschooler_development/language_communication/article/active-listening-power

2. From http://www.trap17.com/index.php/never-listen_t30681.html

3. From http://mentalhealth.samhsa.gov/15plus/

4. Leland Brown, *Communicating Facts and Ideas in Business*, Englewood Cliffs, New Jersey: Prentice-Hall, 1982, p. 380.

5. William F. Keefe, *Listen, Management!* New York: McGraw Hill, 1971, p. 10.

6. Ron Karg, Production Manager, Armstrong Rubber Co., personal interview, Des Moines, Iowa, April 7, 1985.

7. Lee Iacocca [with William Novak], *Iacocca: An Autobiography*, New York: Bantam, 1984, pp. 54–55.

8. Thomas J. Peters and Robert H. Waterman, Jr., *In Search of Excellence: Lessons for America's Best-Run Companies*, New York: Harper and Row, Publishers, 1982, p. 193 (also a program aired on public television).

9. Carl R. Rogers, A *Way of Being*, Boston: Mass., Houghton Mifflin, 1980, p. 142.

10. Russ Canute, Counselor, personal interview, Ames, Iowa, October 5, 1983.

11. Paul J. Kaufmann, *Selected Communication Variables and Their Effect Upon Advisee Satisfaction with Adviser-Advisee Conferences,* unpublished doctoral dissertation, Iowa State University, Ames, Iowa, 1975.

12. Kevin Dobbs, *The Des Moines Register,* January 10, 2006, pp. 1B, 6B.

13. Peters and Waterman, pp. 311–312.

14. Iacocca, p. 58.

15. Scott Miller, Marketing Analyst, Winnebago Industries, personal interview, Forest City, Iowa, November 11, 1987.

16. Harold J. Leavitt and Ronald A. H. Mueller, "Some Effects of Feedback on Communication," in Alfred G. Smith, *Communication and Culture: Readings in the Codes of Human Interaction,* New York: Holt, Rinehart and Winston, 1966. pp. 344–353.

17. Paul J. Kaufmann, "Classroom Instruction and Listening," unpublished monograph, Ames, Iowa, 1989.

18. *Ibid.*

19. Sylvia Porter, "Poor Listening Is Big Problem for Businesses," *The Washington Star,* November 14, 1979, pp. F–B.

20. From *http://www.speaking.com/articles/articles/d/direstaarticle1.html,* "Empowerment Comes from Learning Listening Techniques" by Diane DiResta.

21. Peters and Waterman, Public Broadcasting Program.

22. From http://en.wikipedia.org/wiki/stew_Leonard's

23. "What's He Doing? He'll Kill Us All!" *Time,* April 11, 1977, pp. 28–35.

24. Kristi Koebke, "Engineer says unethical call led to disaster," *Iowa State Daily,* March 4, 1993.

25. From http://www.aerospaceguide.net/spaceshuttle/columbia_disaster.html

26. From http://www.aerospaceguide.net/spaceshuttle/columbia_disaster.html

27. From: *The Columbia tragedy: NASA, Congress, Bush ignored safety warnings* http://www.google.com/search?client=safari&rls=en&q=The+Columbia+tragedy:+NASA,+Congress,+Bush+ignored+safety+warnings&ie=UTF-8&oe=UTF-8

28. http://www.drivinglaws.org/mass.php

29. http://www.wcax.com/story/15259491/how-effective-is-vermonts-new-texting-and-driving-law

30. http://www.cnn.com/2012/0/06/justice/massachusetts-texting-trial/

Chapter One
Awareness Exercises

Name_____   ID#_____

Before responding to these exercises, spend some time paying attention to your listening and the listening of others. Pay particular attention to the amount and type of listening you do and to how others listen to you. Note how much time you spend listening.

    Listening awareness exercise. Please answer these questions thoughtfully.

1. How many effective listeners do you know? _____

    What do they do that makes them effective listeners?

2. How many poor listeners do you know? _____

    What makes them poor listeners?

3. How do you rate yourself as a listener?

4. What do you do as a listener to earn this rating?

5. How much and what type of training (if any) have you had in listening?

6. What problems you have had because of faulty listening?

7. What rewards have you had because of effective listening?

8. How many times in a week do you feel you have listened well? _____

9. In what situations do you feel you listen well?

10. In what situations do you feel you listen poorly?

11. What percentage of your waking day do you spend listening? _____

12. Do you feel you are effective at understanding and remembering information? (a lecture, getting directions) Why?

13. Do you feel you are effective when listening to someone's problems? Why or why not? (Ex. getting a poor job review, the death of a relative)

14. Do you feel you are effective when listening to make a decision? Why or why not? (Ex. buying a car, going to a movie)

15. How much time in a day do you spend listening to enjoy? (watching TV, movies, theatre, concerts, records, tapes, stories, jokes) _____

16. What is your most comfortable situation for listening? (one-to-one, small group, large group)

17. What do you do to make your listening more effective?

18. What people in your life have been the best listeners?

Awareness Database

Name_____   ID#_____

1. What percent of your average day do you spend listening?

   A. Less than 30% B. 30%–40%   C. 50%–60%   D. 70%–80%   E. 90% or more

2. How many people do you know who are effective listeners?

   A. None   B. 1–3   C. 4–6   D. 7–9   E. 10 or more

3. How do you rate yourself as a listener?

   A. poor   B. fair   C. average   D. good   E. excellent

4. Have you had any training in listening?

   A. none   B. some   C. average

   D. above average (a unit or seminar)   E. extensive (a course)

5. How many problems develop because of poor listening?

   A. None   B. 2–6 per month   C. 7–12 per month

   D. 13–19 per month   E. 20 or more per month

6. In the past month, what has been the severity of problems that you have experienced due to listening (problems that resulted in frustration, anger, confusion)?

   A. None   B. 1–4   C. 5–8   D. 9–12   E. 13 or more

7. On the average, how much time in a day do you spend listening for information?

   A. less than an hour   B. 1–2 hours   C. 3–4 hours

   D. 4–5 hours   E. 6 or more hours

8. On the average, how much time in a day do you spend listening to help someone?

   A. none   B. an hour or less   C. 2–3 hours   D. 4–5 hours   E. more than 5 hours

9. On the average, how much time in a day do you spend listening to make a decision?

   A. none   B. an hour or less   C. 2–3 hours   D. 4–5 hours   E. 6 or more hours

10. On the average, how much time in a day do you spend listening to enjoy?

    A. none   B. an hour or less   C. 2–3 hours   D. 4–5 hours   E. 6 hours or more

11. I find listening difficult when I am (choose any two):

    A. tired   B. angry   C. hungry   D. busy   E. other (please specify)

12. My parents or guardians listen(ed) to me

   A. always   B. most of the time   C. usually

   D. seldom   E. never

13. How accurate is the following statement? If everything else is the same, I will spend my money on merchandise in stores where the employees listen to me.

   A. does not matter   B. probably   C. yes, most of the time

   D. the most important aspect

For questions 14 through 20 use these five choices:
   A. very uncomfortable
   B. somewhat uncomfortable
   C. comfortable
   D. very comfortable
   E. thoroughly at ease

14. How do you feel about listening in a one-to-one setting?

   A   B   C   D   E

15. How do you feel about listening in a small group setting? (3 to 6 people)

   A   B   C   D   E

16. How do you feel about listening in a small lecture setting? (12 to 30 people)

   A   B   C   D   E

17. How do you feel about listening in a large lecture situation? (50 to 300 people)

   A   B   C   D   E

18. How do you feel when you are listening to someone who starts telling you a problem s/he is having?

   A   B   C   D   E

19. How do you feel when you are listening to someone who is trying to persuade you—to get you to change your mind, do something, or make a purchase?

   A   B   C   D   E

20. How do you feel when someone starts telling a funny story or joke?

   A   B   C   D   E

21. My friends listen to me

   A. always   B. most of the time

   C. seldom   D. never

Chapter Two

Listening and the Process of Communication

Accurate and thorough communication is essential in any organization. It is the only means we have for understanding people and situations. This ability to communicate is the key to success in our business, professional, family, and personal lives.

In the following example, the head of an insurance company saw a need to restructure the company. For this major change to succeed, he realized the necessity for complete employee involvement. In this description of the restructuring, notice the emphasis he puts on employee involvement:

> Right off, he announced his intention to reorganize the company.
>
> Then he did an even more remarkable thing: He asked employees—yes, employees—to tell him how to do it. . . .
>
> The effort wouldn't have succeeded had it not been for the emphasis that Mr. Craib placed on employee communication. That was a priority from the start. He beefed up Allstate's internal media and used them— *along with his own tireless face-to-face sessions with employees* (emphasis mine)—to inform his workforce of the details of the business, the increasingly competitive environment Allstate was operating in, and the firm's problems and opportunities.
>
> Ironically, amid all the signs of new sophistication, many employee-communication programs nevertheless are putting increasing stress on old-fashioned face-to-face communication.
>
> It may be primitive, but it can still be effective. Surveys reveal that employees prefer to get information first-hand from their bosses. Thus, many companies are emphasizing communication skills in their training courses for middle and line managers.[1]

This example illustrates that successful management involves talking with and *listening* to employees, and that these communication skills are a necessary part of management training. Consequently, to meet these communication concerns, this text offers principles designed to improve listening in five of the most common communication settings: comprehensive, therapeutic, critical, consumer, and appreciative. Before discussing these settings in future chapters, however, we first need to understand the process of communication and listening. In order to accomplish this understanding, this chapter defines communication and describes the process of communication with a descriptive model.[2]

Communication Defined

Simply put, communication is the act of connecting with someone to share ideas. The *connecting* is through any of our five senses—sight, sound, touch, smell, and taste. The *someone* may be ourselves, another person, or a small or large group of people. *When we have communicated effectively, we have created a shared understanding of ideas, facts, or feelings.*

This complex process of communicating is one of the most important aspects of our professional and personal lives. Becoming an effective communicator takes knowledge and practice. The following example helps us understand the complexities of what appears to be a relatively simple communication situation. Notice the detailed decisions that seem to come so easily and naturally in this scene with an experienced and expert communicator—Lewis Lehr, past chief executive officer of the 3M Company. In this description of a morning meeting, Lehr increases the efficiency of the communication with his employees by first preparing for their physical comfort by arranging for refreshments and then preparing for their psychological comfort by sharing a pleasant environment, using preferred names, and creating a comfortable atmosphere for *listening*.

> They came at 8, the caller and five fellow production workers. On the top floor of the 14-floor headquarters of the 3M Company. Lehr was waiting for them in his office, with a pot of coffee. To put the women and men further at ease, he took them to the window, which covers the entire east wall, pointing out 3M's 435-acre industrial complex below and the Mississippi River beyond.
>
> Before the sugar was passed around, everyone was on a first-name basis. The workers got to the point—a festering problem at their plant.
>
> Lehr listened hard. As 3M's chairman and chief executive officer, he was into his major responsibility to the corporation's 85,000 employees: communicating.
>
> "If you can't speak openly about your problems," Lehr contends, "then your problems shouldn't be attended to. And if, as a supervisor or manager, you can't listen to the problems, then you shouldn't be a supervisor or manager."
>
> The fact is that Lehr, 63, presents such an unaffected, easy-to-talk-to sociability that all echelons of employees in the giant manufacturing corporation feel free to stop him in the hall or in the parking lot for a chat.[3]

An analysis of this face-to-face communication shows some of the many details that an effective communicator considers in order to make a meeting successful. The details include planning the time of the meeting, establishing a supportive, friendly climate—both physically and psychologically—developing an openness to listen, and sharing on an equal, first-name basis.

Communication consists of a number of elements, and if any one of the elements is missing, effective communication will not occur. Consequently, using a model of the communication process will help us examine the basic elements involved when we communicate. A model cannot completely replicate the act of communication. However, it will help us identify, understand, and adapt the communication process to meet our needs.

A Communication Listening Model

Before we can discuss and analyze the aspects of listening, we need to understand the fundamental elements operating during the process of face-to-face communication. Technology continues to offer us myriads of electronic ways to connect with others, but our main concern in this text is with people, interacting live and in person. With this backdrop in mind, let's discuss the two divisions of the communication model. The first division discusses four elements that are necessary at the most fundamental level of communication: sender, message, listener, and feedback. The second division of the model addresses three intervening variables: climate, culture, and noise.

Sender

Basically, the sender puts ideas into symbols. This means that the sender is primarily responsible for planning, encoding, and transmitting (through air, light, and touch) a message. The sender has a central role in the communication process. In a one-to-one or small group communication situation, the sending role may go back and forth between two people or quickly change from person to person as the tempo of the communication requires. In a one-to-one or small-group situation, sender planning time may be brief, and the message may be no more than a sentence or a nod.

In a presentational or public speaking situation, the focus usually remains on the sender, who may spend weeks planning a message that might last five minutes to an hour or more. Whether in the one-to-one, small group, or presentational situation, the sender is *primarily* responsible for planning, encoding, and sending a message. However, sender responsibility is not limited to those functions, because the sender is also a *listener* who decodes messages coming back from the receiver of the message. These returning messages from the receiver to the sender are called *feedback*.

Communicators have dual roles: the sender functions as a listener and the listener functions as a sender. *This unique capability to carry out simultaneous sending and receiving in a face-to-face situation allows the potential for constant monitoring for accuracy and understanding of meaning.* The sender is responsible for planning, encoding, and transmitting a message. At the same time, the sender is responsible for listening to the feedback coming from the receiver of the message.

Message

The message is created when the sender puts ideas into verbal and nonverbal codes and transmits them to a listener. The listener decodes the message and attempts to create mental images that represent what the speaker intended. Since we are incapable of mind merging (for example, Mr. Spock of the *Star Trek* series, who could put his hand on someone's head and read thoughts) with other people, we use shared symbols—words and nonverbal cues—to express our ideas. The sender's process of putting ideas into shared symbolic codes is called *encoding*. The listener's process of changing the codes back to ideas is called decoding, and what is being encoded and decoded is the *message*.

A message may be intentionally or unintentionally shared with listeners. An intentional message is encoded by the sender with the intent of reaching a specific goal. The message might be made up of information, questions, repetitions, demands, and affirmations. Even though the sender has a goal she hopes to reach through the intended message, the sender might also be encoding unintended messages that distract the listener from receiving the intended goal.

For example, an intentional message might be to encode approval of a plan that has been proposed: "Yes, I've thought it over, and I think we should adopt the new plan." The unintentional message might come from the tone of voice and facial cues: no eye contact with the listener, and a lack of enthusiasm, or even a hint of doubt in the voice. ". . . I *think* we should adopt the new plan." Several nonverbal messages may be occurring here. Perhaps the facial cues and lack of excitement in the tone of voice, which contradict the meaning of the words, send additional information of insecurity or uncertainty about the idea, or maybe the nonverbal movements are pushing the listener to make a decision. (The discussions of Face-To-Face and Mediated Listening are expanded in Chapters 3 and 4. Communication Movement is discussed in Chapter 5.)

Listener

The listener's primary responsibility is attending to the sender's message, decoding it, and attaching meaning as accurately as possible. Similar to the sender role, listener responsibility in the face-to-face situation will shift back and forth or from person to person. In the presentational or public speaking situation, the listening audience member usually remains in the listening role, and feedback is primarily nonverbal.

The listener's primary responsibility is attending, decoding, and understanding the message. But just as the speaker listens while speaking, the listener is simultaneously sending messages while listening. We

••• **Figure 2.1**   Communication Model

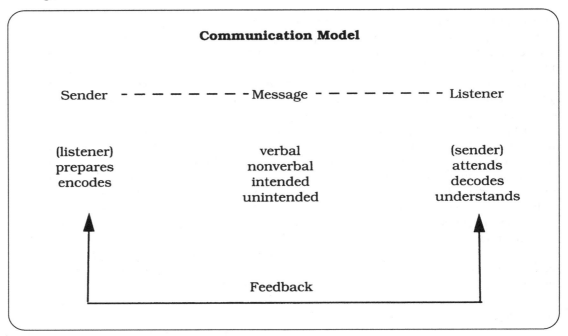

have all experienced listeners who send messages while listening: a smile, a frown, a puzzled look, a nod of affirmation, or even a question to clarify understanding or a paraphrase of the message content.

Feedback

Feedback is the nonverbal and verbal information the sender receives from the listener. The nonverbal feedback can be transmitted from the listener simultaneously, or the feedback may come after the sender has finished the message. In the one-to-one and small group situation, feedback is likely to be verbal in the form of questions and interjections as well as nonverbal—nodding, grunting, smiling. In the presentational or public-speaking situation, feedback during the presentation is usually confined to nonverbal messages—nodding, smiling, frowning, looking puzzled, applause, laughter, texting, or even sleeping. However, time for feedback might be allotted during the presentation or at the end of the presentation in the form of a question/answer period. Figure 2.1 presents the communication model as a table for easy reference.

The first part of the model comprises four ingredients. These are the central elements in our communication model. Communication will not occur if one of these four elements is missing: (1) the *sender*, who originates, encodes, and transmits a message; (2) the *message*—intended or unintended—which is made of verbal and nonverbal codes; (3) the *listener*, who attends, decodes, and attempts to understand or replicate the message; and (4) *feedback*, which is a message that goes back to the sender from the listener.

In addition to the four fundamental elements, there are three intervening variables that are present during the process of communication: (1) climate, (2) culture, and (3) noise. These variables form the second part of the model.

Climate

We usually think of *climate* as closely associated with weather. We can measure many of the weather conditions such as temperature, humidity, barometric pressure, precipitation, and wind that combine to make the climate. These conditions, when combined and measured, give us an overall picture of the climate, which we can evaluate. When we judge the climate as beautiful, perfect, ideal, lousy, or ugly, we are taking an overall view of the conditions and judging them by our expectations.

For example, judging a weather climate "ugly" perhaps is a conclusion drawn from observing the temperature and precipitation as cold, sleeting, and snowing. Our judgment that the climate is "ugly" comes about because the weather conditions are not what we desired. Perhaps we had hopes of skiing, cutting firewood, traveling, or taking a walk.

Ironically, depending on our expectations, these same weather conditions could be judged "beautiful." For example, for mountain vacationers who are ready to relax by the fire in a well-supplied cabin, the conditions might be judged "beautiful." The duck hunter would see these same conditions as "ideal."

Similar to the weather, effective listeners attend to the *communication climate or mood, which is also a combination of events and human expectations.* As members of families as well as the business and professional world, we listen to the communication climate and realize that the climate might also be judged as ugly, uncomfortable, or ideal, and we remember it can change like the weather. We have all experienced a family at dinner enjoying a climate of friendly chatter and joking as they eat their meal, or a sullen, quiet group around a table silently remembering a lost loved one.

In the working world the climate changed when an industry experienced some major dismissals at the highest management levels. One department manager who survived the shuffle, described her experience of the climate as follows: "Until things settle down, I'm taking a low profile. You can literally *feel* the tension in the air. Sometimes I wish I were invisible." The manager was describing an uncomfortable climate.

Frequently, unexpected circumstances happen that can change the climate. For example, the climate might change abruptly to a positive mood when you hear the news that, "Hal got an 'A' on that English test," or "We landed the BIG contract." Or it might change to a negative mood with the news that "The stock market has crashed," or "There will be no Christmas bonuses," or "The first shift is canceled for Monday." Climate, then, is an intervening variable that affects the sender, message, listener, and feedback.

Culture

Culture is the second intervening variable that we need to consider in the process of communication. Culture is a strongly held system of shared values, traditions, legend, and folklore. Unlike climate, culture is more permanent in the organizational setting. Where the *climate* might vary on a daily or even hourly basis, the culture remains a stable set of behavioral guidelines within the organization.

Every country, every town, every family, every department, and every organization has its own distinct culture. *Culture is a system of shared values and expectations initiated and maintained by the leadership in the organization.* Peters and Waterman's *In Search of Excellence* illustrates the reality of culture in businesses and professions:

> All the companies we interviewed, from Boeing to McDonald's, were quite simply rich tapestries of anecdote, myth, and fairy tale. . . . Nevertheless, in an organizational sense, these stories, myths, and legends appear to be very important, because they convey the organization's shared values, or culture.

Culture is not only present in the business and professional setting, but it also has significant impact on the *communication* within the organization. Peters and Waterman continue their discussion of culture by describing how it becomes the structure for effective communication.

> . . . the stronger the culture and the more it was directed toward the marketplace, the less need was there for policy manuals, organization charts, or detailed procedures and rules. In these companies, people way down the line know what they are supposed to do in most situations because the handful of guiding values is crystal clear. One of our colleagues is working with a big company recently thrown together out of a series of mergers. He says: "You know,

the problem is *every* decision is being made for the first time. The top people are inundated with trivia because there are no cultural norms."[4]

Culture can have a very specific impact on communication in a variety of ways. For example, one professional leader has developed the cultural value that clients are the top priority. Consequently, a shared cultural norm is that employees in her organization will always be positive and accepting. In this merchandising enterprise, the customer is so highly regarded that one of the shared cultural values is that no one comes to the job in a bad mood. In fact, coming to work in a good mood is part of the job description. Needless to say, with this expectation as a cultural value, the employees are generally positive and helpful to the customers.

These examples further demonstrate that culture is a system of shared values and traditions that are unique for every business and professional setting. Culture, as a variable in the communication model, affects who communicates to whom, how they communicate, and even the comfort level of the communication.

Culture and climate are intervening and interdependent variables that function along with noise within the communication process. Noise, the third variable is any interference in the communication process.

Noise

Noise is any interference in the communication system, and a major mission of this text is to minimize communication noise. Specifically, Chapters 6: *Listening to Ourselves*; 7: *Listening and Personality*; and 8: *Listening and Stress*, explore noise as it's generated from ourselves, our personalities, and stress.

Noise can stop communication, so that no understanding takes place. For example, two people may become so angry that they walk away from each other, or the noise can be minimal in an effective communication situation, where people put their feelings aside and exchange information. Much of our communication energy is spent in reducing noise, which might externally or internally affect the sender, listener, message, feedback, climate, and culture.

Sender/Listener Noise

Although speaking and listening focus on two different communication roles in the communication process, much of the noise that affects both sender and listener is common to both. Noise affects the communication of the sender and the listener externally and internally.

External sender/listener noise is any outside distraction. External noise might be noticed with any of the senses: competing sounds coming from machines or voices, cell phones, interruptions, or visually distracting movements, gestures, colors, or texts. Some other less common sources of external noise could be odors, uncomfortable temperatures, or cramped and confining spaces. We have all experienced external noise in rooms that are too warm or cold, or where chairs are uncomfortable.

Internal sender/listener noise is a distraction within the sender or listener. The noise might be physical or psychological. Physical noise could be hunger, headache, lack of sleep, a cold, a sore throat, pain, or any physical discomfort that competes for our attention. The physical noise might be mild, taking little energy and concentration to overcome, such as being thirsty or a bit hungry, or the noise might be severe, a migraine headache or sharp pain, making any meaningful communication difficult or impossible.

In addition to physical internal noise is psychological noise, which is in the mind. Psychological noise can range from minor internal messages—"I've got to give Arnie a call about Jan's marketing plan" or "Did I leave my keys in the car?" In the cases of minor internal noise, the psychological messages can be dismissed and the sender or listener can attend to the message. However, severe psychological noise can effectively stop communication. Internal concerns like: "Dad's health is going downhill fast and I feel so helpless," or "I'll have to fire my friend Bill if he continues his heavy drinking," or "Jake's been avoiding me, I wonder if he's seeing someone else?" can become so distracting that communication can stop. Psychological noise, like physical noise, pulls the attention of the speaker or listener away from the communication focus and lowers efficiency.

Message Noise

As already noted, external and internal physical and psychological noise can affect the speaker's and listener's encoding and decoding of a message. The effects of this dysfunctional encoding and decoding result in message noise.

For a number of reasons, *message noise* might lie in the words or the nonverbal cues being encoded. The words may be technical jargon, or words that are not part of the listener's field of experience; therefore, the listener might decode them differently from the sender's intended meaning. Common words that we use to designate meals can be misinterpreted. For example, "supper," "lunch," and "dinner" might carry different meanings to different people in terms of meal time and the amount of food being served. *Supper* to some people means a light meal served in the evening. To others, *supper* means a large meal served at noontime; others think of *supper* as an afternoon snack between the noon meal and the evening meal.

Noise can also enter the message with words that have changed over a period of time: computer technology has created different meanings for "hardware," "software," "on line," "twitter," "text," and even the simple word "down." Time has also changed the meanings of words such as "pot," which has changed in meaning from a vessel to carry water to a plant that is smoked, or "cool," which used to be an aspect of temperature, but is now a measure of desirability.

Noise can distort the message nonverbally. One type of nonverbal noise occurs when the sender encodes mixed messages. The words may be giving a message of calm reassurance, while at the same time, the gestures, facial expressions, and tone of voice are sending messages of concern and anxiety. The nonverbal messages of calmly, quietly, and politely saying, "I'm very angry," or in a flat, monotone saying, "That was fun," or "That was a good idea," might send confusing, mixed messages where the words do not match with the vocal emphasis. In these examples, the sender has encoded two different messages. The words are the intended main message, but the accompanying nonverbal cues create noise by presenting a message that is inconsistent with the words. Therefore, the listener is confronted with the different meanings of two messages: the verbal message and the noise of the nonverbal message.

Message noise can be verbal or nonverbal. Verbal noise comes from jargon, words from different fields of experience, and meanings that have changed over time. In addition, noise can be created by mixed messages where the nonverbal and verbal meanings are in apparent disagreement.

Climate Noise

As discussed earlier in this chapter, climate is a combination of conditions and expectations. Climate can be a source of noise and cause dysfunction in communication when the atmosphere changes unexpectedly or does not meet expectations. For example, you arrive at your office with plans to review a complex procedural change with a colleague. When you arrive at your office door, you are surprised to see it has been covered with balloons and messages of "Happy Birthday." The whole climate in the office is festive, and this climate certainly changes the communication with your colleague, at least for the time being. Another example of climate noise occurs when you are at a store discussing a purchase that you have been considering for a month. To your surprise, the manager announces that the store will be closing in ten minutes; that it has shortened its day by an hour. Your discussion becomes rushed and confused, and you delay your purchase.

In both of these examples, climate noise disrupted the communication. In the first example, the unexpected, festive, birthday climate made serious discussion difficult or impossible, for the time being. In the second example, the unexpected early store closing precluded meaningful discussion of the purchase, and the shortened time created pressure that caused delay of the purchase. In both of these cases, climate noise made communication dysfunctional.

It should be remembered that communication climate is not always noise. In fact, climate can encourage functional communication, and how we choose to deal with the climate can determine how effective the communication will be. An example of building a comfortable communication climate is discussed in an article titled "The Manager's Open Door and the Communication Climate," which focuses on the impact of climate and how it can support or threaten communication.

> In general climates are on a continuum from supportive to defensive. Supportive exchanges invite openness, but defensive remarks result in resentment or lack of communication. We would venture that traditional principles of management unintentionally reinforce or initiate defensive climates.[5]

This example emphasizes that climate can encourage or discourage communication. It also points out that we typically want to be supportive of effective communication, and we need to look carefully at the climates we create to determine if they are actually supportive.

Culture Noise

We have defined culture as long-term shared values, traditions, and expectations within an organizational unit, and that culture is generated by the leadership. When the cultural values are not shared, understood, or known, or when they conflict with other shared values from another culture, inefficient communication results.

Through organizational leadership, every group establishes its culture: its own set of values and expectations. We are effective in our communication if the rewards and punishments are consistent within the culture.

Cultural noise exists when there are conflicting cultures. For example, in manufacturing organizations, there are sometimes differing cultures between salaried positions, which are usually supervisory employees, and employees paid by the hour, who are typically involved in production. Noting these cultural differences, one supervisor remarked that when she was visiting with another supervisor in a one-to-one situation, she was relatively comfortable and at ease; however, when a production worker was present, neither supervisor felt comfortable, and the communication became difficult because of mixed cultural values. The supervisors went on to disclose how the different cultural expectations hampered effective communication:

> It was as though we couldn't be ourselves. We shared some important ideas about the job and the company, but the ideas and values that we were interested in were somewhat different from the concerns of the production people. One difference I remember was emphasized in a remark I made about a new marketing strategy we were considering which I thought was terrific. The man in production had just the opposite view. He felt the marketing idea would just cause massive procedure changes and do nothing but hurt production output. We certainly didn't share the same values on that topic, and our communication stopped immediately.

From this example, we see that the supervisor and production cultures differed greatly. One value difference dealt with marketing programs. The supervisors saw the new marketing idea as making the product more visible and increasing sales. The production worker saw it in terms of difficult machine changeovers and revised procedures.

Culture is a stable part of an organization. When the leadership at any level changes a valued tradition, it will create communication noise. For example, one large manufacturing organization had, for twenty-five years, given its employees a turkey before the Christmas holiday. One year, with no explanation, the week of the Christmas holiday arrived without the expected turkey. A tradition had been broken. As a result, rumors, speculation, and low morale created cultural noise that affected the communication in the organization. Communication broke down because of value differences. The employees speculated that the turkey was withheld as punishment for any number of difficulties, which ranged from low production and poor quality control, to high numbers of accidents. However, management simply believed the tradition was outdated and not important anymore. The cultural value that made the communication confused was based in the idea that the employees had come to value the holiday turkey as a cultural expectation, and management had failed to inform them that the outdated tradition of giving a turkey was going to be stopped: it was not a punishment; it was just not important anymore. *From this example, we can see that cultural noise occurs when values or traditions are abruptly changed or ignored,* and the resulting dysfunctional communication can spread throughout the entire organization.

At this point, our communication model looks like Figure 2.2.

••• **Figure 2.2**   Revised Communication Model

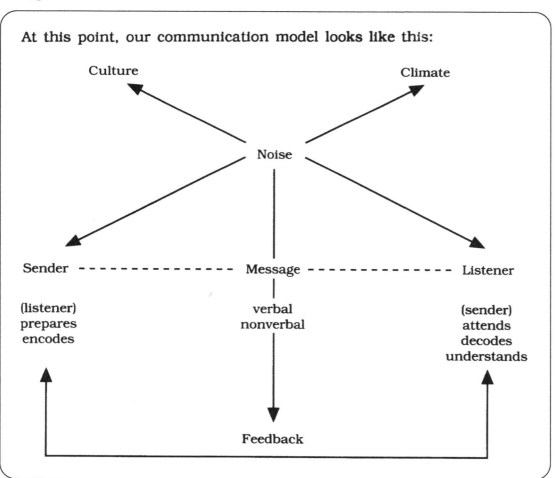

At this point, our communication model looks like this:

Culture   Climate

Noise

Sender – – – – – – – – – – – – – – – Message – – – – – – – – – – – – – Listener

(listener)   verbal   (sender)
prepares   nonverbal   attends
encodes   decodes
                                                                understands

Feedback

Summary

This chapter discusses the complex process of communication and defines communication as the act of connecting with someone to share ideas. To help understand the process of communication, a model elaborating on the communication elements and intervening variables is developed. The elements are sender, message, listener, and feedback. The intervening variables are climate, culture, and noise. Noise is discussed as any internal, external, physical, or psychological interference in the communication process. Noise brings dysfunction into the communication process at any point it occurs.

In Chapter 3, we will expand the message component of the model by discussing *holistic* listening, which is listening to nonverbal messages with both brain hemispheres and all five senses.

Notes

1. William H. Miller, "More than Fish Stories Now," *The Business Management Magazine,*" vol. 234, no. 4, August 24, 1987, pp. 39–41.

2. Warren Weaver, "The Mathematics of Communication," *Scientific American*, vol. 181, pp. 11–15, 1949. Reprinted in *Communication in Culture*, Alfred G. Smith, editor, New York: Holt, Rinehart and Winston, 1966, pp. 15–24.

3. Del Marth, "Keeping all the Lines Open," *Nation's Business*, October, 1984, p. 85.

4. Thomas J. Peters and Robert H. Waterman, Jr., *In Search of Excellence: Lessons for America's Best-Run Companies*, New York: Harper and Row, Publishers, 1982, pp. 75–76.

5. Charles E. Beck and Elizabeth A. Beck, "The Manager's Open Door and the Communication Climate," *Business Horizons*, vol. 29, January–February, 1986, p. 15.

Chapter Two
Awareness Exercises

Name _____   ID# _____

Before responding to these questions, spend some time paying attention to your listening and the listening of others. Notice the amount and type of listening you do and to how others listen to you.

1. Define communication noise.

2. Give an example of external noise that has interfered with your listening in the past week.

Example #1

1. Situation

2. Give an example of internal physical noise that has interfered with your listening.

Example #1

1. Situation

2. Give an example of psychological noise that has interfered with your listening.

Example #1

1. Situation

2. Give an example where a confusing word interfered with your listening.

3. Give an example where a mixed message interfered with your listening.

4. Briefly describe someone who gives you clear feedback.

5. Briefly describe someone who gives you vague feedback.

6. Describe a communication situation where climate noise existed.

7. Describe a communication situation where cultural noise existed.

8. Give three cultural values of an organization in which you are involved.

    Name of organization:

    Values

    a.

    b.

    c.

Chapter Two
Awareness Database

Name_____   ID#_____

While you are listening, how often do you:

1. feel aware of external noise?

    A.   B.   C.   D.   E.
    often   seldom

2. feel aware of internal physical noise?

    A.   B.   C.   D.   E.
    often   seldom

3. notice psychological noise?

    A.   B.   C.   D.   E.
    often   seldom

4. pay attention to nonverbal messages?

    A.   B.   C.   D.   E.
    often   seldom

5. focus on the exact meanings of words?

    A.   B.   C.   D.   E.
    often   seldom

6. consciously give the sender feedback?

    A.   B.   C.   D.   E.
    often   seldom

7. try to become aware of cultural values and expectations?

    A.   B.   C.   D.   E.
    often   seldom

8. pay attention to the climate?

    A.   B.   C.   D.   E.
    often   seldom

Chapter Three

Listening Holistically

The title of this text—*Sensible Listening: The Key to Responsive Interaction*—highlights some necessary ingredients for effective listening. Two of these ingredients are tied in with the word *sensible;* a third lies in the meaning of *responsive.* The word *sensible* is used with two meanings: the first meaning implies logical and reasonable: that is, listening with good sense. The second use of *sensible* means activating all of our senses while listening, and the third key idea is *responsiveness,* which is being active, alert, aware, sensitive, in the moment, and "with" the situation—these last two ideas are discussed in this chapter.

The definition of listening is *assigning meaning to all sense input,* which means our goal is to gather as much meaning as possible from each message. Understanding holistic listening will help us reach this goal. The term *holistic* is frequently applied to medicine. It implies that health is the product of a number of factors such as genetics, diet, stress, exercise, and environment. At a given time, any one of these factors may affect health more than another, but they all work together to contribute to our overall health.

Listening is also holistic, and its factors include all senses—sound, sight, smell, taste, touch, and both brain hemispheres. When we listen holistically, the five senses and the brain work to assign accurate meaning, and our listening becomes synergistic—where the combination of senses and brain hemisphere each *multiply* the effects of the others rather than merely adding to them.

The following narrative offered by a city manager exemplifies the power of holistic listening.

> On a city council I was working with, there were five members: a physician, an attorney, a teacher, a business-man, and a factory worker named Joe. During the course of a meeting, Joe said little, but he listened. He listened to the words, spoken and unspoken, and the flow of the meeting; he took it all in. When Joe finally spoke, usually at the end of the meetings, everyone gave him full attention, because his comments incorporated the important ideas and feelings of the whole group. Because Joe listened at all levels—not just the words but the feelings as well, he could put his finger on the heart of the problem and come up with helpful, acceptable solutions to their problems.[1]

Holistic listening is defined as *assigning meaning to all sense input, using both brain hemispheres.* This definition means that we listen to messages through our senses: ears, eyes, noses, skin, and tongues, and we interpret and evaluate the messages with the right and left brain hemispheres to create meaning. This chapter examines the concept of holistic listening by first discussing the role of the left and right brain hemispheres in the listening process, and second, the role of the five senses in the listening process.

Listening with Both Sides of the Brain

In our society, we are educated to use primarily the left side of the brain. The creative demands of holistic listening, however, require that the right side be activated as well. Consequently, listening is difficult because by choosing to listen actively, we have decided to activate the less-used right hemisphere of the brain to work together with the regularly used left hemisphere.

A comparison of left and right hemisphere characteristics will help explain the brain functions as they relate to holistic listening.[2] While reading the left brain/right brain comparisons in Figure 3.1, notice that the left brain hemisphere functions are practical, rational, logical, evaluative, and concerned with symbols in the form of words, gestures, and numbers. The right brain hemisphere is spontaneous, aware of the whole scene, creative, nonevaluative, playful, unconcerned with symbols, and intuitive. The left hemisphere is logical and evaluative; the right hemisphere is creative and nonverbal.

As this left–right hemisphere comparison shows, each side of the brain is primarily responsible for processing different types of input. The left side responds to structured information in an analytic and logical way using numbers and words. The right side is creative and processes nonverbal input working mainly in images and pictures.[3]

To some extent, our culture and educational systems emphasize the logical and sequential left brain functions. For example, emphasis is placed on developing knowledge in mathematics, grammar, science, and logic, as opposed to the right brain functions of music, art, poetry, creative writing, and dance. Consequently, through conditioning and habit, the left hemisphere is used more than the right hemisphere. The fact that 80 to 90 percent of meaning is created in the

••• Figure 3.1

Left	Right
Verbal: Using words to name, describe, define	*Nonverbal:* Awareness of things, but minimal connection with words
Analytic: Figuring things out step-by-step and part-by-part	*Synthetic:* Putting together to form wholes, aural sounds
Symbolic: Using a symbol to stand for something	*Concrete:* Relating to things as they are, at the present moment
Abstract: Taking out a small bit of information and using it to represent the whole thing	*Analogic:* Seeing likenesses between things, understanding metaphoric relationships
Temporal: Keeping track of time	*Nontemporal:* Without a sense of time
Rational: Drawing conclusions based on reason and facts	*Nonrational:* Willing to suspend judgment, fun loving, playful
Digital: Using numbers as in counting	*Spatial:* Seeing where things are in relation to other things, and how parts go together to form a whole
Logical: Drawing conclusions based on logic: one thing following another in logical order—for example, a math theorem or well-stated argument	*Intuitive:* Making leaps of insight, often based on incomplete patterns, hunches, feelings, or visual images
Linear: Thinking in terms of linked ideas, one thought directly following another, often leading to a convergent conclusion	*Holistic:* Seeing whole things all at once; perceiving the overall patterns and structures, often leading to divergent conclusions

right hemisphere from nonverbal input,[4] helps us understand the importance of right hemisphere activity when listening.

As an example of the importance of nonverbal, right hemisphere listening, picture a morning scene at your workplace. Your usually upbeat, energetic partner says the words, "Good morning," as expected, but something is uncomfortable in the *way* the words are said. His tone of voice connotes a somber feeling. How do you interpret this? In actuality, the nonverbal message in the voice has more impact than the words, "Good morning." Your right hemisphere is sensitive to this nonverbal message and creates a meaning that something is wrong.

What if a co-worker says nothing when a greeting is appropriate or expected? In this instance, the entire message is nonverbal. The right hemisphere attempts to attach some meaning to the silence, so we respond internally by asking ourselves, "What is wrong with Dave today?" Then we may do a quick mental search of personal interactions: "Did I do something to cause him to react this way?" or, "Were there procedural changes that could have been responsible for the uncomfortable atmosphere in the office?" "Is he having problems at home?" The point is that holistic listening involves assigning meaning from *all* senses, not just hearing, as the last example demonstrates. Sometimes there is nothing to hear, yet several meanings are generated from the silence.

Holistic listening relies on all working senses for input: it is a combination of the five senses working together. Listening holistically processes significantly more information input than senses working independently, because our senses and brains are functioning cooperatively, giving a more reliable meaning to the message-receiving process. Listening holistically can be compared to a basketball team. Each of the players represents one of the five senses: sound, sight, smell, touch, taste. The patterns and movements of the players are interdependent, and there is a rational and emotional bond between the players, similar to the bond between the right and left brain hemispheres. The players, like our senses, come together to form a team that accomplishes tasks that none of the players would achieve if playing independently.

People who are totally deaf can listen. Even though they cannot hear sound, they give meaning by listening with their other working senses—sight, smell, touch, and taste. The idea that listening is holistic means that listening is the integration of all of our working senses and seldom relies on assigning meaning from only one sense.

To emphasize further the concept that we listen to more than words, imagine yourself as a plant manager. A forty-year-old woman who was fired yesterday by one of your supervisors tells you the following:

> Yesterday I was talking with one of the punch-press operators when my boss storms in and begins raking me over the coals for a work stoppage I had nothing to do with. I stood there in shock. I was so angry that I wanted to yell back at him, but I kept my cool. But all day I couldn't get it out of my mind. No matter what I was doing, it haunted me. I finally got so angry that I burst into his office and told him just what I thought of him. I even let him have it for a few lousy things he's done in the past. He fired me on the spot. Last night I was pretty depressed, and all day today I've been trying to figure out where I can get a new job or maybe how I can get my old job back.[5]

What is missing that would help us get a better understanding of the situation? Would we get more meaning if we could listen to the tone of the voice? If we could listen to the facial expressions? If we could listen to the gestures and movements? It is frustrating not to be able to include these other nonverbal listening cues in the listening process, because we know how crucial they are in helping to form *complete* meaning.

Listening with All the Senses

An estimated 65 to 90 percent of our listening is directed toward nonverbal messages.[6] We listen to space, to touch, to smell, to dress, to the environment, to time, to facial expressions and eye movements, to bodily movements and gestures, and to the tone of voice. The successful communicator is actively listening to the verbal and nonverbal cues.

Holistic listening is the process in which we actively obtain meaning from information received through all of our working senses, as we consciously use the right and left hemispheres of the brain. In addition to listening to sounds and words with our ears, we also listen to visual messages with our eyes, to smell with our noses, to taste with our tongues, and to touch with our skin.

Listening with Our Ears

The sense most commonly connected with listening is hearing—using our ears—and certainly hearing is an extremely important part of holistic listening. Hearing is sometimes called "the watchdog of the senses," because when we are asleep or daydreaming and the other senses are not actively listening, we can still be awakened by a smoke detector, a child's cry, or a siren. When crossing a street, we remind children to, "Stop, look, and listen." In this reminder the word *listen* means using the ears to function along with the eyes. The warning before crossing the street would actually be more accurate in the holistic sense if it were stated, "Stop, listen with your eyes, and listen with your ears."

Hearing is the mechanical and neurological process of noticing various incoming signals. *Listening* takes the incoming signals to another level and *assigns meaning to the signals*. To increase our understanding of the process of listening, we need to recognize the function of semantics and vocalics in order to assign meaning to these sounds.

Semantics

Although signals have been thoroughly studied and understood as parts of communication, meanings are the least understood and analyzed, because a substantial difference between signals and meanings exists. Signals—particular words, sentences, or gestures—can be recorded on CD or DVD, but the meanings of these signals cannot be recorded, since meanings are inside the listener and are much more complex and subjective than signals.

Meanings we give to signals are psychological and learned from culture.[7] The study of meanings is called *semantics* and focuses on how situations, social systems, and cultures form the meaning we put on language. A primary function of listening with our ears in a face-to-face interaction is to listen to words and put an accurate meaning on those words. However, in addition to the semantic meaning we give words, we use our ears to listen beyond the words. The *voice itself* saying the words contains messages that may or may not be related to the dictionary meaning of the words themselves. In addition to using our ears to hear signals, we also use them to hear vocal intonations that add meaning to the signals. These added meanings that come from the voice are called *vocalics*.

Vocalics

The vocal aspects of holistic listening are called *vocalic paralanguage*, which means there is vocal meaning embedded in the words themselves (we hear the words, but what is the voice saying?). We have all listened to messages where the meaning of the words changes completely because of the tone of the voice. Someone saying, "That's just a *wonderful* idea," with a sarcastic vocal emphasis on the "wonderful" can completely reverse the meaning of the sentence. Vocalic meanings are derived from voice volume, pitch, rate, pauses, quality, and vocalization.

Volume.   Volume is the strength or loudness of the voice. A message sent very quietly might convey a meaning of secrecy—this is just for you—or it might convey the meaning that the sender is shy, or the receiver might infer that the sender has a cold. A loud message might mean that the sender is angry or wants others to hear the message, or the sender is hard of hearing and cannot adjust the volume appropriately.

Pitch.   Pitch, the highness or lowness of the voice, also carries meaning. A higher than usual, tight sounding voice might imply a nervous, tense sender. A lower-pitched, relaxed, steady voice might be more believable and credible. For example, newscasters with their trained voices speak at a lowered and less-varied pitch in order to deliver an objective message.

Rate.   Rate, the speed at which the sender speaks, carries meaning. For example, someone who speaks at a slow rate can give the additional message of being thoughtful, slow-witted, or tired. Consequently, as with any paralanguage, the slow rate of speaking may mean nothing at all—this person just talks slowly. Words that are spoken at a rapid rate can carry the meaning that this person is busy, intelligent, hyperactive, angry, a compulsive talker, or nonthinking. These are just a few examples of how rate can affect the meaning of a message.

Pausing.   Pausing is defined as one to five seconds of silence, and these pauses can add meaning beyond that of slow rate speaking. Pauses might send a meaning of wisdom, thoughtfulness, methodical thinking, or a lack of preparation. Long periods of silence, which are more than a few seconds, might send a message of anger, boredom, comfort, thoughtfulness, or nervousness.

Quality.   Over time, a person's voice can be recognized by its unique sound. For example, a child can recognize a parent's or family member's voice quality, and eventually, grows to identify friends' unique voice qualities. The voices become extensions of personalities. The low voice with little variety might be perceived as more authoritative and masculine. A high-pitched voice with variation might be perceived as artistic, or feminine.

Vocalizations.   Vocalizations are signals that are not specifically categorized as words. "Hmmm," "uh huh," "uhm," and "ugh" are sounds that might offer some meaning. "Hmmm" and "uhm" might indicate that the sender is thinking; "Uh huh" might signal agreement; and "ugh," distaste or physical effort.

Vocalics involve listening with our ears to the vocal aspects of loudness, pitch, rate, pauses, quality, and vocalizations. Attending actively to vocalics can add greatly to the meaning of the message being received. Moreover, vocalics can help us determine if someone is telling the truth. Research indicates that voice pitch is a better indicator of lying than facial expression.[8] Perhaps this is the reason the statue of justice has her eyes covered.

Listening with Our Eyes

Our eyes listen to space (*proxemics*), body movement (*kinesics*), physical appearance, *artifacts*, and facial expressions and *oculescics*.

Proxemics

Proxemics is a general term for space. Proxemic listening is assigning meaning to space. In listening to space, we are first concerned with the organization of space, placement of objects, and the directions and distances between people and objects. The general meanings derived from space usually lie in one of two categories: affiliative or private. With affiliative space, we might listen to the space and decide that the sender wants to connect with people; the sender uses space to say, "I'm interested in you. Won't you join me?" Or we might listen to the space and assign the meaning that the sender wants some privacy, or some distance. This private space is saying, "Don't get too close"; "Leave me alone. I need some time to myself." Space can be manipulated and managed to be affiliative or private.

Observing how space can be managed is very informative. One chief executive officer (CEO) of a large manufacturing organization thoughtfully arranged her office space. The CEO placed a large, tall desk and heavy leather padded chair in the back of the office near picture windows overlooking wooded hills. The desk faced the office door. A few feet in front of the desk stands a glass covered table that is short and round. The table is surrounded by short, plush-looking chairs.

Upon entering this office, one might observe through listening to the organization and placement of objects that this woman is powerful and distant. A person invited to have a seat in one of the plush low chairs at the low round table might find that this position has the effect of exaggerating the CEO's size. This same person standing in front of the desk, finds himself eye-to-eye with the sitting CEO. Eventually, the visitor sits in a short, plush chair looking three feet up to the CEO. Consequently, depending on the nature of the discussion, the CEO might stand, walk around her desk, and sit with the person in one of the low seats at the round table. This change in space is dramatic. Proxemic listening at this point might tell us that this woman is not so powerful, but very average in many ways, and friendly.

Territory is space that includes ownership of specific locations or geographical areas. All animals, as well as humans, have a need to control and sometimes defend territory to achieve a balance between their affiliative and private needs. Individuals set up their homes, studies, offices, or rooms to meet specific needs. Affiliative or public territories would include a chair in a classroom, a place at the lunch table, a table at the restaurant, or a seat in a break room. Private needs would include offices, study rooms, and parts of the home.

We listen with our eyes to determine if people have *marked* or laid claim to some territory. The mark may be as obvious as a name plate on a door, or in the case of public space, territory may be marked by the placing of personal possessions which imply, "This place is mine at this time." If one were to walk into a restaurant and put a briefcase on a table and coat over the back of the seat at the table, she would have marked that territory as "hers." If she left for a moment, she would be surprised and perhaps a little disturbed to return finding her case and coat had been moved to another table. In this situation, the person who moved the belongings either did not listen carefully enough to the visual mark of the territory, or the meaning was ignored and the items were moved anyway.

Personal space is another aspect of proxemic listening. This is space that we, as senders and listeners, carry with us. Personal space is like an array of circles around us. We stand in the middle in a tight circle around us, and the diameters of the circles become greater as they get further from us. Imagine personal space as a stop-action picture of waves after a stone has been thrown in the water. We are the stone, and the waves are personal space that moves with us wherever we go.

We allow someone to enter our personal space depending on the situation and the relationship, and, of course, as listeners, we assign meaning to personal space. If we were to view the same people—same clothing, same room—in different situations, we could probably determine accurately whether they were being inducted into an honor society (a formal situation), or whether they were attending a family reunion. For example, at a reunion family members would greet and maybe hug each other—distance would be close. At an induction ceremony for an honor society, honorees might stiffly shake hands with each other and officials conducting the ceremony—distance would be greater. One of the variables used in making this determination would be listening visually to the personal space.

Just as we develop different languages in different cultures, and even different meanings for the same words within a culture, the meanings we attach to personal space become part of our culture, and the meanings can vary from culture to culture. Within family cultures, some members can function comfortably at close range and some function better at a greater distance. That is, members of one family may speak softly and closely, while members from another family might speak more loudly at greater distance. When members of these different families get together for the first time, they are likely to listen to the space and misinterpret it—assign inaccurate meanings. A family member who is accustomed to close interactions might think, "He is certainly unfriendly"; a family member who is accustomed to more distant interactions might think, "He is pushy; a little too friendly." Therefore, it is best to observe and listen to the proxemics for awhile in order to determine a more accurate meaning.

Becoming aware that holistic listening includes visually assigning meaning to space, helps us realize that space affects communication. We assign meaning to space as it involves the arrangement of an office, the type of territory, and the distance we create between people. We also listen with our eyes to body movement, or *kinesics*.

Kinesics

Kinesics is the name given to body communication. We can imagine walking into our supervisor's office. She smiles and offers a chair. As the conference begins, we notice that she is relaxed, and we interpret this relaxation as a sign of her security and self-confidence. We also notice that she is attentive because she is leaning slightly forward, facing us directly. We interpret this posture as showing interest, involvement, and even respect.

In another scene, we imagine ourselves walking into our supervisor's office. She glances toward us and waits for us to sit. As we begin the conference, we notice she is fidgeting with her pen and darting her eyes around the office, and we interpret this nervousness as a sign of insecurity. We feel that she is not paying attention because she is leaning away and is facing her desk. We interpret this posture as showing disinterest, uninvolvement, and disrespect.

In both instances, we are listening with our eyes and assigning meaning to body communication, particularly body movement. We listen to the way people move when we are interacting with them, but we also form impressions of people when we are not interacting with them. For example, we put meanings on walking styles. Long, solidly planted strides might indicate confidence and security. Short, choppy steps, might indicate uncertainty and insecurity. Heavy, rocky steps might convey toughness.

Physical Appearance

Physical appearance and artifacts are also observed with the eyes. We listen to physical appearance in terms of body build and condition, as well as artifacts: clothing, make up, jewelry, hair style, and tattoos. Some of the labels we assign to body build might include wrestler, football player, basketball player, gymnast, runner, swimmer, or model. Some meanings from body build might be expressed as, "She really must feel good about herself. She stays in shape and keeps her weight just right." "He must be having problems, look at the weight he's put on."

In addition to physical appearance, we listen to artifacts. Most artifactual listening lies in clothing and accessories. The style of clothing and accessories a person chooses can tell much about the organizational culture. For example, International Business Machines, IBM, has a white shirt, tie, and leather briefcase culture. Apple Computer Corporation artifacts indicate a blue jeans, sweatshirt, and tennis shoes culture, which indicate a more casual workplace. These written or unwritten dress codes tell us something about the formality and expectations of the culture. Moreover, on a daily or weekly basis, we listen to the meaning derived from the clothing worn at certain restaurants or theaters—some are casual, relaxed, and informal; some are formal.

Many job roles we play require a uniform. For example, an airline stewardess' or steward's uniform quickly informs us of their role. In fact, the symbolic impact of some uniforms carries such strong meaning that the occupation becomes synonymous with the uniform. For example, a badge is closely identified with a police officer, as is a fire hat with the firefighter, or a mail bag with the mail carrier. The businessperson's suit and the mechanic's coveralls, although not as strictly defined, are also uniforms that give occupational meaning.

Just as we can assign inaccurate meanings to words, we can also process inaccurate meanings for artifacts. For example, some years ago a twenty-five-year-old friend named Ron was getting ready to go to a wedding. In those days, one fashion that was popular for young men was to wear a black turtleneck sweater and black pants. Accompanying this outfit, the appropriate jewelry was a gold or silver medallion about three inches in diameter (it usually looked like a sunburst or rays radiating from a circle) dangling from a chain around the turtleneck.

At the wedding reception, Ron was dressed in black with the medallion hanging from his neck. Another man of a different generation, age about sixty, listened with his eyes to Ron's appearance. To this older man, the medallion, which looked somewhat like an Olympic medal, meant something: Ron must have won that medal. So he approached Ron with a question:

Man: "What did you win it for?"

Ron: "Win what for?"

Man: "That medal." Pointing to the medallion.

Ron: "Oh, that. No, it's just some jewelry."

Man: "Come on, pal. Really, what did you win it for?"

Ron: "Seriously, nothing. It's just a decoration."

In the older man's world of meaning, when a man wore something that large around his neck, it was a medal, and it *had* to be an award. The older man had listened with his eyes and had assigned meaning. However, the meaning was wrong; it was inaccurate, and as is often the case with inaccurate communication, the miscommunication caused some discomfort and frustration. In fact, as the festivities progressed through the evening, the gentleman became more insistent on knowing the nature of the award. To put an end to the questions, Ron finally invented an act of heroism to satisfy the older man's certainty that the medal was won for something.

Tattoos

Body tattooing has been around for at least 5000 years, and today tats have become popular visual artifacts. Tattoos express simple to complex messages about relationships, family, aging, immortality, religion,[9] independence, rebirth, fertility, power, and gang affiliation.[10] Like any other expressive art form, tattoos offer us an array of visual messages with a fantastic range of shapes, colors, and body placements. Visually listening may give us a fairly clear message quickly; while other tattoos may require deeper knowledge of the decorated person as well as substantial research into the background of the design.[11]

CALVIN AND HOBBES © 1988 Watterson. Reprinted with permission of UNIVERSAL UCLICK. All rights reserved.

Facial Expressions and Oculesics (Eye Movements)

We listen to facial expressions and eye movements, and when we do not have access to this visual input—when we are on a phone, for example or on the Internet—we lose an important source of listening input. Facial expressions and oculesics supplement, clarify, and amplify interpretation of spoken words. This additional input is called *metacommunication*, which is messages about messages.

As holistic listeners, we can look at the other person's face and eyes to determine the intensity of what is being expressed. For example, an emotional expression, like a smile, is probably the most obvious, and when linked with direct eye contact, a smile can show genuine warmth in the accompanying words. Along with facial expression, the eyes can have a powerful metacommunication impact. During struggles for racial equality, people identified what they called a "hate stare," which was an expression of intense eye contact that furthered the intensity of hate by focusing on a person as if he or she were a *thing*.

Women and men communicate differently with their eyes and faces. Generally, women are more expressive than men. They tend to smile more frequently, and their messages are more pleasant and positive. Consequently, when a woman's eyes and facial expressions are somewhat unpleasant or negative, she is viewed as much more harsh than a man who sends the same kinds of unpleasant and negative eye and facial messages.[12]

The eyes and face also send meanings that can coordinate interaction between people. Imagine yourself sitting across from a friend at a table in the library, and an acquaintance sitting one chair away from you. You know something about the newcomer and want to share this information with your friend. To get your friend's attention, you quickly connect your eyes with hers, and she knows you want to talk to her. You both casually walk over to the drinking fountain where you can converse.

Changing amounts of eye contact can also have meaning. Decreased eye contact might mean, "He doesn't want to talk to me anymore." or "Something is distracting her from our conversation." You may be conversing with your supervisor and notice that she is shifting her eye contact away from you. From this change in eye contact, you arrive at the meaning that it is time to close this meeting, so you thank the supervisor and leave.

At another time you may be in your supervisor's office when a secretary enters quietly and puts a memo on the side of the supervisor's desk. Neither you nor your supervisor gives the secretary acknowledgment through eye contact; instead, you continue your conversation. This unspoken agreement not to establish contact with the secretary is called *civil inattention*, and it allows the secretary to function without disrupting the communication.

In addition, increased eye expression can help us determine whose turn it is to listen and whose turn it is to speak. As the sending role is ending, the sender will begin to look at the listener more. These increased eye signals tell the listener that it is his turn to speak.

We have discussed holistic listening as a whole brain activity that processes meaning from ear and eye input. The next sense input that adds to meaning is *haptics*, which is listening to touch.

Listening with Our Skin

Tactile or touch communication is called *haptics*. Touch may be the basis for all communication, because without direct or indirect touch, we cannot send or listen to one another. For example, with speech, the sender's vocal bands vibrate the air, and the air is formed into words by the articulators (the tongue, teeth, lips, and nose). These words go through the air, and the vibrating air *touches* the listener's eardrums and sends them into motion. The mechanical energy of the vibrating eardrums is converted into neurological energy and presents itself as sound to the brain. In the process, if the air in the room where we are talking is removed, we can no longer hear the sound, since the shared air is what carries the voice frequencies to the receiver. The air, then, is a means for the sender to touch the listener.

Visual communications are also based on touch. Light is reflected from the sender and *touches* the cones and rods of the listener's eyes. This touching vibrates the eye receptors and presents a visual image to the brain. As with air touching the eardrum, the light touching the eye is an extension of the sender. If the light is removed and we are in the dark, the sender can no longer touch visually, and the message is lost.

Of course, direct skin-to-skin physical touch also communicates, as this narrative highlights:

> I went through high school and college with a good friend named Greg. I knew his family well and spent a good deal of time with them. Our senior year in college, Greg's father died. When I arrived at the funeral home, there was Greg with his brothers and sisters standing at the coffin. As I approached Greg, words would not come. So without thinking, I took his hand and held it tightly. As I look back on this spontaneous act, I realize that touching is the basis for all communication: that is, direct physical touch works when no other communication channels seem appropriate or available.

Touch is a basic means of communication, and even though the channels of air and light are available as extensions to touch, other variables in the communication setting might require direct touch for effective communication. For example, a father hears the baby crying, picks the child up, and cuddles and soothes her through touch. It would be unreasonable for a parent to attempt to reason with the baby or discuss the situation—"What seems to be the trouble? Does your diaper need to be changed?" Instead, the parent communicates to the child by comforting her through closeness and stroking. When touch through air and light is removed as an extension of the sender, the only communication option that remains is direct person-to-person touch, which is the core of communication.

The rules that regulate touch, and all communication symbols, are defined within every culture; consequently, the meanings assigned to various touches are different from culture to culture. One researcher proposes that there are five categories of touch. Each category is described by the quality of touch, the body area that is touched, and the touch response from the listener.[13]

1. *Functional-professional touches* are basically without relational meaning; they are an expected part of the profession. The barber or hairdresser cutting, styling, and shampooing, the doctor touching to diagnose, and the tailor fitting clothing are examples where touch has no meaning beyond accomplishing a task.

2. *Social-polite touches* are regulated by the expectation of the social situation. Examples of social-polite touches would be an approving pat on the back for a job well done, or a social hug as a greeting.

   One of the most common social-polite touches is the handshake. Some researchers report that they can assign categorical meanings to different handshakes. These categories of handshakes and the meanings they give are self-explanatory: Bone Crusher, Pump Handle, Limp Digits, Dead Fish, No-release, and Winning.[14]

3. *Friendship-warmth touches* occur between family members and good friends. The relationship is not sexual, but it is one of deep caring. Depending on the situation, the friendship-warmth touch could be misinterpreted as a relational advance beyond that of friendship.

4. *Love-intimacy touching* progresses from the friendship-warmth relationship. This touch communication occurs between very close family members and lovers.

5. *Sexual arousal* is touching that leads to and occurs during sex.

Listening to touch can be extremely rewarding, because touch messages are usually connected with professional and social behavior, friendship, love, and sexual behavior.

The next sense is listening to smells, *olfactics*. Listening to olfactics is responsible for providing us with substantial meaning, but it has not been as thoroughly researched as have other areas of holistic listening.

Listening with Our Noses

Listening to smell, *olfactics,* is one of the most basic senses, and it consumes a good deal of our time and money. Americans spend millions of dollars every year on changing how they smell and how their territory smells. Mouthwashes, deodorants, perfumes, colognes, sprays, furniture polish, and air fresheners are some of the marketed items designed to alter smell.

Three general meanings are given to smell: (1) identification, (2) identification/attraction, and (3) attraction.

We listen to smell for *identification.* For example, to expedite identification, the obnoxious smell of natural gas is added to the fuel by the utility distributors as a warning, since natural gas in its normal state is odorless. Chemists and physicians smell various compounds to determine the formula or composition. Certainly, if all of our other senses were not functioning, we could identify a musty basement, or a hospital, or a spring rain shower. Even books can be identified olfactically:

> I was walking across campus with Clay, a blind friend of mine. We were taking a route we didn't usually use and visiting about a number of things. As we walked, Clay was unsure where we were and asked me,
>
> "Where are we going? Are we headed back to your office?"
>
> Before I could answer, he said, "Never mind. I know where we are."
>
> I was puzzled. I wondered how he knew our location and asked him how he figured out where we were. He told me we were near the library, which, in fact, we were.
>
> "How did you know that?"
>
> "I can smell the books."
>
> "You can smell the books?"
>
> "Yeah, can't you?"
>
> I stopped, and sure enough, from a ventilation outlet near the building came the smell of books—a smell I never noticed before. I'd been past that spot hundreds of times and never got the olfactic message that belonged to the library.

We may listen to smell and assign a combined meaning of *identity and attraction.* We identify the smell of caramel popcorn coming through a shopping mall, and we are attracted to buy some. We smell a hint of hardwood smoke, and we are attracted to the fire in the living room, or to the roast turkey in the kitchen, as the aroma moves through the home.

We might also identify a smell and be repulsed by it—the smell is so foul that we are not attracted to it—maybe even nauseated. The smell from a bus or a car burning oil might be easily identifiable as something we want to avoid. One smell that is repulsive is that of cigarette smoke. Our society is educating us to have increasing negative reactions to it. More and more families and businesses do not allow smoking in their homes or buildings because of the immediate infiltration of smoke and because of the residual smell long after the smoker is gone. All government buildings have banned smoking altogether.

Listening to some smells creates meanings that are attractive or repulsive. The smell may be coming from an unknown source, yet it conveys meaning: "I don't know what they're cooking in there, but it sure does smell good." "Mmmm, I really like the smell of what you're wearing." On the repulsion end, "By the smell of things, there must be a culture in its golden age living in the refrigerator. I think we have liquid lettuce again"; "There's a real bad odor coming from the sewer in the basement."

A final thought about listening olfactically lies in the fact that *smell is closely linked to taste.* We listen to the taste of food with our tongues, and if our ability to smell is impaired, taste is also impaired. Consequently, the variables that apply to smell also apply to taste, and we put meanings of identification, attraction, or revulsion with certain tastes.

Identification is as simple as tasting and noticing, "This has onions in it." Attraction comes from a good tasting meal and might reflect meaning about the cook: "He is a good cook," or "She cares about me because she cooks my favorite meals." Revulsion is also a possibility with taste: "What! garlic in the chili again?" The taste of garlic might mean, "He doesn't care about *my* dislikes." Someone might take a sip of wine and notice: "This wine tastes watered down." To the taster, the weak taste of the wine means, "Man, is he tight with his money." We listen to taste and assign meaning.

Multisense Listening

We have discussed how we listen with our ears, our eyes, our skin, our noses, and tongues. The final aspect of holistic listening is applying multisense holistic listening to four aspects of our daily lives: time (chronemics), immediacy, power, and responsiveness.

Chronemics

Listening to time can be a visual interaction with a clock, a calendar, an appointment book, or the familiar list of things to do. Time also can be intrapersonal. For example, "When is the best time for me to do this?" "My best time to put together an outline for my report is in the morning; I can concentrate better then." Listening intrapersonally, people learn that efficient use of time will vary. Some people wake up ready to begin a project; others slowly gain momentum as the day moves along. So we listen to time as it affects us from the outside, and how it affects us within ourselves.

We listen to interpersonal or interactive time with our eyes and ears. When two people are going to have a meeting, they need to coordinate their views of time. They listen to each other's concerns and commitments about time to decide if they are going to meet in the morning, afternoon, or evening. Having determined when they are to meet, they need to decide the length of the meeting. For example, if someone is willing to meet, even though the particular time is not optimal for that person, we might assign the meaning: "She's really interested in this project and really wants to get it finished." Moreover, if someone says, "No, I can't meet with you tonight; I have to organize my CDs," you might assume that the project is not one of the higher priorities."

Listening to interactive time gives meaning about our interpersonal relationships. For example, when someone in a relationship wants to spend the best quality time in the relationship, a listener might conclude that the relationship is important to that person. However, if someone in a relationship wants to spend his or her best quality time outside the relationship with other people or projects, the listener might conclude that the relationship is not the highest priority for that individual.

Often, people cannot choose how to use their time. Jobs, family responsibilities, and various other commitments determine the use of time. However, when the use of time can be chosen, the listener can observe what choices are made and draw conclusions. Observing how people choose to use their time can give a great deal of meaning about what they value. The idea that time use indicates priorities is illustrated in the following narrative:

> When I was working on my doctorate degree twenty-five years ago, I was involved in some demanding statistical analyses. Fortunately, one of my committee members, Dr. Warren, was an expert statistician who was willing to give me some of his much sought-after time. He would meet with me on Saturday mornings and Sunday evenings, and whenever he could squeeze me in. Today, I cannot recall the specific problems we discussed, but I remember him fondly for sharing his time and helping me. By giving me his time, he was telling me that I was important, and he believed in me.

When we listen to how people choose to use their time, we can begin to understand their personal priorities. When we listen to how people respond to cultural expectations of time, we can gain insight into their willingness to conform and adapt to cultural pressures. The North American culture is time conscious. If someone arrives late for a meeting, we might assign a negative, neutral, or positive meaning: "He doesn't care about this project," or "He's not prepared for the meeting," or "He must have had car trouble," or "He's probably been busy on something more important." Also, if someone keeps us later than the expected time for a meeting to end, we might assign the meaning, "She sure is insensitive," or "Doesn't she know I have to be in the shop now?" or "She cares enough about my understanding this procedure that she's willing to go overtime to explain it," or "I respect her for not being overly concerned about the time pressure to finish the report."

Time, when listened to carefully, gives additional meaning to intrapersonal, interpersonal, and cultural communication. Intrapersonally, it might tell us when it is best to perform a certain task. Interpersonally, listening to time can give meaning to the quality of a relationship and what someone values. Culturally, time gives us insights into a person's view of cultural pressures in relation to other values and expectations.

The three final multisense aspects of holistic listening are immediacy, power, and responsiveness.[15]

Immediacy

Immediacy describes attraction, and it is measured by approach or avoidance behaviors. When listening holistically for immediacy, we are processing sense input that might indicate attraction or avoidance. For example, note the immediacy in the following statements: "He really likes that car"; "She seems very fond of that puppy"; "They seem really attracted to each other"; and "She loves her job." There are conclusions drawn from listening to sense input that indicate attraction or approach behaviors, resulting in high immediacy. The following statements indicate avoidance behaviors and low immediacy: "She certainly keeps him at arm's length"; "He hasn't been inside a church for ten years"; "He wouldn't buy one of those if it were the last one on earth."

Power

Power is the amount of control a person has in a situation. It can be physical, psychological, or both. Physical power is determined by the use of strength and skill. We can listen holistically, for example, and come to the conclusion that one team or person overpowered the other. In relationships between adults or children, physical power is sometimes used to control.

Psychological power comes from arranging and manipulating situations to gain control. It attempts to control through offering rewards or punishments that can be quite subtle. As listeners, we might assign meanings of power to a large office, a person's title—president, doctor, manager, supervisor, CEO, and the amount of space and money a person controls. A subtle message from a person with a large, expensively decorated office would be: "If you go along with my ideas and plans, I can reward you"; "If you don't go along with me, I can punish you."

Responsiveness

Responsiveness conveys the idea that someone is alert to what is happening. A responsive person is someone who is listening actively and effectively. When we listen to someone who is reacting to others quickly, adjusting eye contact appropriately, and attending in movement

and gestures, we come to the conclusion that this person is alert and aware of what is going on. This person is listening with a high level of responsiveness, and *responsiveness is the highest priority in active listening.* Conversely, when we observe someone who is not listening attentively, who does not react, whose comments do not reasonably follow the flow of ideas, and whose eye contact and gestures are not appropriately adapted to the situation, responsiveness is low.

Holistic listening requires us to combine the senses working interdependently with the effects of time, immediacy, power, and responsiveness. In fact, responsiveness is the most important aspect of listening, and when we actively listen with all available senses, we are responsive to the meanings. In fact, the title of this book, *Sensible Listening*—listening with common sense and all of our senses—reflects that such listening leads to responsive interaction—the ultimate goal of human connecting. In turn, one can obtain an accurate meaning to the messages.

••• Figure 3.2

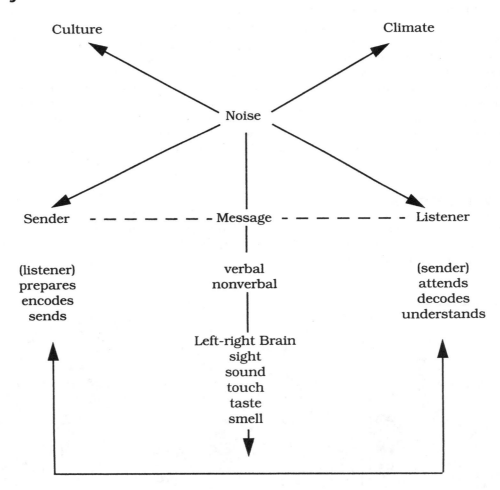

Summary

This chapter defines holistic listening as a creative process using both the right and left hemispheres of the brain and all sense input to assign meaning. It discusses the differences in right and left brain functions, noting that the left hemisphere is responsible for the logical and practical, while the right hemisphere is responsible for the creative and nonverbal.

The chapter examines the principles of holistic listening skills using all of the senses: sound, sight, touch, smell, and taste. Auditory listening includes semantics, vocalics, vocalizations, and silence. Visual listening includes proxemic, kinesics, artifacts, facial movements, and eye movements—oculesics. Haptic and olfactic listening include the meaning of touch and smell. In addition, holistic listening requires that we apply our multisense meanings to four aspects: chronemics, immediacy, power, and responsiveness. *Responsiveness* is the goal of face-to-face human interaction.

Holistic listening principles provide us with an awareness of how we use all of our senses in the listening process to make it more effective. We listen with all senses and process information with all of our abilities to gather information to form complete and detailed meanings. Therefore, if we apply holistic listening, we will achieve the success that comes with clear and complete understanding.

This chapter discusses Holistic Listening in face-to-face settings where all the senses are available. Chapter 4, *Listening and Media Communication*, examines listening with Cell and Smart Phones where visual, haptic, and olfactic messages are not typically available, and vocal volume, pitch, and quality are distorted.

Notes

1. Dave Benson, attorney, personal interview, May 7, 1987.

2. Betty Edwards, *Drawing on the Right Side of the Brain: A Course in Enhancing Creativity and Artistic Confidence* (Los Angeles: J. P. Tarcher, Inc., 1979).

3. Albert Mehrabian, *Silent Messages*, 2nd ed. (Belmont, Calif.: Wadsworth Publishing Co., 1981).

4. Stephen Michael Kosslyn, *Ghosts in the Mind's Machine: Creating and Using Images in the Brain* (New York: W. W. Norton & Company, 1983).

5. Gerard Egan, *Exercises in Training Skills: A Training Manual to Accompany the Skilled Helper* (Monterey, Calif.: Brooks/Cole Publishing Company, 1985).

6. Mark L. Knapp, *Nonverbal Communication in Human Interaction* (New York: Holt, Rinehart and Winston, 1972), p. 12.

7. Alfred G. Smith, *Communication and Culture: Readings in the Codes of Human Interaction* (New York: Holt, Rinehart and Winston, 1966).

8. Daniel Goldman, "Can You Tell When Someone Is Lying to You? *Psychology Today* (August 1982), pp. 14–23.

9. http://www.propheticevangelism.com/

10. https://aca.academy.reliaslearning.com/Interpreting-Gang-Tattoos--EL-TAT-CORR-NMGTF.aspx

11. https://www.psychologytoday.com/blog/swim-in-denial/201310/if-tattoos-could-talk

12. Jean Stockard and Miriam M. Johnson, *Sex Roles: Sex Inequality and Sex Role Development* (Englewood Cliffs, N.J.: Prentice-Hall, 1980).

13. Stephen Thayer, "Close Encounters," *Psychology Today* (March, 1988), pp. 31–36.

14. Doug Harms, *The First Thirty Seconds*, unpublished monograph, Ames, Iowa, 1985, pp. 27–31.

15. Mehrabian, pp. 43–47.

Chapter Three
Awareness Exercises

Name_____ ID#_____

Before responding, spend time paying attention to the holistic aspects of your listening and the listening of others.

1. Describe someone you know who listens holistically.

2. Describe an office that uses space to communicate.

3. Describe an instance when you assigned an inaccurate meaning to a nonverbal message.

4. Describe an instance when you assigned meaning to olfactics.

5. Describe an instance when you assigned meaning to chronemics.

6. Describe an instance when you assigned meaning to vocalics.

7. Describe an instance when you assigned meaning to haptics.

8. Describe an instance when you assigned meaning to territory.

9. Describe an instance when you assigned meaning to proxemics.

10. Describe an instance when you assigned meaning to artifacts.

11. Describe a right-brain-hemisphere activity you enjoy.

12. Describe a left-brain-hemisphere activity you enjoy.

13. Give an example of when you listened to smell for identification.

14. Give an example of when you listened to immediacy.

15. Give an example of when you listened to responsiveness.

Chapter Three
Awareness Database

Name_____ ID#_____

1. How am I at drawing pictures?

   A.　　　　B.　　　　C.　　　　D.　　　　E.
   very good　　　　　average　　　　　　poor

2. How am I at math?

   A.　　　　B.　　　　C.　　　　D.　　　　E.
   very good　　　　　average　　　　　　poor

3. When recalling a lecture or conversation, I can hear the voice of the sender in my mind.

   A.　　　　B.　　　　C.　　　　D.　　　　E.
   seldom　　　　　　　　　　　　　　　frequently

4. When recalling a lecture or conversation, I can visualize the sender in my mind.

   A.　　　　B.　　　　C.　　　　D.　　　　E.
   seldom　　　　　　　　　　　　　　　frequently

5. I find a good deal of meaning in what people are wearing.

   A.　　　　B.　　　　C.　　　　D.　　　　E.
   seldom　　　　　　　　　　　　　　　frequently

6. People tell me that I am an effective listener.

   A.　　　　B.　　　　C.　　　　D.　　　　E.
   seldom　　　　　　　　　　　　　　　frequently

7. Being on time is

   A.　　　　B.　　　　C.　　　　D.　　　　E.
   not important　　　　　　　　　　　very important

8. The appearance of someone's office tells much about that person.

   A.　　　　B.　　　　C.　　　　D.　　　　E.
   definitely　　　　　　　　　　　　　not at all

9. I find meaning in voices.

   A.　　　　B.　　　　C.　　　　D.　　　　E.
   seldom　　　　　　　　　　　　　　　frequently

10. I touch.

    A.　　　　B.　　　　C.　　　　D.　　　　E.
    seldom　　　　　　　　　　　　　　frequently

11.   I am conscious of smells.

A.   B.   C.   D.   E.
seldom   frequently

12.   I remember my dreams.

A.   B.   C.   D.   E.
seldom   frequently

13.   I am aware of power in settings.

A.   B.   C.   D.   E.
seldom   frequently

14.   I try to find quiet time for myself.

A.   B.   C.   D.   E.
seldom   frequently

15.   I listen for responsiveness.

A.   B.   C.   D.   E.
seldom   frequently

16.   I am responsive when I listen.

A.   B.   C.   D.   E.
seldom   frequently

Chapter Four

Listening and Mediated Communication

In Chapter 2, we explored the four fundamental elements of communication: Sender, message, listener, and feedback. We also described three intervening variables: climate, culture, and noise. Chapter 3 extended the topic by discussing nonverbal messages from sight, sound, touch, taste, and smell as we listen to them in Face-To-Face settings. In this chapter we'll first explore the nonverbal changes—and the reasons for those changes—that occur when we switch from Face-To-Face Communication to Media Communication, and second we'll discuss some listening adaptations to optimize listening while using the cell phones.

Throughout the chapter "FTF" stands for "Face-To-Face Communication," and "MC" stands for "Media Communication with any kind of cell phone"—which 91 percent of adults use daily for voice and text communication.[1]

Nonverbal Changes When Moving from FTF to MC

Picture a situation where you're visiting with five friends in a restaurant. The meal is served, and you're talking back and forth about the day's happenings. A couple of them had been working, one at a training session, and two had taken a short canoe trip on a local river. Stories are told, some jokes go around, and there's general good-natured chatter. You listen to the words, the smiles, the gestures, the pats on the back, the tone of the jokes, the pauses, the smell of the buffalo wings, and, of course the taste of the food. In fact, someone mentions there's so much going on, it's hard to take everything in.

Toward the end of the meal, one of the folks gets a text from a friend who couldn't make it to the restaurant but will be able to make it next time. She takes the time to disengage from the group and texts back, "OK," and then continues visiting. You're in a FTF setting where all your senses are at work listening to the whole scene. The listening is responsive and complete, and even a bit too much sometimes.

When you're home later that evening, one of the friends gives you a call to tell you about a funny incident that happened on the canoe trip that he forgot to tell at dinner. He's an exciting and animated storyteller, and you want to hear the story.

In this Media Phone setting, he's relating the incident, and you wish you were with him so you could take in his gestures, and all the vocal paralanguage—the volume variations, the pitch changes, the quality of his unique voice. The story is great, and you get the details of the incident, but the visual part is lost, and the subtle voice variations are minimized and sometimes missing in this phone conversation.

From these descriptions of the dinner and the later phone call, we see the major differences between FTF and MC: In the FTF restaurant setting all participants are together where they have access to all the senses—sound, sight, smell, touch, taste, and all those sense messages can become a bit overwhelming. In the MC setting, participants can communicate remotely, but the trade-off for the distance between them is the loss of the touch, smell, and taste senses, leaving the listener with only voice and visual texts; moreover, the phone voice quality is distorted.

Before we begin a further examination of Media's effects on nonverbal messages, some background of these wireless text and voice technologies will help us understand and appreciate their advantages and limitations.

Wireless Communication Development: Text

"Wireless Telegraphy," which was primarily developed by Guglielmo Marconi in the late 1800s, was the beginning of today's text communication. Before Marconi's wireless radio, text messages were sent and received by Morse code from fixed stations that were connected by cables.[2] Local folks would come to the telegraph station to send and pick up messages, and often telegraph employees would hand-deliver messages to customers. The process was burdensome by today's standards, but a hell of a lot faster than sending letters by stagecoach or ship.

Now, with wireless technology, these visual texts could be sent and received to and from roaming stations. Logically, the shipping industry was intensely supportive of this wireless texting, which kept ships communicating anywhere. In fact, shipping's wide use of wireless communication led to the first slang text anagram: the coded letters, "SOS"—Save Our Ship—became the universal emergency signal used for all types of emergencies. Today, a ship in trouble might text: "SOS"/"OMG."

Texting has become faster and remarkably efficient since Marconi's time, but the basics are the same. Texts are efficient, short, non-voiced, visual messages using letters keyed onto phone screens. They are convenient and extremely useful because they shorten talk time by getting right to the point, and messages can be stored in the "in box" for later reviewing.

Wireless Communication Development: Voice

By the late 1800s texting was established as viable wireless media. Wireless voice media was close behind, and in 1900 Reginald Fessenden accomplished the first wireless voice transmission. On December 23, while working for the Weather Service, he was able to transmit: "One-two-three-four, is it snowing where you are . . . ?" from an island in the Potomac River to a colleague a mile away. Now, the basics were in place for wireless text and voice media communication that would eventually affect almost every aspect of people's lives worldwide.[3]

Over a hundred years later, wireless cells have made amazing progress, having spanned the world and outer space. The voice quality is acceptable, but still lacking the fidelity of FTF. In fact, we use cell/smartphones so often, we forget what we're giving up in voice fidelity. Even our grandma's old wall phone, and the early analog cells had much better voice quality. And none of them—even the best—can offer the audio fidelity of FTF.

The voices coming from the cell can usually supply us with recognizable words that carry some meaning for us, but the channels that carry innuendo and deeper, more subtle human content are limited and often distorted. Reviews of cells highlight a number of variables that influence fidelity, and two of the major ones are: (1) the small size of the phone and (2) the diverse message routes taken from phone to phone.[4]

Phone Size—As smartphones keep getting smaller and smaller, in addition to the microphone and speaker, they become more packed with a host of goodies that have nothing to do with talking to someone—they take pictures, send and receive texts, scroll the Internet, play music, direct us to locations, wake us up, remind us of appointments, and so on. All the hardware and processing involved in these functions take up space and erode the quality of talking and listening. Not surprisingly, basic flip phones do have somewhat better voice fidelity—far from perfect—but measurably better than the multifunction smartphones.[5]

Message Routes—Messages don't go directly from phone to phone; they are broken into tiny bits and piggybacked on microwaves, and then like tiny puzzle pieces put back together in the receiving phone. In-between, these message bits hop from cell tower to cell tower, sometimes through weather sunspot distortions, bouncing into windmills, trees, buildings, and mountains. In addition, they get split apart on the trip, and these different pieces reach the receiving phone at slightly different times resulting in that annoying cell echo. As one reviewer concludes: "It's miraculous that voice calls sound as clear as they do." ". . . the bottom line is, don't expect much, and be thankful for what you've got."[6]

Wireless voice communication grew from texting technology, and today cell phones combine both text and voice communication. Cells are totally portable: we can take them anywhere, and this can create some awkward social challenges as well as some dangerous visual and attention distractions when driving.

MC and Social Challenges

Our cells go along with us like little friends. Sometimes we dress them in colored covers, change their voice tones, and pamper them with screen diapers to keep them clean and dry. They've become part of our identity—lose it or leave it at home, and we can't rest until we retrieve it.

This strong attachment we have is generally good—our cell is a tool to keep us connected with people. In many settings the cell is our healthy priority for communicating across distances to make schedules, gain information, and maintain relationships.

The challenge comes when we need to prioritize FTF and MC. The motivation to develop wireless communication was to create an FTF-like technology to communicate from any distance. Now, having cells with us most of the time, we have some important listening choices when we're around other people.

It's tough to prioritize. The current theme of this chapter—actually, the entire text—is that FTF has the potential for the most rewarding listening. It follows, then, that when people are together, they need to consider carefully their choices to use media or not use it.

If folks have gathered for a social event—a wedding or movie—the choice is clear: silence the phone. If they gather for a meeting or a visit, they should attend with all senses, to ensure a rewarding connection with each other.

As one writer put it: "Of course, I am not anti-technology and am in awe of the iPhone just like the next gadget freak. But when my friend chooses to tap on his iPhone while we are out having dinner, I feel like I'm having dinner for three: me, him, and the iPhone. We often joke about his techno-habit and how hard it is to break, but the joke gets old when it becomes reality."[7]

Source: From "How Cell Phones Are Killing Face-to-Face Interactions" by Mark Glaser, *Mediashift,* October 22, 2007.

MC and Driving

Studies have shown that cell phones cause accidents by diverting our visual attention from the road. Here's what happens: We look around to find the phone—it's usually in the cupholder but not always—while we're looking, we notice the thermostat, and since we're a little chilly, we turn the heat up; we find the phone and enter a number; then we talk and browse a bit, and end the call. As we're putting the phone away, we accidently drop it on the passenger side floor. Five minutes later, we get a call—there's that feeling of urgency . . . "Where's the phone?! Can I unbuckle and reach it?"

All these tasks significantly increase the percentage of time we take our eyes off the forward roadway, and a little time can go a long way. The time it takes to answer the phone when it's in the cupholder is about 4.6 seconds; at 56 miles-per-hour we've gone the length of a football field—a lot could happen.[8]

Studies related to talking on a cell phone and driving safety are mixed: one study concluded that the sole act of talking was not associated with an increased safety risk; rather, all the associated maneuvering that accompanies the talking is the culprit. Other findings linked negative effects with MC and driving: poor speed maintenance, reduction in the area of visually scanning, slower reactions to unexpected events, and increases in stoplight violations.

Interestingly, some evidence found that regularly talking on the phone increases alertness when driving in boring, monotonous conditions.[9] (So talking in rural Nebraska or southern Texas might be allowed.)

It is important when driving to focus our listening—mainly with our eyes—on the driving situation—the road ahead, rear and side mirrors, flashing lights, warning signs, lane markers, traffic, and so on. Visual input is the priority.

An FTF–MC Case Study

A general summary of what we've covered so far about FTF and MC is this: In the FTF setting all senses are available within limited distance, and, consequently, FTF gives us the potential for a complete listening experience. The MC setting connects at any distance, but the messages suffer from nonverbal losses and distortions.

The case study below takes us on a geographical and relational journey that will highlight and enrich the discussion of these FTF and MC differences. As we listen with our eyes to this story, notice the benefits, the shortcomings, the adaptations, the dangers, the excitement, and sadness as they are influenced by FTF and MC. When it's finished, we'll expand on some of the key issues as they relate to nonverbal changes and adaptations as Lee and Andrea switch back and forth between FTF and MC.

The case was created from the journal of Dr. Lee, a thirty-five-year-old physician who recently completed training on "Listening to Patients' Concerns—in the Office or on the Phone." He ties in this listening training with experiences a year before he entered medical school. He titled it:

Staying Connected

Ohio to Omaha

I had driven my motorcycle from Dayton, OH, to Omaha to meet-up with an old buddy, Chris, who was starting a new business and wanted me to join in. Omaha was new to me, and the only people I knew there were Chris and his wife.

But after socializing in the city a couple months, I met Andrea, and we began to date. Well, one thing led to another, and after about a half-year, we moved in together. The relationship was pretty good for about six months, but then it was noticeably falling apart. We'd get along for short periods; then something would aggravate one of us, and arguments would take over. This running hot and cold life-style began to wear on us more and more, and by this time we'd been together for over a year, and we had basically built all the trappings of a home together.

All our stuff was in the apartment, and we finally realized we were both overwhelmed—we both had new jobs, a new residence, and, of course a relatively new relationship. Not only were we trying to resolve our own problems, but her father also became involved as well as her sister. It was just too much. We loved each other, but the atmosphere had become really toxic, and we needed some time and space. We tried explaining our concerns to each other, but all the talk erupted into more drama and anger. I hoped after things cooled off we could reconnect and hopefully agree on a solution to our relationship troubles.

Omaha to Ohio

Not knowing how to solve our problems, I decided to take a break to figure things out. So I sold my cycle, packed what I could fit in a backpack and caught a flight back to Dayton. Andrea was really pissed, and looking back, she had every right to be—I was like a little kid running home. I had abandoned her, with no real plan in mind, so she threatened to get rid of my belongings and move to a new place. My goal at this point was to get our relationship to where we could speak calmly and take charge of our own belongings—she was basically holding my stuff (clothes, electronics, computer, etc.) hostage, and I was holding our future hostage.

Here I was 750 miles from her trying to do hostage negotiation for my stuff, and maybe repair our relationship. She was angry and resentful, and I was too, but I was also sad and missed her, and I'm sure she missed me, too. We cared deeply for each other, but it just wasn't working.

Believe me, diplomacy from this distance is really difficult, but it sure wasn't getting better when I was with her, either. Now I was in Ohio; she was in Omaha, and she wouldn't answer the phone. I would email, text, and post on Facebook.

After many, many tries, she did answer the phone, and after numerous calls, I thought maybe we were at the point of beginning to discuss getting my belongings back. I say "maybe" because I didn't know where we really agreed or disagreed.

Often our phone conversations left me wondering if she was softly laughing, crying, or being sarcastic, and I couldn't catch those little inflections that would hint of sadness, hope, frustration, impatience, or anger. And she was having similar confusions—accusing me of not paying attention to her, mocking her, or getting impatient.

Since we weren't physically together where we could get all the nonverbal cues, we tried to overcome the limits of phoning by asking each other to state simply how the other was feeling. She would say, "I can't tell if you're impatient now. Are you?" Sometimes I could pause, take a breath, and acknowledge, "Yes, I'm frustrated. This isn't getting us anywhere."

Other times, I'd lie. It was unintentional; it just came out: "No, I'm good. Go ahead." Had we been in the same room, she'd have known instantly I was lying.

Another thing we'd try was to ask for repetition or rephrasing for clarity. I remember one time saying, "I really hoped we could get back together."

She came back with: "I can't read you. Was the 'hoped' in past tense? The hope is gone, then? Or is the hope for our relationship still there?"

I think I had been intentionally vague about our future together. "I'm not sure," went into the phone.

"I'm not either," came from her.

These strategies of questioning, paraphrasing, and repeating gave us some insights into where we were in this partnership, and they really did help us understand many of our issues. And we became aware that we could talk more objectively without some of the emotional overtones. Knowing where we stood gave us enough common ground to keep connected. I even began to think about planning a face-to-face visit, to discuss more emotionally-charged concerns.

Even though we were communicating better, something happened that undid some of the progress we had made: Since I was still a little worried that meeting directly might bring us to where we were when I went back to Ohio, I tried to put together a practical plan to get my belongings back. I thought maybe once that was settled, we could focus on our relationship.

My plan was to send her enough money so she could box up my stuff and UPS it back to me. When I mentioned this plan to her, her message back to me was clear—I think I could have heard her without a phone—and she told me what I could do with that idea. As I look back on her strong reaction, I can see it really made sense—she knew we had to meet face-to-face to reach some decisions about us, and she reasonably saw mailing my belongings as a possible way to avoid a live meeting.

Well, at this point I was confused and needed to visit with someone just to discuss my situation. I was pretty close to my cousin, Jemin, and she lived about a half-hour from Dayton. I gave her a call and we planned to meet at a coffee shop. It was a quiet place, and we met mid-morning when it wasn't busy.

Jemin is a couple years older than I, and had just been promoted as head buyer at a clothing retailer. She was busy but agreed to meet. We met; it was really great to see her, and after the usual chatter about relatives and general "catching up" stuff, I began to unfold my situation. Jemin listened as I poured out my story.

Then her phone chimed, letting her know she had a text. She guiltily glanced at the phone:

"Sorry, Lee, I need to respond to this."

She read and sent back a fairly long text.

"We just ordered from an Italian clothing source, and one of the items isn't available. We need it for the spring line-up."

"Oh, sure," I affirmed. "Have to stay on top of it."

"Tell me more about Andrea."

"Well, she's lived in Omaha all her life; has a degree in Civil Engineering, and has worked for two years with a mid-size construction outfit. She enjoys her work and and . . . "

Chime—Jemin's phone. Another text break—about five minutes.

Our conversation was punctuated with her texts and responses for about an hour, and we both agreed this probably wasn't a good time for our conversation. We were glad to be together, but our mind traffic patterns were going in different directions: Jemin was physically with me; mentally at work. I needed her to be here for me, and I was a little resentful that she would drive to meet me but not shut off her phone for an hour.

Even though we wanted to visit more, Jemin's job was a priority, and her back-and-forth texting wasn't satisfactory for either of us, so we ended our visit. One conclusion we did reach, however, was that I should keep trying to connect with Andrea by whatever means possible.

Ohio to Omaha

After days of these attempted negotiations with Andrea, I came to the conclusion that media communication—cell phone, text—wasn't going to cut it, so I rented a car and headed west to Omaha. I only had the car for two days, so in those forty-eight hours I had to travel round-trip and negotiate and figure out the state of our relationship—hopefully with the option of getting back together later—and get my stuff in the car.

While on the road, I texted her so she knew where I was, and we could exchange information about the weather, and generally how the trip was going. It was mostly informational stuff, but it did keep us in contact, and she knew my driving conditions, time of arrival, but not how nervous I was about the whole meeting: texting gave us zero information about where the hell the other was emotionally, but that was okay—I'd find about that later.

Text and talk did let me know she was still there and apparently hadn't trashed my stuff. (We didn't talk about this specifically, but our conversations were neutral and responsive, and her not mentioning it was a good sign.) Once we could talk in person, we would have some chance to work things out, because it seemed weeks of phoning, and texting had at least calmed us emotionally.

My arrival back in Omaha after communicating only by phone and text for a month came to a major transition when she opened the apartment door, and we met face-to-face. The days of phoning and texting reminded me of the times I'd stand on the beach in Hawaii looking into the water—interesting and informative but limited, removed, and safe. Opening the apartment door and seeing Andrea and our apartment was like jumping in the water and experiencing all the colors and multiple forms of life—and the vulnerability, threats, and need for vigilance.

We settled in and visited. We consciously and unconsciously listened to the paralanguage of all the subtle nuances of vocal tone, volume, pitch, pauses, facial and eye movements, body positions/gestures, touch, smells. With all these channels available we were able to listen and interpret messages.

After some awkward moments over a couple hours, we slowly came to realize a sad reality about our relationship—it was over. Even though our actual words never said it, all the overtones of this face-to-face visit came together to confirm where we were as a couple, and the physical removal of my stuff became a tangible symbol of our emotional removal from each other.

Omaha to Ohio

I was back on the road the next morning. It was really difficult, but at least we had been able to work out a plan to retrieve my stuff, understanding that we would continue communicating whenever appropriate.

With all this fresh on my mind, the driving time back to Akron let my thinking wander and finally organize around Andrea and our relationship, and on media's role in the whole experience—and I mean the whole experience, because I believe media damn near killed me near Chicago. Here's what happened:

Heavy rain started about a hundred miles west of Chicago, and it was twilight and rainy when I got just south of Chicago. Interstate 80 had new blacktop with no lane-paint or markings, and traffic had slowed, being funneled from four lanes to two. Someone had pulled on the right shoulder, and the car in front of me stopped suddenly to let that person back onto the highway.

I stopped just short, glanced into the rearview mirror and saw headlights about seventy-five yards behind me coming right at the back of my car! I didn't have time to do anything, and I figured that car was going 45–50 miles per hour. When he was not more than ten or fifteen feet from me, he swerved left—missing me by about two feet—into the left lane; then skidded, hydroplaning on the wet surface and spinning almost a hundred and eighty degrees, smashing the right front fender on the heavy concrete barrier which separated the eastbound traffic from westbound.

Now, headed at an angle toward me, he slid forty or fifty feet before stopping with his driver side window about a foot from my window. I looked directly at him slumped over the bloody steering wheel, his body sponged-in with his air bag. I could easily see every detail, and the one sight I'll never forget was his right arm bent over the top of his head almost touching the windshield, his bloody hand holding a smartphone which was trapped between it and the windshield.

If he had he hit me at that speed, I would have been crushed between him and the car in front of me—severe injury, maybe death. The low light, the rain, and the unmarked lanes made driving tricky, but they didn't cause this accident—there were numerous warnings and flashers to alert drivers. I'm convinced this accident resulted from driver inattention, probably while texting. Luckily, he looked up from his phone in time to swerve away from me. He was badly injured, but I don't know how badly. As the ambulance came, I pulled ahead and continued east.

I was back in Akron by midnight.

Final Thoughts

I have to remember the crucial role media played in Andrea's and my story. After face-to-face discussions spiraled into unmanageable arguments, media gave us the chance to look at our relationship from a distance, and we had private time with the option to phone or text. After my flight back to Akron, we probably would have had a much harder time finding out where we were as a couple if we couldn't toggle between voice and text.

Not only did media keep us communicating, but phoning and texting also provided a clear comparison and contrast between limited and full sense listening. Actually the sense and fidelity limitations of media were helpful sometimes because they were unable to transmit nonverbal cues that might be upsetting or misunderstood, and allowed us to focus on more objective information.

Media's sense limits and low fidelity kept us from revealing emotions that were sometimes better off not being expressed at the time. They kept reactions at a minimum, and I would welcome the fact that we could listen with limited senses even though I knew I wasn't listening to the entire message.

There were times, however, when we needed more vocal and visual nonverbal cues, and sometimes when we tried to paraphrase and repeat for clarity, we could understand the issues, but we felt empty of the feelings about it. In the final run, we needed all of our senses to get a complete reading of our situation; the only way to get that was being present with each other.

When I came back to Omaha and opened the apartment door, the full spectrum of listening senses enveloped me. Our communicating went from mainly voice and text to complete holistic listening, and we were ready and able to read the whole situation and face the reality of where we were. Certainly, we could have broken-up over phone calls or text messages, but that would have robbed us of the full human experience—it would have been a hollow, cold, incomplete ending, like shutting an outside light off with the flip of an inside switch.

I think relationships are substantially affected by transitioning from being together to being apart. Together, we get to know each other at many possible levels. Apart, we listen to ourselves and judge if the knowledge we have gained when together is meeting personal goals. If so, we make adjustments and stay in the relationship. If we question whether personal goals are being met, we try different strategies; if goals are clearly not being met, we begin to pull away.

Whatever the decision—stay, experiment with new strategies, pull away—the judgment is based on how we function when we're together. Even at its best, media cannot replace being present with another human being. I guess that's why the big moment with online dating is the actual face-to-face meeting of the individuals—it can either make or break all the media build-up to that moment.

As I learned when studying listening, "It's easier and simpler to put a person on the moon than to figure out human relationships. The moon shots are done with textbook Newtonian physics and the tools of applied technology. But the only manuals for figuring out people are the ones about listening."

Final Step: Applying the Theory

Hopefully, the Case Study was interesting, and you could identify the communication limits in the FTF and MC settings as Andrea and Lee worked through their relationship. The Case Study is included to connect FTF and MC theory with a real-life happening to reach three goals: the first goal is to recognize the FTF and MC situations, sense limits, and strategies; next is to identify some similar events, situations, and interactions as they have occurred in your own life; last—and this is the ultimate learning goal—to apply your knowledge of FTF and MC directly in your own life.

Go through these steps with as many of the scenes in the story as you can find. Often, Lee and Andrea provide strategies that they've worked out through their experiences. Then use the steps with scenes from your own life that will help you optimize your MC listening.

Of the many possible scenes that involve FTF or MC, we'll go through the steps using the scene where Lee meets his cousin, Jemin:

Step 1: Recognize the FTF and MC situations, limits, and strategies.

Jemin listened as I poured out my story.

Then her phone chimed, letting her know she had a text. She guiltily glanced at the phone:

"Sorry, Lee, I need to respond to this."

She read and sent back a fairly long text.

"We just ordered from an Italian clothing source, and one of the items isn't available. We need it for the spring line-up."

"Oh, sure," I affirmed. "Have to stay on top of it."

"Tell me more about Andrea."

"Well, she's lived in Omaha all her life; has a degree in Civil Engineering, and has worked for two years with a mid-size construction outfit. She enjoys her work and and . . ."

Chime—Jemin's phone. Another text break—about five minutes.

Lee grasped the importance of these texts, but he was ". . . a little resentful that she would drive to meet me but not shut off her phone for an hour."

The word "resentful" might indicate a feeling of emotional distance from Jemin as a result of the text interruptions.

Remembering the incident, Lee would remember to quiet his cell in a similar situation.

Step 2: Identify some similar events, situations, and interactions as they have occurred in your own life.

Last Tuesday, I was meeting with a carpenter about putting some hardwood flooring in my office. We were discussing the measurements, type of wood, cost per board foot, and installation. Every few minutes, he'd get a text, turn his back to me and text back. I've known him for years, and I told him to either shut the thing off or put it in his truck until we were finished. He put it in the truck, and we finished.

Step 3: Apply your knowledge of FTF and MC directly in your own life.

Tomorrow I'm meeting with a friend whose brother just died. He probably just wants to talk and share memories and express his feelings. I'll meet him at 11:00; my phone will be off.

Summary

Most of us have cell phones; we take them for granted—and we should: they're portable, dependable, and they can do what FTF can't—they can regularly connect us to anyone, anywhere. However, MC's trade-off for long distance performance is noticed in lowered sense involvement and poor voice fidelity.

This chapter explores listening in FTF and MC settings and uses a Case Study to connect the theory with real situations. Moreover, it suggests a three-step process to help optimize MC listening in our lives.

Notes

1. http://www.pewresearch.org/fact-tank/2013/06/06/cell-phone-ownership-hits-91-of-adults/

2. Erik Larson, *Thunderstruck* (New York: Crown Publishers, 1960).

3. http://transition.fcc.gov/omd/history/radio/ideas.html

4. http://www.consumerreports.org/cro/news/2014/05/3-reasons-voice-quality-on-smart-phones-still-sucks/index.htm

5. http://www.npr.org/templates/story/story.php?storyId=122018496

6. http://www.consumerreports.org/cro/news/2014/05/3-reasons-voice-quality-on-smart-phones-still-sucks/index.htm

7. http://www.pbs.org/mediashift/2007/10/how-cell-phones-are-killing-face-to-face-interactions295/

8. http://www.distraction.gov/download/81175.pdf, p.5

9. *Ibid.* pp. 4, 6.

Recommended Reading

"Did a Text Kill My Brother?" *The New York Times*, February 15, 2015.
    http://www.nytimes.com/2015/02/15/opinion/sunday/did-a-text-kill-my-brother.html?_r=0

Chapter Four
Awareness Exercises

Name_____   ID#_____

1. Use your phone log to add-up the number of voice calls and texts you've sent and received on an average day and record the numbers below.

   Voice calls dialed_____

   Voice calls received_____

   Texts sent_____

   Texts received_____

2. Describe a time when you were confined to MC, but felt FTF would be more effective.

3. Describe a FTF setting where communication would be more effective in a MC setting.

4. Describe a FTF setting where MC disrupted the communication.

5. Describe a setting where MC created a real or potential hazard.

Chapter Four
Awareness Database

Name_____   ID#_____

1. I turn my phone off before entering a casual FTF setting_____% of the time.

    A. Never   B. 25   C. 50   D. 75   E. Almost always

2. I turn my phone off before entering a more formal FTF setting—example: interview, lecture, conference_____% of the time.

    A. Never   B. 25   C. 50   D. 75   E. Always

3. I text when the car is stopped_____% of the time.

    A. Never   B. 25   C. 50   D. 75   E. Whenever I need to

4. I text when the car is moving_____% of the time.

    A. Never   B. 25   C. 50   D. 75   E. Whenever I need to

5. I talk on the phone when the car is stopped_____% of the time.

    A. Never   B. 25   C. 50   D. 75   E. Whenever I need to

6. I talk on the phone when the car is moving _____% of the time.

    A. Never   B. 25   C. 50   D. 75   E. Whenever I need to

7. I have "hands off" phone capability in my car (Bluetooth, headset).

    A. Yes   B. No

Chapter Five

Listening to Communication Movement

This chapter focuses on *communication movement,** which is the energy or force behind the message. Communication Movement is part of every interaction, but more apparent in face-to-face settings where more senses are being used. Nevertheless, whether on the cell or in person, it adds substantial meaning to the message. This chapter will first explain the general idea of communication movement; second, define and explain the five communication moves, and third, relate movement to holistic listening.

Communication Movement

If we try to communicate with someone who is unconscious, or in a deep sleep, we quickly realize that movement is necessary for a response. If the unconscious person is capable of even slight movement, we can listen and assign some meaning to the movement. The smallest muscular twitch can give some cue, some signal that could be the basis for interaction. For example, there are stories where a paralyzed person's movement is so limited that all the person can do is blink once for yes and twice for no in response to questions. In this situation, some minimal communication can take place. However, where there is *no* movement, there is no meaningful interaction. Consequently, a reasonable conclusion is that movement is required for interacting with others.

The idea that human behavior is predicated on some kind of muscular movement cannot be overemphasized, because *listening to movement gives significant meaning to the total message.* People will use the phrase "make some moves on someone," to indicate they are going to attempt to relate to someone by *moving on* or *moving toward* that person.

The idea that communication is anchored in movement becomes evident when we follow the evolution of behavior from infancy to adulthood. A newborn infant moves randomly, only slowly learning to bring muscles under control. Kicking, squirming, and grabbing evolve from reflexive to purposeful movements. The baby learns that certain movements help in picking up desired objects or in knocking down blocks or in getting a cracker. As we all know, movement of vocal muscles comes early, as well. At first cries may simply register general discomfort, but by degrees they soon indicate specific needs: food, diaper change, attention. Through the use of her arms and voice, the baby discovers a world to move on and a world which moves on her.

As children, we begin to learn to move more effectively as social beings. That growth continues through adulthood, where we learn more sophisticated behaviors that are based upon both physical and vocal moves.

As this discussion points out, in early life, movement is random. Later, it becomes purposeful, and it is used to communicate goals and desires. As we grow to maturity, a variety of verbal substitutes is developed to replace some of the physical movements used in infancy. Among these substitutes are words. As babies, we might throw a rattle out of the playpen for attention, but as adults, we would simple say, "Please come here for a minute." The goal would be the same. With maturity, we substitute words for gestures or touches.

As adults, we communicate with infants through physical movement, which is the only language babies understand. The seven-month-old might get a touch on the hand for pulling an electrical plug; the two-year-old might be *told* not to touch it. In the latter case, the words are a verbal substitute for the touch on the hand.

By replacing words for physical movement, we reach goals. In effect, words function as physical muscular moves, but words are more efficient. Taking an example to a ridiculous extreme, picture a father wanting his daughter to drive the car into the garage. He could say, "Please put the car away." This is more efficient than taking her hand and leading her to the front door, taking her to the car, opening the door, ushering her into the car, and finally getting her to drive the car into the garage. Saying the words gets the same results with much less energy. Yet in saying, "Please put the car away," the father is efficiently moving on her. It is apparent, then, that speech is a form of movement: speech enables people to move on others, prompting them to change and to behave in a certain way. Speech is movement in our interactions.

We listen to silent moves in many situations: athletic events, music performances, art, drama, and just watching people in various settings. An example where silent moving occurs can be seen at some auctions where the bidders substitute subtle physical moves for verbal ones: a tug at an ear, a nod, a finger at the forehead. A verbal move, "I'll bid $200," could be used, but in this case, silent moves are used instead.

So, verbal and nonverbal messages grow from movement. Early in life the movement is random and unmeaningful, but later it becomes goal oriented.[1]

Definition of Communication Moves

Communication movement, then, is inherent in the communication process. Consequently, awareness of the five basic move categories—place, push, pause, please, and pull—will lead to a more complete understanding of the message.

The Place Move

The place move places ideas, facts, or feelings in front of the listener. It is usually a noncontroversial move, and the goal in placing is to inform, describe, explain, and add to the listener's understanding. Below are some examples of place moves that might be made during a conversation. In the place move pairs, the first is placing of an idea or fact; the second is placing a feeling.

Place

Idea or fact—"Maybe I'll go fishing later this week."
"A bolt on the landing gear of the tow plane is broken."

Feeling—"I'm *delighted* with the new procedure."
"I am *angry* because John ignored my suggestion."

Just as with physical objects, facts and feeling can be placed near or far from us. Imagine yourself as the listener, and notice the removed, distant nature of these place moves:

Distant Place

Idea or fact—"I think I'll wax the car this weekend."
"The low temperature a year ago was 41."

Feeling—"I was *upset* because women couldn't be in marching band when I was in college."

Again, as a listener, take note of the closeness of these place moves:

Close Place

Idea or fact—"I started a new job today."
"We shipped the complete order to your warehouse this morning."

Feeling—"I'm *confused* about the changes in procedure that came down from your department."
"Our classmate Gretchen loves her new apartment."

Of course, communication movement is not confined to conversations. It exists in all settings, including speeches. Listen to the repeated place moves of fact and belief at the beginning of this speech titled "Restructuring America: Focus on the Core Business." Notice that each sentence is a place move.

> My talk today is about Corporate America's problems and what I see as solutions to those problems. Corporate America is in the middle of a major overhaul that is long overdue.
>
> We are seeing a transformation of Corporate America. We're seeing a new focus now that's where it should have been years ago. It's a focus on results, where size becomes meaningless. The emphasis is on creating value instead of empires.
>
> Corporate America's problems started soon after World War II with the emergence of professional managers. The professional manager was trained to minimize the risk and maximize the upside.[2]

Place moves do not ask or demand; rather, the sender is objectively placing facts or feelings in front of the listener.

The Push Move
. . . .

The Push move is just that—an attempt to exert force or pressure on the listener. Instead of physically pushing, the sender puts directional energy behind words and nonverbal symbols. Push moves are muscling, compelling, pressuring, or insisting. In the following examples, compare the dynamic energy of the push move with the calm static feeling of the place move:

Push—"Okay, get out on that floor and play the second half like you did when you beat Iowa!"

Place—"We have fifteen minutes of game time left."

Push—"Please shut the door."

Place—"The wind is blowing all the papers off my desk."

Push—"Drop everything, and put all your people on this project."

Place—"We're two days late on this shipment."

Push—"Get out of bed!"

Place—"It's already 7:30."

Push—"Let's try to beat last quarter's excellent record."

Place—"I see that our productivity is on the rise."

Push—"You start getting here on time, or you're OUT!"

Place—"I notice you've been late the last five days."

Push—"Stop, or I'll shoot!"

Place—"I'm pointing a loaded pistol at you."

Push—"Would you please come here?"

Place—"I'd feel better if we could discuss this."

Push—"Give me a raise."

Place—"I feel unappreciated when I don't get a salary increase."

There is a definite feeling of directional force in the push move when compared to the place move, and not only can we push people in a lateral direction—"Check the mail," or "Preflight the plane," but we can also push upward or downward. An upward push affirms someone; it is a type of please move. It encourages: "Keep up the good work!" "Complete that last page, and we'll be finished."

A downward push is discouraging and can lower self-esteem: "Can't you come up with anything better than that?" "Any third grader could solve that problem."

To help understand the directional force of the push move in a speech, we turn to the speech cited earlier, "Restructuring America: Focus on the Core Business." Recall that in the introduction, the speaker used mainly place moves. Now, near the end of the speech, he moves away from the place moves and starts pushing for action. Notice his plan—push and then place the direction he wants his listeners to take.

Let's go back to the transformation we are witnessing in Corporate America [Push]. There's a group that's fighting change, and they're being left at the station. This crowd is easy to identify [Place moves]. Watch for them in your proxy material [Push]. They have very little stock. They have a big salary, they have a big bonus and they have a big mouth about the many "constituencies" of the corporation [Place]. They make a lot of speeches about short-term and long-term strategies [Place].[3]

The Pause Move

The pause move is actually no movement in relation to the listener. The pause is *intentionally* being unaware, ignoring, not responding, not reacting, letting things go, or not consulting. Here are some pause examples:

Pause—You are conversing with a co-worker about a job-related subject, when he makes an untrue and inappropriate comment about one of the secretaries. You pause the comment by continuing the discussion, so you can reach your initial goal—agreement on the job-related subject.

Pause—You are passing a string of traffic on the Interstate, and another driver moves up quickly and follows you closely. Your goal is to pass comfortably and get into the right-hand lane, so you pause the car behind and continue passing at your chosen speed.

Pause—You are involved in a discussion with three other people. One of them keeps interrupting one of the other speakers. You pause the interrupter by keeping your attention focused on the interrupted speaker. Your goal is to give an equal chance for everyone to talk.

Pause—In your office you are having an important discussion with your oldest daughter, a college freshman. Your phone rings; you pause the phone caller by shutting off the ringer, and continue toward your goal of working out a solution to her problem.

Pause—You are a department manager responsible for making a decision that will greatly affect nine of your people. Your goal is to get the decision finalized fast, so you pause discussing it with the nine and make the decision quickly by yourself.

We have discussed the three basic communication moves: place, push, and pause. The intent of the place is to inform by placing fact or feeling close or distant from the listener. The intent of the push is to energize the listener to act, agree, or conform. The intent of the pause is to ignore and avoid reacting. Two other moves, the please and pull, are subcategories of place, push, and pause.

The Please Move

The please move is often a subcategory of the place move. It is an idea, fact, or feeling that is positive or helpful to the listener. It can be a compliment, an affirmation, sharing, understanding, showing friendship, listening, or making things easier. The please move attempts to establish a positive connect between the sender and the listener. Below are some please moves that are subcategories of place moves:

Please (place)

Idea or fact—"I want to work on this project together."

"All indications show that you did an excellent job."

"Could I help you carry your groceries into the house?"

Please (place)

Feeling—"I feel confident that you can handle the plane by yourself now."

"I was sorry to hear that your uncle died."

"It gives me confidence to know that you're back there."

The please move can also be a subcategory of the push move when it directs that listener toward a desired goal, or it pushes upward in a friendly manner:

Please (push)

"Keep up the good work!"

"Let's show them what *we* can do."

The please move can be a subcategory of the pause move. Pausing something that might be embarrassing or uncomfortable is a please move:

Please (pause)

Someone ignores (pauses) the fact that I'm wearing braces.

Someone ignores (pauses) the fact that I'm a half-hour late.

As with any of the moves, the please move is not limited to conversation. Listen to the please moves at the beginning of this speech, "The Truth About Savings and Loan Institutions." One can almost feel the sender patting the listeners on the back for their good work.

> As I look around this room this afternoon I see people who have devoted their working lives to the savings and loan business—successful managers who can be proud that, day in and day out, they deliver on the promise that is the savings institutions charter: To make it possible for American families to realize the dream of home ownership.
>
> Ours is a worthy, necessary pursuit and one that has made this nation the best-housed of any in the world.[4]

The Pull Move

The pull move is a special type of place or pause move. It is a move that arouses curiosity and attracts the listener. A pull move might be offering a reward, inducing, hinting, seeking elaboration.

Pull

(Place/Idea or fact)—"I've been thinking . . ."
(The listener is pulled in: ". . . About what?")

"I have a plan that might get us out of this mess."
(The listener is pulled in: "Let's hear it.")

"Number two engine is really acting strange."
(The listener is pulled in: "How? In what way?")

"I need a favor." In question form:
"Would you do me a favor?"
(The listener is pulled in: "How can I help? What is it?")

(cell phone)—"Ring"
(The listener is pulled in . . ."who could it be??")

(cell phone)—"Text chime"
(The listener is pulled in . . ."what's this about?")

"I wonder why you made that decision." In question form: "How come?"
(The listener is pulled in: "Well, I just thought . . .")

"You'll never believe what's going on at the Johnson house!"
(The listener is pulled in: "What *is* happening over there?")

"I'm curious to know what you said in response." In question form:
"And you said . . .?"
(The listener is pulled in: "Well, I started by mentioning the incident last May, when . . .")

Sometimes conjunctions by themselves are pull moves:

"And . . ."
(The listener is pulled in: ". . . and I overshot the runway.")
"So . . ."
(The listener is pulled in: ". . . So I told her what was on my mind.")
"But . . ."
(The listener is pulled in: ". . . but it quit ringing before I could get to it.")

Pull moves are sometimes difficult to identify, because they are frequently questions. However, all questions are not pull moves. Sometimes questions are push moves where the sender is trying to push answers out of a listener: "Will you *please* tell me what has been going on?!" is pushing, not pulling, for a response.

In addition to words and questions, being silent and not reacting might be a pause move, but the silence also can pull the listener toward a goal. Maybe the goal is to keep someone talking to find out what happened or get another view of a situation. Examples of silent pull moves are in this conversation between two pilots:

1. "The howling got louder and louder."

2. "——————————silent pull——————————."

3. "Well, I don't know what it was."

4. "——————————silent pull——————————."

5. "So . . . I shut it down."

The Role of Movement in Communication

All messages fit into five basic move categories—place, push, pause, please, or pull. Consequently, we could record all of our conversations and speeches, and put each sentence into one of the basic communication move categories:

Instructor, Placing:	—"We need to know the wind velocity and direction."
Student, Placing:	—"Well, an hour ago it was twelve knots, out of the south."
Instructor, Pausing:	——————silent ——————
Student, Placing:	—"I guess we should use runway one-nine."
Instructor, Pulling:	—"Well, I . . ."
Student, Pulling:	—"What . . .?"
Instructor, Placing:	—"There's that construction at the south end."
Student, Placing:	—"Just some little dirt mounds; the machines are gone."
Instructor, Placing:	—"Yes, that's right, the big stuff is gone."
Instructor, Pushing:	—"Preflight the ship."
Student, Placing:	—"Okay."
Instructor, Placing:	—"I'll check the traffic."
Instructor, Pleasing:	—"You're coming along pretty well."
Instructor, Pushing:	—"Hang in there!"

Now with the moves identified, we can expand our understanding of listening by discussing the role of movement as it relates to the basic parts of the model: message, sender, listener, climate, culture, and noise.

Here are some examples of this functional relationship.

Sender/Listener

Movement enters the communication process as the sender prepares and encodes the message, and as the listener decodes and understands the message. The sender may *intend* to place, push, pause, please, or pull, or not even think about the moves she is making, but whether intentional or unintentional, the movement is there. Look at these examples of movement's relationship with the sender and listener.

Sender, Placing: "It's about ten after six." Listener recognizes that the information has been placed in front of her.

Sender, Pushing: "Please clean up this work area." Listener recognizes that she has been pushed to clean up the work area.

Sender, Pausing: Does not acknowledge that the listener has entered the room. Listener recognizes that she has been paused (ignored).

Sender, Pleasing: "Your report was excellent!" Listener recognizes that she had been pleased.

Sender, Pulling: "I'm out of ideas for promoting this project." Listener recognizes that he is being pulled for some ideas to help with the promotion.

Noise

Movement can become noise in the process when it is misunderstood by the listener. For example, noise is increased when a manager intends a place move, "I appreciate employees who get to work on time," but an employee, who has been late a few times, misinterprets the intended place move and feels uncomfortably pushed. Consequently, movement is noise when the sender's intended move is misinterpreted by the listener. Look at some examples of noise caused by misinterpreted moves.

Sender, *intends* a place move: "It's getting late, and I have a 4:00 appointment."
Listener, *interprets* a push move: "He wants me to help him finish."

Sender, *intends* a push move to get some help: "It sure is awkward for one person to carry this."
Listener, *interprets* a place move: "Yes, I'll bet it is difficult to carry."

Sender, *intends* a pause move by ignoring the salesperson.
The salesperson *interprets* a pull move and continues to explain the qualities of the products.

The sender *intends* a pull move: "I'm not sure what to do next."
The listener *interprets* a place move: "I have trouble deciding what to do sometimes."

Climate

Communication movement can create the climate. We can listen to the relatively objective, matter-of-fact climate of a discussion where placing is the predominant move. We can listen to the heightened energy in the climate where pushing is the main move. We can listen to the controlled pace and measurable timing where the pause move is a common part of the climate. We can comfortably listen to the climate that is supportive with please moves. Finally, we can sense when we are being pulled in a certain direction. An example of a pull climate is a meeting where the leader establishes open, nonjudgmental communication. She offers the background to a problem to be addressed and uses questions to prompt ideas and suggestions. The climate is one of pulling for solutions. Look at these examples of movement and climate.

Place Climate

As I walked into the board room, I could sense the tone of the meeting. There was not a great deal of excitement or irrelevant talk. The speaker was just placing some information and some ideas for us to look over in the next two weeks. The atmosphere of the meeting turned into a factual exchange, and we shared a large amount of information.

Push Climate

Just listening to his footsteps in the hall told me we were in for a real "motivating" meeting. The latest information had clearly shown that deliveries were catching up, but not fast enough. Some clear-cut directives were on the way—they would be heavy handed and blunt: "We will put every available person on loading and shipping." "If we need to work overtime for the next three months, we will do it!"

Pause Climate

We watched as she read the report and waited for her reaction to the problem. But there was no reaction. She thanked us for coming to the meeting and told us we were free to go. A month later, she told us that she knew we were working on the project as well as possible, so she paused it and worked on some other projects.

Please Climate

As soon as I walked through the door I felt a warm, almost festive mood. The big computer print-out read "HAPPY B-DAY, JIM!" I could smell the goodies and hear the relaxed conversations. The mood was warm and pleasing, and we all stayed and visited for over an hour.

Pull Climate

The supervisor began the meeting by detailing the deadlines we were under. Then she gave us a hand-out with the deadline information, spread her arms with hands open and said, "What do you think?" This open gesture and question encouraged us—pulled us—to give feedback, and whether we did or did not give feedback, we all felt obligated to try to offer some suggestions.

Culture

Communication movement is a cultural value. The movement that is valued by the leadership becomes ingrained in the culture. One need only look at the leadership of one of America's most successful men, the late Sam Walton. At the inception of his business venture, Walton emphasized the please move culture in his Wal-Mart stores. He believed in pleasing the customers by developing the attitude with his employees that the customer comes first. This please move culture encouraged the customers to return.

The place move culture exists in the law firm where the founding partners value giving and obtaining information. Upon entering the firm, the client is acknowledged by a receptionist who places, "Mr. Benson is with another client and will be free in five minutes. You may hang up your coat and have a seat if you wish." The receptionist then announces, "Mr. Benson will be out in a moment to show you to his office." Mr. Benson then arrives and places, "Good morning. I'm ready to discuss your case. I have coffee and tea in my office."

When in the office, Mr. Benson places, "I'm interested in listening to the facts involved in this case. I'd like you to start at the beginning." The client responds by placing the facts and events that are pertinent to the case.

The push move culture is experienced in a clothing store where the salespeople are on commission. Since they are paid a percentage of each item they sell, the management encourages pushing articles of clothing to be purchased. The push culture is noticed by such comments as: "Take that one into the dressing room and try it on"; "You can't possibly get along without that"; "I'll get the green tie that goes with that"; "You can't wear that skirt with those high heels—put these flats on"; "Oh, that hat is YOU; you just can't get out of the store without it."

The pause move culture is experienced in a typical department store. At this store, the salesperson greets the customer and says, "If you have any questions, I'll be happy to help out." After that, the salesperson responds only if the customer requests help or information.

A pull move culture can be found where there are attempts to draw us into the organization by arousing our curiosity. Probably the most commonly experienced pull cultures are shops and stores with window displays and entries that attract our interest. Once pulled inside, other messages might tell us, "Elegance at an affordable price," and we are pulled to find out the price, or "Unequaled power and performance," might arouse our interest in an automobile's performance figures. Simple messages reading, "Ask us about our low interest rates," pull us toward the possibility of making a credit purchase.

These examples show that movement is a basic part of organizational culture. Even though the leaders that formed the culture may not have consciously decided to create a place, push, pause, please, or pull culture, a culture valuing one or more of the moves evolved under their leadership. As listeners, we need to be aware of the movement that the culture values, so that we can adapt to it.

The listening model is now complete and is presented in Figure 5.1.

••• Figure 5.1

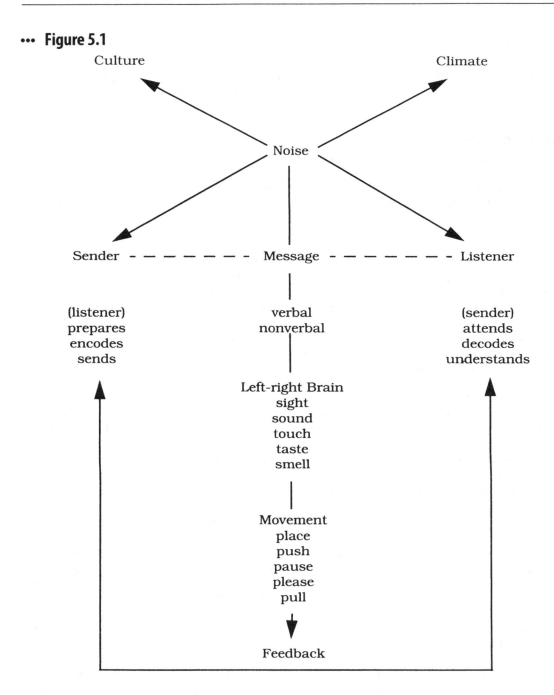

Summary

Movement is the last variable to be discussed as part of the communication process, and it is a basic component of human interaction. Listening to movement, which occurs in the form of gestures and speech, can add substantial meaning to a message. Movement is broken down into five categories: (1) the place move, (2) the push move, (3) the pause move, (4) the please move, and (5) the pull move. Moreover, movement affects each element and variable in the process of communication: sender/listener, noise, climate, and culture.

Notes

1. Paul J. Kaufmann, *Basic Communication Behavior: The Impact of Movement on Interpersonal Communication* (Ann Arbor, Mich.: Management Dynamics Corp., 1980).

2. T. Boone Pickens Jr., "Restructuring America: Focus on the Core Business," General Partner, Mesa Limited Partnership. Speech delivered before the Economic Club of Detroit, Detroit, Michigan, May 2, 1988. *Vital Speeches of the Day,* Vol. LIV, no. 22 (September 1, 1988), p. 676.

3. *Ibid.,* p. 678.

4. Theo Pitt Jr., "The Truth About Savings and Loan Institutions: State and Federal Bungling." Speech delivered at the Third Regulatory Policy Conference of the U.S. League of Savings Institutions, Washington, D.C., June 28, 1988. *Vital Speeches of the* Day, Vol. LIV, no. 22 (September 1, 1988), p. 674.

Chapter Five
Awareness Exercises

Name_____   ID#_____

1. Write three place moves.

    A.

    B.

    C.

2. Write three push moves.

    A.

    B.

    C.

3. Describe a situation where a pause move was used.

4. Write three please moves.

    A.

   B.

   C.

5. Write three pull moves.
   A.

   B.

   C.

6. Explain how movement might be a part of a culture.

7. Explain how movement can be a source of noise.

8. Explain how movement can affect the communication climate.

9. Briefly describe a time when you listened to place moves.
   A. The setting

   B. The place moves

10. Briefly describe a time when you listened to push moves.
    A. The setting

    B. The push moves

11. Briefly describe a time when you listened to pause moves.
    A. The setting

    B. The pause moves

12. Briefly describe a time when you listened to please moves.
    A. The setting

    B. The please moves

13. Briefly describe a time when you listened to pull moves.
    A. The setting

    B. The pull moves

14.   Describe three instances when noise occurred because of misunderstood moves.

A.

B.

C.

Chapter Five
Awareness Database

Name_____   ID#_____

Identify the predominant move.

A. Place   B. Push   C. Pause   D. Please   E. Pull

1. Would you please shut the door?

    A.   B.   C.   D.   E.

2. The oil isn't at running temperature, yet.

    A.   B.   C.   D.   E.

3. There's something very interesting going on in the production manager's office.

    A.   B.   C.   D.   E.

4. The mail just came.

    A.   B.   C.   D.   E.

5. You put on an excellent program.

    A.   B.   C.   D.   E.

6. Smoking is not allowed in this building.

    A.   B.   C.   D.   E.

7. We've got to move; jump in!

    A.   B.   C.   D.   E.

8. Look. I'll do my job; you do yours.

    A.   B.   C.   D.   E.

9. Can I give you a hand with those packages?

    A.   B.   C.   D.   E.

10. The power just went off.

    A.   B.   C.   D.   E.

11. This stew is terrific!

A.   B.   C.   D.   E.

12. Wait till you see what they've done to your office.

A.   B.   C.   D.   E.

13. I feel relieved that the whole business is finished.

A.   B.   C.   D.   E.

14. Would you mind getting that knife for me?

A.   B.   C.   D.   E.

15. I'm so angry I could spit!

A.   B.   C.   D.   E.

16. Your department's final report was clear and thorough.

A.   B.   C.   D.   E.

17. I think you'll find the solution very interesting.

A.   B.   C.   D.   E.

18. Last year we put on four ground towing workshops.

A.   B.   C.   D.   E.

19. Start the engine.

A.   B.   C.   D.   E.

20. We'll be in your office at half past ten.

A.   B.   C.   D.   E.

Chapter Six

Listening to Ourselves

These next three chapters discuss listening to ourselves. This chapter, 6, discusses listening to our needs; Chapter 7, listening to our personality; and Chapter 8, listening to stress. Before we can give our complete attention to another person (interpersonal listening), we must first become aware of our own needs through *intrapersonal listening*. In this chapter, we will discuss (1) the intrapersonal listening role, (2) listening to personal needs, (3) our self-esteem and listening to others, and (4) changing internal messages.

The Intrapersonal Listening Role

The *intra*personal listening role involves shutting out external messages and *listening to ourselves*. This personal listening time allows us to become aware of our own needs, and if they are unmet, to plan to satisfy them either immediately or in the foreseeable future. Satisfying personal needs is like putting our house in order for visitors. When our house is in order, we can shift our attention to the visitors.

Similarly, when our personal house is in order, that is, when our needs are met, we are free to give our listening energy to others. The idea that recognizing and meeting personal needs precedes listening to others is illustrated in this narrative, told by a supervisor. Notice how the employee, Russ, is unable to listen effectively to his supervisor because of Russ's unresolved personal needs.

CALVIN AND HOBBES © 1986 Watterson. Reprinted with permission of UNIVERSAL UCLICK. All rights reserved.

A few years back I was in charge of a department with eleven employees. I had gotten to know each of them fairly well, and we seemed to be getting along fine. One morning, one of them, a man named Russ, walked past my office door, and I gave a loud and friendly, "Morning, Russ!" He shot a glance in my direction, didn't say a word and went on to his office. I was puzzled and thought about what the problem might be.

I reviewed his job assignments and requests for time off and vacation time but found nothing that would prompt his disturbing behavior. The next morning's encounter really took me back. My "Good Morning," this time was warmly returned, and the next thing I knew he was in my office with a cup of coffee and all sorts of chatty news. His behavior was just the opposite of the day before.

After several more experiences with Russ's responsive and nonresponsive mornings, I came to realize that *I had nothing to do with his responses to my, "Good Mornings."* What Russ was listening to inside himself was affecting how he listened to me.

It turns out that Russ was having some serious personal problems, and on the mornings when these problems were bothering him the most, he was so preoccupied that he couldn't listen to my simple greeting. On the mornings when he had apparently thought about his problems and had either solved them or put them aside, he could listen to my "Good Morning," and we would visit.

These experiences with Russ taught me that what's going on inside people directly affects how they listen to those around them.

Intrapersonal listening takes place at any time: when we first wake up and begin to assess how we feel and what needs to be satisfied; when we are alone and away from work and other responsibilities; or when we take a short break to determine how we are feeling when we are with other people.

We are in the intrapersonal listening role whenever we listen to our feelings, which are reactions to physical or emotional needs that have been met or unmet. Examples of physical reactions are: "My stomach was churning when she called my name"; "This pain in my left shoulder is getting worse"; "I wanted to get into some warm clothes and rest." Some emotional reactions are: "I felt a glow of joy when I saw the kids having such a good time"; "I smiled to myself as I realized how much fun the ride was"; "Now, more than ever, I had to get out of there and make some decisions of my own"; "I wanted to talk to her about the loss"; "I really need to get this done on time." In each of these intrapersonal messages, some reaction to personal needs is being expressed. These emotional and physical reactions could be spurred from specific personality traits, which are examined in Chapter 7 or from stress, which is discussed in Chapter 8.

Just as individuals listen intrapersonally to determine need satisfaction before listening to others, successful family, social and business organizations listen internally before reaching out to serve others. Before an organization can successfully adapt to the needs of those it serves, it must listen to its own internal needs to be sure it is well structured and running smoothly with confidence and high self-esteem. After this internal listening, it can listen to the expectations, problems, and needs of others.

The importance of internal organizational listening is highlighted in this sequence of internal listening events that led to the establishment of a very successful restaurant:

Gina, the owner and manager of a popular and financially rewarding restaurant, decided to open another restaurant with totally different menu offerings—she was going from a meat, French fries, and salad menu to an array of Mexican offerings. She had surveyed other Mexican restaurants in the area and had a good sense of the competition. Moreover, her years of experience had taught her to listen internally to her organization before attempting to open the doors of her second restaurant to the public.

She listened carefully to the *internal* needs and limits of her current staff of cooks, servers, washers, managers, and other support personnel. She then organized the new staff around a core of her experienced employees. Listening to the needs and limits of her cooks, she began with a very small menu, which consisted of a combination of only eight items, and because of her staff's uncertainties about the new business, she began by serving dinners only. Setting up for lunch service would come when her internal listening told her the organization was ready.

By listening carefully to internal needs, she opened a restaurant with a confident, well-organized staff and a small but competently prepared menu. Listening internally helped her build a smooth and well-organized operation, which made it possible to begin the process of *external* listening to customers' additional requests and needs.

Internal listening, whether it is personal or organizational, is the first and most important step toward effective external listening. The discussion now turns to need areas that should be considered when listening intrapersonally.

Listening to Personal Needs

To the extent that our personal needs are met, we will be effective listeners. For example, before I can concentrate on what you are saying, I must satisfy my need for food and shelter. If I were hungry, wet, and cold, I would find it difficult to turn my listening energy to you. However, if I am relatively comfortable, well fed, and warm, I can more easily listen to you. Intrapersonal listening is the first step in recognizing and satisfying needs. Once these needs are satisfied, we can listen more effectively to others.

To structure this discussion the needs are numbered from one to five; however, number one is not necessarily the most important, because the relative importance of the needs will vary with time and each individual. Consequently, for some people, need five, the need for fun, will be more important than need number one, the need for survival. The needs are: (1) survival, (2) belonging—to love, share, and cooperate, (3) power, (4) freedom, and (5) fun.[1]

Survival

The first need to be discussed is survival. We listen to ourselves for physical survival to determine our state of nutritional satisfaction, environmental comfort (temperature, humidity, noise, and light), and health (amount of energy, pain, ability to rest, or physical well being). Intrapersonal messages related to physical survival are: "I'm feeling hot"; "The noise from that train is giving me a headache"; "I find the waves washing on the shore relaxing"; "I feel rested and ready to finish the painting."

In addition to physical survival needs, we listen to emotional needs, which include feelings about relationships—family members, spouses, lovers, parents, friends—feelings about decisions or events which affect our self-worth, success, and failures, and our general outlook on life. Some intrapersonal messages that relate to emotional survival needs are: "I'm happy she sent me that birthday card"; "I feel great about the raise I got"; "I think I'll stay away from him—I'm not worth anyone's time"; "I feel like crawling in a hole and disappearing"; "I'm glad mom and dad called this morning"; "It was a tough decision, but I feel good about it."

Love and Belonging

The second need is love and belonging. This need is satisfied when people or projects that we care about help us feel comfortable and welcome. The need might be satisfied through family and friends whose company we enjoy, or through people who share the same hobby such as boating, jogging, basketball, tennis, flying, writing, or quilting. The need for love and belonging is not met when a person has chosen to spend time where there is little shared respect or concern for each other: a family setting where nothing in common is shared; or a work environment where there is no sense of caring or belonging, and the only reward is a paycheck (which *does* help satisfy the need for survival). In this case where the work environment does not meet the need for love and belonging, it is reasonable to conclude that the worker's listening energy will not go beyond the minimum to get the job completed.

By listening intrapersonally, we become aware of what needs are being met, as well as those that are not met. Moreover, we discover that at any given time different needs will be a priority. Sometimes the need for survival might be more important than the need for love and belonging as in the case of the worker who puts up with a cold, uncaring environment for a paycheck.

As we survey our personal needs and how they impact our listening, we need to keep our priorities in mind. In the following description, imagine how the person describing the priority of his need for love and belonging might listen to others.

> As I look inside myself, I find that the need for friends, family, and love—best described as the need to belong—occupies as large a place in my mind as the need to survive. It may not be as immediate as thirst or hunger, but if, over the long pull, I did not have the close, loving family and friends that I almost take for granted, I think that the idea that life is hardly worth living would come occasionally to mind. Even if we have friends and family, many of us also enjoy a sense of belonging with pets, plants, and even an inanimate object like a "beloved" boat or computer.[2]

From this example, we can understand that as circumstances change, needs will have varying importance in our lives. The person who wrote this description gives listening attention to people he loves. If his situation were to change, or if he were from a country where war is a constant threat, his concern for survival would become a high priority, and he would shift his listening focus to matters of survival.

Power

The third need, the need for power, has a clear and strong impact on how we listen to others. This need to control other people and our environments can be felt on a daily basis. Concerns for power range from physical to psychological. From a physical standpoint, certain personality types engaged in the routine of preparing for a day outside the home, are quite concerned about how they appear in comparison with other people. A number of popular books exist on dressing for power, and they address questions like: "How do I look?" "Am I in style, well groomed?" "Do I have the *right* shoes?" "Am I good looking?"

Moreover, some people will exercise to become a physical model of strength and what they think they should look like. (They might also exercise for survival: lower the blood pressure, cholesterol, and other health factors.) When these people are comfortable intrapersonally with how they look, they increase the probability of listening to someone else comfortably, because they have satisfied their needs for physical power.

Psychological power needs are concerned with emotional and mental control. Someone exploring this power need might ask herself: "Are my feelings calm and positive about this matter?" "Can I let go of the anger I feel about this?" "Can I control the happiness I have about this?" "Do I have the information I need for this discussion?" "Is my mind alert and ready to think?" "Is my stress level acceptable?"

As with the needs for survival and love and belonging, the need for power varies with each individual personality type. Some people have little concern for physical power, either in appearance or strength. Some have little interest in psychological power, but whatever the need level, power, like the other needs, must be listened to internally before the individual can attend effectively to others.

Freedom

Freedom is the fourth need. As physical creatures, we need freedom of movement to stay alive and to communicate. At the most basic level, freedom of movement allows us to find shelter, to prepare food, and to express our ideas. At a higher level is physical freedom which allows us to gain access to social and educational opportunities.

As physical freedom increases, effective listening increases. One well-known example of this lies in the biography of Helen Keller, who early in life lost her sight and hearing, which at the time ended her freedom to listen and express. With the help of her nurse and her parents, Helen learned to communicate through touch, and was able to listen to her needs and ultimately listen to others and express herself.

In addition to physical freedom, we need psychological freedom. We have all observed youngsters growing up and asserting themselves for their "freedom," as well as parents who need the freedom that "being away from the kids" occasionally gives them. Sometimes people feel psychologically trapped in a relationship or an occupation.[3] Their listening loses effectiveness, and their intrapersonal messages tell them they need some time away from each other or a vacation away from the job.

Fun

The fifth need is the need for fun. Fun is doing something for enjoyment—something that gives pleasure without hurting anyone else. As Mark Twain wrote, "Fun is what you do when you don't have to do it." Our culture, which is based on the Puritan work ethic, at times views fun as unacceptable behavior; it tells us that fun is all right for kids but not for adults. However, fun is an important need which can keep our lives balanced, help us learn, and help us become better listeners. In a lecture titled "Listening and Counseling," Dr. Russ Canute, a counselor for thirty-five years, offered these ideas about fun and listening:

> People who have a life balanced with fun are better listeners. They listen to their own need for fun, and even though the work is piled sky high, they decide to leave it for awhile and have some fun. (And, by the way, when they get back to it, they're better at it.) And whenever they have fun, they're learning something. Think of the last time you had fun. What did you do? Did you go waterskiing? What did you learn from that? Did you go to a movie or a play? What did you learn from that? Did you run, walk, play basketball, swim, play chess? What did you learn from that? Did you go visit with some friends? What did you learn from that? Did you go to the library and read some journals? What did you learn from that? I honestly don't think you can have fun without learning something. And, in order to learn, you have to listen with your ears and your eyes. But keep the fun thing in balance. There are things in life we need to do that we don't like, but when you can, listen to your need for fun, it'll make you a better listener to the people and things around you.[4]

Listening intrapersonally for these five basic needs—survival, love and belonging, power, freedom, and fun—is the first step in satisfying needs. Once these needs are met our self-esteem rises, and we are ready to reach out to others.

Self-Esteem and Listening to Others

Intrapersonal listening gives us a grasp of what needs are being satisfied, and to the extent that they are satisfied our self-esteem is formed. If we listen to ourselves and find that our own needs are satisfied, we can listen to others in a comfortable and responsive manner. If we listen to ourselves and find conflicting needs and discomfort, we cannot effectively reach out to someone else's world and listen.

The type of internal messages we listen to stems from a complex catalog of perceptions we have about ourselves. Depending on how well we are working to meet our needs, these perceptions fall into two categories: first, the amount of *value* we have for ourselves, and second, how *competent* we perceive ourselves to be. Our self-esteem is anchored in our sense of *value* and *competence.*

If we experience a high sense of personal value, we see both our strengths and shortcomings. We accept who we are and work to improve our shortcomings. So when we value ourselves, we send positive messages to ourselves. Although not in so many words, these messages say, "I like who I am"; "I'm not perfect, but I'm a good person who's getting better all the time." Valuing ourselves means we accept ourselves, and this acceptance frees us to accept others as they are.

When we experience low self-esteem, we do not value ourselves, and listening effectively to others becomes difficult, We may become defensive in order to hide our nervousness, fear, feelings of insecurity, or inadequacies. Many of these defensive messages are rooted in the feeling that we are not of value in this particular situation: "I've always been lousy at this"; "No one really cares about how I feel, anyway." Defensive messages come from a hidden belief that we are bad, unlovable, unworthy, and not respected for who we are.*

---

* The goal here is not to detail all of the types of defenses linked with self-esteem—there are volumes that do that in detail; rather, the purpose is to discuss some common defensive messages in order to raise awareness of their impact on listening.

So instead of listening attentively, a person with low self-esteem might avoid the situation all together: "Well, I don't want to talk to her; she never has anything interesting to say"; "This report's going to be stupid. I can't ever figure out what he's getting at." If already in a listening setting, a person with low self-esteem might be internally saying, "You're just talking to me because you have to"; "You don't really care if I understand this or not"; "You're just here to show how much you know and how little I know."

A listener with high self-esteem listens attentively without becoming defensive. People who respect themselves do not need unhealthy defenses, because defenses are put up to protect weaknesses; they are not needed where there is strength and adequacy.[5] With high self-esteem, the listener's internal messages might say, "Sure, I'll listen to her—I usually learn something interesting from her"; "This guy's vocabulary is difficult to understand, but I'll take good notes and figure out what he's getting at"; or "I'm not sure why John came in to visit, but I'll keep listening to see what's on his mind."

The sense of value we have for ourselves at any given time has some impact on the way we listen. Our sense of competence also plays a role in our internal messages.

Imagine the following office scene: Behind a large walnut desk sits an executive, about forty-five years old, white shirt, dark tie, and suit coat. A new employee comes and is introduced by a secretary. The executive looks the new employee in the eye, reaches over the desk, and shakes his hand.

The executive appears confident, but for some reason he does not seem to *feel* confident. Sometimes we are fooled by false confidence, but at this time, the nonverbal messages show the executive's discomfort. Maybe a hesitancy, an exaggerated gesture, or some visible tension reveal a lack of competence and confidence. Perhaps the handshake was a bit too long and tight; the voice too loud; the eye contact too direct and mechanical.

At the time, the executive's internal messages might be saying, "I'm not good at this"; "I hate meeting new people"; or "I can't let this guy get the best of me." The executive is giving the *appearance* of confidence rather than *being* confident, and his internal feelings of insecurity come to the surface and lower the effectiveness of the communication.

Listeners who are sending themselves messages that say, "I'm not competent," or "I'm really afraid," find it particularly important to appear competent and courageous on the outside. However, listeners who send realistic internal messages of, "I'm nervous, but I can handle this," or "I'm looking forward to this interaction," have no need to present a flawless image to others, because they accept themselves as they are.

Listening to ourselves honestly will give us a realistic picture of who we are. We will find that we are worthwhile and competent in some areas and that we fall short in others. What is important is that we recognize our strengths, face our weaknesses, and work to improve.

How we value ourselves—our self-esteem—determines how we will behave with others. If we feel positive about ourselves, we will have more self-confidence and will communicate with people effectively. If we are feeling negative about ourselves, we will shy away from others; our communicating will not be effective.[6] Moreover, people who feel good about themselves—that is, people with high self-esteem—are willing to take risks: they will try new things, meet new people, and listen to new and unusual ideas. They see involvement with the world around them as an exciting opportunity to learn.[7]

To increase the effectiveness of our listening to others, then, we need to listen to ourselves to determine the kinds of *intrapersonal* messages we are sending. In general, to the extent that these internal messages tell us that we are meeting needs and we are likable, worthwhile, competent, and confident, we will be more effective listeners.

Changing Internal Messages

Our self-concepts—how we view ourselves—grow and change throughout our lives. We take on new tasks, new responsibilities, and we experience some degree of success and failure. Since some aspects of our self-concepts are learned, we can capitalize on these successes and failures and use this knowledge to build more confident, positive self images.

To raise our self-esteem we must have positive experiences. As adults, we can look back on our parents and our upbringing and praise or possibly criticize some of those experiences. This looking back to understand why we are what we are is healthy and normal, but it probably will not change our listening behavior. What *will* help, however, is listening to ourselves as we are *today.*

The one person in the world you should not avoid is yourself. If we listen to ourselves, and if we need improvement, we make some changes. Maybe there are certain listening settings where we feel less confident. We might be confident and at ease in a family or business meeting, but in a social setting wish we were somewhere else.

To be effective listeners, we need to operate confidently in a variety of settings. If we do not feel comfortable in a particular setting, the first step in changing how we feel is being *aware* that the discomfort exists.

Facing internal discomfort is important, since it is the first step in preparing for the listening situation. For example, a person may be fearful of a staff meeting where a particular idea she has been promoting will be discussed at length. Because of the amount of thought and time put into the proposal, she feels personally attached to it, and she is concerned that the idea might not be accepted. Because of the stress, she wants to avoid the meeting.

After recognizing how she feels about this meeting, the next step is accepting the fear she is experiencing: "I'm afraid to walk into that meeting room." After recognizing and accepting her fear, she can now begin to minimize it.

As one author comments:

> We are always stronger when we do not try to fight reality. We cannot make our fear go away by yelling at it, or yelling at ourselves, or indulging in self-rebuke. But if we can open to our experience, stay conscious, and remember that we are larger than any one emotion, we can at minimum begin to transcend unwanted feelings, and often we can dispel them, since full, sincere acceptance tends, in time, to dissolve negative or unwanted feelings such as pain, anger, envy, or fear.[8]

After facing and accepting her fears, she can imagine the people and the situation until she feels more comfortable. Now, even if the reality of the upcoming meeting is dreadful, she can attend it with more confidence. By consciously engaging intrapersonal listening she first, became aware of her fears, and second, minimized them by imagining the people and dynamics of the meeting.

So, we first listen to our needs to put our own feelings in perspective before we can listen to others. These four steps offer a structure for listening to ourselves:[9]

1. How is my self-esteem? How am I feeling about myself? Are my needs for survival, belonging, power, freedom, and fun being met?

2. How do I treat these feelings? Do I accept them as my own, or blame someone else for how I feel? Do I cover up my feelings or do I pretend I have feelings that are not there?

3. When I feel this way, how well do I listen to others? How well do I communicate?

4. How comfortable am I in this new listening situation? Am I comfortable enough within myself to take the responsibilities of listening to others?

To illustrate this four-step process, we can look at a professional, Nancy, a junior vice president of a bank.

Nancy is thirty-eight years old, and she works with two other junior vice presidents, three senior vice presidents, and of course, the bank president. In addition, there are three loan officers and fifteen other employees working as tellers and performing miscellaneous jobs around the bank.

Nancy is a college graduate who has been with the bank for six years. In this relatively short time, she has advanced through the ranks of teller, to loan officer, to junior vice president. Her performance reviews consistently highlight her effective communication skills, particularly her listening abilities, as the key to her promotability.

Nancy acknowledges that listening was a failing at her last job, so she took it upon herself to work consciously on improving her listening skills. This is her narrative of the process when she first started her job at the bank:

Step 1. How Is My Self-Esteem? Are My Needs of Survival, Belonging, Power, Fun, and Freedom Being Met?

In the morning, while I was getting ready for work, I would assess how I was feeling about myself today. Usually, I felt fairly worthwhile and confident, and needs were being met. But there were some areas of uncertainly. This bank job was new, and I wanted to do well. One consistently recurring feeling I experienced had to do with meeting with the other junior vice presidents. One VP was a woman eight or nine years older than I; the other, a man of about my age. I had just started as a teller, and the first meeting I had with those VPs was not comfortable, to say the least.

Without giving too much detail, let me say that the first meeting was at best intimidating. I felt that I had no power in the situation, and it certainly allowed me no freedom or *fun*.

At this first meeting, we met in Mrs. Borman's office, and instead of taking the form of a meeting, it was more like a military briefing. I sat while the *both* of them stood and explained the policies I would be following.

But that first meeting was a long time ago, and this morning as I faced another meeting with them, my feelings were ones of anger and fear, and I didn't want to go. I was a little disappointed in myself, too, for letting these feelings take control, but I couldn't forget how helpless and powerless I was at that first meeting!

Step 2. How Do I Treat These Feelings? Do I Accept Them as My Own, or Blame Someone Else for How I Feel? Do I Cover Up My Feelings or Do I Pretend I Have Feelings That Are Not There?

My next reaction, after admitting how I felt, was to blame the two VPs for their insensitivity, lack of preparation, and demeaning behavior at that first meeting. I was saying to myself, "It's *their* fault that *I* feel this way." This was an old rule from my past—put the blame for my feelings on someone else. But this morning I threw that old rule out, and simply acknowledged, "I feel angry and afraid. I DO NOT want to go to that meeting." No putting my feelings on someone else; no blaming someone else; just "These are my feelings. I needed to face them, period."

Step 3. When I Feel This Way, How Well Do I Listen to Others? How Well Do I Communicate?

At this point, I decided not to communicate my feelings directly to the VPs, but rather to imagine the reality of the meeting, put my anger and fear aside, and concentrate solely on LISTENING to the information. Instead of communicating my feelings of powerlessness and frustration, I decided to communicate my interest in the information they were to give me. Information that might help my job performance.

Step 4. Am I Willing to Take the Risk of Actively Listening When I Feel Like I Don't Belong in This Intimidating and Restricted Setting?

This was a new and different approach for me. It was risky, because in the past I used to go through all the motions of listening—fake listening, I guess—just to make the meetings bearable and make myself look good. Now I put my feelings of frustration and anger aside, and didn't worry about anything except listening to and understanding the information.

My anger and fear aside, I was able to focus on the positive aspects of listening—"I'm good at it"; "I'm able to attend to these people and understand what they are saying to me." I faced the reality of the situation—simply, what was expected of me was to listen—and played the role of a listener, and it worked! I came out of the meeting with some helpful information, and the VPs actually thanked me for my attentive listening.

Dr. William Glasser, author of *Control Theory*, points out that we emphasize different needs in our lives, and if we listen to ourselves we can begin to understand these needs and listen with respect and understanding to the needs of those around us:

To gain effective control of our lives, we have to satisfy what we believe is basic to us and learn to respect and not frustrate others in fulfilling what is basic to them. All you will ever know is what drives *you*, just as I will know only what drives *me*. We cannot look into other people's heads and see what drives them. We can listen to what they tell us and look at what they do, but we should not make the mistake of assuming that we *know* what drives them. This means that we can never be sure of satisfying anyone else no matter what we do. It is reasonably safe, however, to assume that what drives us is similar to what drives other people, so there is no harm in trying to satisfy another person. But if what we do does not work, we should be careful not to persist or we run the risk of losing that person for a friend or lover.[10]

Dr. Glasser is advising that we probably will never reach a perfect understanding of another person. If, however, we listen sensitively to ourselves, we can begin to listen to others and understand their motivations and feelings.

Summary

Intrapersonal listening is listening to ourselves, and it is the first step in becoming an effective listener. As we listen internally, we can determine which of the five needs: survival, love and belonging, power, freedom, and fun, should be satisfied before we can turn our energy to listening to others. Need satisfaction results in higher self-esteem, and the more we value ourselves as competent individuals, the easier it becomes to listen to others.

A four-step process for improving intrapersonal communication and listening effectiveness is discussed: first, listening internally to feelings; second, deciding what to do with these feelings; third, determining how these feelings affect communicating with others; and fourth, taking the risk to listen actively. Chapter 7, "Listening and Personality," and Chapter 8, "Listening and Stress," expand the discussion of intrapersonal listening by focusing on personality traits and the effects of stress on listening.

Notes

1.   William Glasser, *Control Theory, A New Explanation of How We Control Our Lives* (New York: Harper & Row Publishers, 1984), pp. 5–15.

2.   Glasser, pp. 9–10.

3.   Glasser, p. 10.

4. Russ Canute, "Listening and Counseling," lecture given October 14, 1982.

5. Dorothy Corkille Briggs, *Your Child's Self-Esteem* (Garden City, New York: Doubleday & Company, Inc., 1975), p. 29.

6. Sveri Wahlross, *Family Communication* (New York: Macmillan, 1974), p. xi.

7. Caroline Donnelly, "Writing an Advertisement for Yourself," *Money,* vol. 4 (January, 1974), p. 308.

8. Nathaniel Branden, *How to Raise Your Self-Esteem* (Toronto: Bantam Books, 1987), p. 48.

9. Virginia Satir, *Making Contact* (Millbrae, California: Celestial Arts, 1976).

10. Glasser, pp. 13–16.

Awareness Exercises

Name_____ ID#_____

Before responding to these questions, spend some time paying attention to your intrapersonal listening and how you listen to others.

1. Describe a listening situation that is uncomfortable for you.

2. What messages do you give yourself to make the situation bearable?

3. What listening situations do you avoid if possible?

4. What listening situations do you enjoy?

5. When are you most aware of listening to yourself?

6. Describe a survival need that you have (either physical or psychological):
    A. satisfied

    B. not satisfied

7. Describe a love and belonging need that you have:
    A. satisfied

B. not satisfied

8. Describe a power need that you have:
    A. satisfied

    B. not satisfied

9. Describe a freedom need that you have:
    A. satisfied

    B. not satisfied

10. Describe a fun need that you have:
    A. satisfied

    B. not satisfied

11. Describe someone you believe has high self-esteem.

12. Describe someone you believe has low self-esteem.

13. How does self-esteem affect your listening?

Chapter Six
Awareness Database

Name_____   ID#_____

1. I consciously make efforts to listen to myself.

   A.   B.   C.   D.   E.
   frequently   seldom

2. I am aware of my feelings toward various listening situations.

   A.   B.   C.   D.   E.
   frequently   seldom

3. I believe that I know myself.

   A.   B.   C.   D.   E.
   frequently   seldom

4. I feel that I can be myself when communicating.

   A.   B.   C.   D.   E.
   frequently   seldom

5. I am aware that how I feel about myself impacts how I listen to others.

   A.   B.   C.   D.   E.
   frequently   seldom

6. I feel comfortable in most listening situations.

   A.   B.   C.   D.   E.
   frequently   seldom

7. I feel a strong need for love and belonging.

   A.   B.   C.   D.   E.
   frequently   seldom

8. I feel a strong need for physical power.

   A.   B.   C.   D.   E.
   frequently   seldom

9. I feel a strong need for psychological power.

   A.   B.   C.   D.   E.
   frequently   seldom

10. I feel a strong need for freedom.

    A.   B.   C.   D.   E.
    frequently   seldom

11. I feel a strong need for fun.

    A.   B.   C.   D.   E.
    frequently   seldom

Chapter Seven

Listening and Personality

In Chapter 6, Listening to Ourselves, we discussed the importance of *intra*personal listening as a key to improving *inter*personal listening. We noted that self-observation helps us understand when our needs (survival, love and belonging, power, freedom, and fun) are being met. When needs are met, we attend more effectively to others; if not met, these needs must be temporarily put aside if not satisfied, before we can give full listening attention to someone else.

In this chapter we move beyond the five basic human needs to the needs of our personality type. The intrapersonal process remains the same, but we are adding the potential to listen for the status of our personality needs. To reach an understanding of the relationship between personality type and listening behavior, we will first discuss personality types so we can identify our own type, and then explore how our personality influences our listening.

Personality Types

Personality is the product of all the observable behaviors and traits that distinguish one person from another. Each personality has its positive and negative traits, and self-awareness can optimize the best parts. Different folks might be described as having a perfectionist personality, a giving personality, a productive personality, a romantic personality, a philosophical personality, a trouble-shooting personality, an adventurous personality, a bossy personality, or a peace-making personality.

A Google search using the words "Personality Types" yielded millions of hits, and within these hits are dozens of personality tests, descriptions, and traits. Much of the information directed toward personality spins off the psychoanalytical work of Sigmund Freud, who is considered the father of psychoanalysis, Carl Jung, who developed analytical psychology, and William James, an influential American psychologist.

Although these psychologists have made significant contributions to personality disorder therapy, our purpose in this chapter is not to psychoanalyze—that is, go into the deepest meanings of motivations and behaviors—but rather to become aware of personality traits that can be applied to improve listening. With this purpose in mind we turn to a descriptive rather than psychoanalytical personality system called the *Enneagram*.

The Enneagram[1]

The Enneagram describes nine personality types. Its name is derived from the Greek words *ennea* (nine) and *grammon* (lines or points). The Enneagram, then, is a nine-pointed diagram showing as many personality types:

1. The Perfectionist
2. The Helper/Giver
3. The Producer/Get it Done
4. The Tragic Romantic
5. The Observer
6. The Trouble Shooter
7. The Visionary
8. The Boss
9. The Mediator

By becoming aware of these nine personality types, we can determine which personality type most closely fits each of us, and ultimately apply this knowledge to our listening behavior.

Personality Type One, the Perfectionist: A person who is not pleased by anything that does not meet very high standards.[2]

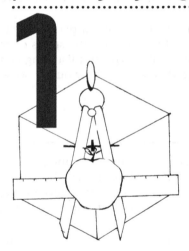

Also known as: the Reformer, the Purist, the Judge, the Visionary.

The Perfectionist's view of the world: *I have the right way, so let me help you get it right.*

Self-description: "My life's goals are aimed at making the world a better place—the very best it can be."

Positive characteristics: principled, committed, disciplined, detail oriented, scrupulous.

Negative characteristics: judgmental (of self and others), self-righteous, indignant, inflexible, unforgiving.

Notable Ones: Julie Andrews (Mary Poppins), Tom Brokaw, Hillary Clinton, Confucius, Harrison Ford, Jodie Foster, Joan of Arc, John Kerry, The Lone Ranger, Martin Luther, Harry Truman,[3] Mahatma Gandhi, "Mr. Spock" (Star Trek).[4]

Overview: Type One, the Perfectionist

Many Ones report that, as children, they were obedient, responsible and wanted to do things just right in the eyes of others. They came to believe there is only one right solution to a problem, and whenever possible, problems should be solved before relaxing and having fun.

Perfectionists work toward far reaching goals, adhere to high principles, make strong commitments, exhibit stability and honesty, are detail oriented, disciplined, objective, and principled. When Ones know they are on the right track, they pour large amounts of energy into their work, and to be sure that their goals are given high priority, they carefully schedule times for work, exercise, visits, and meetings.

Perfectionist can be pompous, self-righteous, ruthless, coldhearted, arrogant, rigid, and judgmental of themselves and others. As these attributes indicate, Ones' leadership style is "Follow the rules," "Go by the book," and "Follow my example."

Type One's Communication Style. Perfectionists are prone to listen to messages that have themes of *duty, ethics, approved procedures, the Golden Rule.* Messages that suggest a quick fix and seem to compromise the integrity of the outcome, or suggest that something should be done because the sender "says so," will be rejected by Perfectionists.

Perfectionists listen to their powerful internal critics. Their intrapersonal messages are highly judgmental because they want to be correct and perfect in the eyes of others. When listening to others, Ones focus on correctness; they look for the *right way* to approach a project or idea so their communication is precise, to the point, detailed, process oriented, and task related.

Ones' content focuses on the correctness of a plan or outcome: "We *should* follow that plan," "We *ought* to check into that," "We *must* find the source of the problem," "The *correct* way would be . . . ," "That was an *excellent* outcome," "That would be a *good* move," "He took the *wrong* approach," "It was the *right* thing to do." Their communication is quickly responsive and precise, concise, and detailed, and they may become defensive if challenged.

Ones are often unaware when they are angry. Even when others are "listening" to Ones' nonverbal messages of anger—tight jaw, red face, pursed lips (as if trying to contain angry words)—Ones are unaware of their anger.

Jason's Thoughts

I'm definitely in the Perfectionist category. As an airplane mechanic, rules and procedures are important, and that's the way it should be. When I sign off the work I've done, it must be right in every detail. If there is anything vague or unclear in what should be done, I'll take it to the extreme detail of correctness. Someone might tell me, "Just look it over; it's no big deal," but if I have even the slightest doubt, I will dismantle it and inspect every part, even if they're not crucial to the safety of the plane. What's right is right, period!

This perfectionism carries into my hobbies. I'm a pianist and love to play. And here, again, my need to have it *just so* takes over. The piano must be in tune—I even have a tuning fork and wrench to keep it in tune. I feel morally compelled to have the music sound exactly right. I guess I'm a purist in that regard, too.

In my relationships, like everything else, I look for what things *should* be like. It must be difficult at times for my friends and family. My inner critic is constantly judging and evaluating: "We really need to be ready to go by 6:00," "When you turn you shouldn't wander into the other lane," "I'll need to touch-up the paint around the woodwork."

Once I figured out that I was a One—a Perfectionist—I had the awareness to break out of the perfectionist borders I was putting around myself. For example, I was never aware of how much anger I had in me. That inner critic of mine was always on my back, hounding me about what was right or best, or the way something should be, and all that striving for perfection was pissing me off.

Now that I've talked about this stifled anger of mine, people will tell me how mad I'd look sometimes. They told me my face would be red, my jaw clamped tight, even my hands clenched, but I'd never acknowledge that I was angry. Now that I have observed that anger in myself, I can let it go. In fact, when I'm around people, I can relax those perfectionist boundaries and get away from listening for the rights/wrongs, shoulds/ought tos, and attend to the content of what's being said without constantly judging it.

Knowing my personality type has made me a much more flexible, open, and adaptable listener, both when listening to myself and others. Here I am, nearly forty years old, and just beginning to see how my personality type worked its way into my listening and general communication style.

Here's a partial list of what I learned about listening from understanding my perfectionist personality type:

- Don't over-focus on the what's right or wrong, attend to the content of the message instead
- Listen for other people's feelings toward criticism
- Let my anger out when it's appropriate
- Accept what's "Good enough"

- Forgive myself
- Mind my own business—I'm not responsible for your morality
- Get out of my judgment mode and just be present to listen
- Acknowledge that I'm human, I make mistakes

Personality Type Two, the Helper: **Someone who devotes herself/himself completely; "there are no greater givers than those who give themselves."[5]**

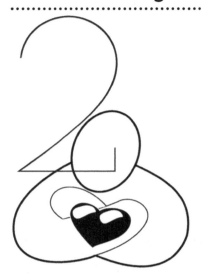

Also known as: the Care Giver, the Manipulator, the Guardian Angel, the "Power Behind the Throne."

The Helper's view of the world: *I will support and encourage others. They certainly can't do it without me.*

Self-description: "I am considerate, giving, and thoughtful; people are grateful for my help and care."

Positive characteristics: friendly, encouraging, optimistic, praising, enthusiastic, loving.

Negative characteristics: manipulative, seductive, flattering, martyr-like, self-sacrificing, plotting.

Notable Twos: Carolyn Hax, Jimmy Carter, Danny Glover, Roosevelt Grier, Melanie Griffith, Jesus Christ, Jerry Lewis, Jennifer Lopez, Nancy Reagan, Mr. Rogers, Mother Teresa, Ann Landers, Florence Nightengale, "Dr. McCoy" (Star Trek).[6]

Overview: Type Two, the Helper

As children, many Twos report they were rewarded with warmth, love, and security for helping others meet their needs. Their sense of listening to nonverbal messages is remarkable in that they have a finely developed radar-like awareness of others' moods and preferences—a disapproving look, an ignored comment, a slight nod of approval, the quiver of a smile.

They are tuned-in with all senses to subtle messages and cues that offer clues for helping someone. In fact, Helpers frequently put their own needs in the background to address the needs of others.

This "selfless" approach to life has Twos taking on characteristics that they believe will enhance their ability to accommodate the needs of the important people in their lives. In relationships, whether job related or personal, Twos will reach such a high degree of identity with their partners that they take on the personality traits that they believe will be most acceptable to the partner and situation. They can be warm and loving.

Helping, however, is not always the end goal of Helpers; rather, helping might be a means to gain approval and control. Twos expect efforts to be acknowledged and appreciated, because this is where they get their power, "The power behind the throne," and Helpers are devastated if efforts are not approved or are ignored.

Twos' sensitive attention to nonverbal messages is equally active in determining feedback. If the feedback is positive and affirming—"They needed me for this one," "They were lost without my help"—Twos are fulfilled. If, however, feedback shows a lack of appreciation—"He totally ignored what I did," "What was that frown about?" then Twos are compelled to regain that approval, since their self-worth is dependent on how others view them.

Twos are highly gifted verbal and nonverbal listeners who can use their listening abilities to either support or destroy. Consequently, they might be a source of inspiration and power in the background of a successful person. If, however, the Helpers' contributions are not recognized or are downplayed by the person they've been helping, the Twos can withhold support and contribute to the collapse of that success.

Type Two's Communication Style. Helpers are intensely observant and sensitive to the needs of people they consider important. They are prime examples of people completely immersed in the Listening Role. Twos engage all their senses and attend to feedback with such intensity that they lose themselves in the process: they feel and think like the sender.

Twos ask personal questions to gain information that will increase their ability to adapt. Their intense listening nonverbally and verbally enables them to be quick with a compliment and gives them a sense of what needs to be done to proceed toward success. While helping and giving in this manner, they work to strengthen their relationship to the point that they become indispensable to the person in charge.

Once Twos have listened and adapted, they can offer a lighthearted touch into exchanges and keep the relational and project energy moving forward by kidding and cajoling in a way that keeps energy directed toward these goals. Helpers will at times also use their charm to communicate seductively—not necessarily in a sexual manner, but any maneuver to get people to like them—in an effort to tighten their bond to further the goals of the project and the relationship.

As Helpers listen to themselves they come to realize that they have many selves, because they change their persona to match the needs of important people in their lives. When Twos begin the intrapersonal process of examining themselves, the exact nature of their personality becomes blurred, since they frequently alter their identity to fulfill the needs of the person being helped.

With further self-listening, Twos realize that they might be fooling others, perhaps so they won't be judged for who they really are, and they risk losing their personal authentic feelings. Helpers' intrapersonal listening reveals that being rewarded and acknowledged for meeting others' needs is necessary for them to continue this relationship or project, and if their help is ignored, Twos are likely to use knowledge to derail the relationship.

Maggie's Thoughts

It's been a long walk for me. I've been wandering around being so many people that I honestly had no idea who I was. Things really came to a head when the guy I had practically given my life to sent me on my way without (what seemed to me) a second thought. I met him four years ago; he was a handsome, witty pharmacist who had opened three new drug stores in the last five years. We were at a Christmas social for volunteers in our North side suburb. I saw him chatting with some other guys, one of whom I had done some volunteer work with. Anyway, we were introduced and we started to get to know each other.

I hung on every word, cueing in on his facial expressions, figuring out what he liked and disliked, his hobbies, his social world, his family background, his education, favorite TV shows, sports, drinks, food, art, vacation spots—you name it, I took it all in.

As I got to know him and we dated, I dressed the way he liked, familiarized myself with his hobbies, movies, and on and on. And (yes, you guessed it), I even studied pharmacy texts and articles on building businesses.

Well, long story short, when he slammed the door on me, I was shattered. Empty, empty, empty. My head felt like a merry-go-round, and something else was happening: I was searching for answers to my crazy handing over of myself to this other person.

One of the books I unearthed somewhere was about the Enneagram. I read it and came to realize that I seemed to fit in the Two category. As I studied more I realized I fit the Two mold pretty well; very well, in fact.

Anyway, when I first tried to listen to myself, *there was no self to listen to!* I didn't know who the hell I was. As I self-observed, insight slowly trickled into my mind. I discovered I did have my own private person, even though it was hard to find since I had given it away so often. Now I listen to myself, and here's what I listen to:

Most importantly, I listen to be aware when my real feelings are being replaced by the feelings of someone else. I don't want to lose myself again. "Don't put myself on a shelf," I reminded myself, and when I listened to myself and found I was doing that, I took a time-out to analyze what I was doing and where I was going. This shift of listening to myself kept me from losing myself by obsessively listening to someone else. It balanced my listening behavior.

Intrapersonal listening made me aware of issues that were problems that Twos like me need to face: wanting to act like someone else; fantasizing various ways of being loved; figuring out which of my selves is really me; staying in relationships with the one who "needs me more," rather that the one I really want to be with; fear of not having a real self; feeling insecure without the protection of other people; feelings that I've "bought" into relationships, that I've fooled people to become their friend; feeling that gaining approval is gaining love; fear that if I'm independent I can't be loved; playing power games by pursuing relationships that are unrealistic or hard-to-get.

All these were important, but one of the biggest insights for me was my compulsive attraction toward difficult relationships. I was challenged to go after the hard-to-get. It was like a game to see if I could bury myself into someone's thoughts and use that information to conquer affection and respect. This game playing became more important than really getting to know someone intimately and having a real relationship, because it turned into, "I won this one, now what's next?" In the end I might have won, but there was no deep relationship or commitment.

Personality Type Three, the Producer: A person who acts and gets things done; "a principal actor in this affair"; when you want to get something done get a "producer"; "a miracle worker."[7]

Also known as: the Performer, the Doer, the Manager, the Achiever, the Motivator.

The Producer's view of the world: *Life is a contest—a competition—and I can win if I appear successful and work hard.*

Self-description: "I know how to project an image that will lead me to success; I know how to get things done."

Positive characteristics: competent, industrious, ambitious, goal oriented, high achieving, organized, motivating, enthusiastic.

Negative characteristics: vain, unemotional, image centered, self-promoting, self-deceiving, status seeking, corner cutting, unauthentic.

Notable Threes: F. Scott Fitzgerald, Jesse Jackson, Michael Jordan, Demi Moore, Elvis Presley, Diane Sawyer, Arnold Schwarzenegger, William Shatner, Will Smith, Sylvester Stallone, George Washington, Oprah Winfrey, Tiger Woods. Bill Clinton, Jane Pauley, Tom Cruise, Barbra Streisand, Sharon Stone, Madonna, Sting, Paul McCartney, Ted Danson.[8]

Overview: Type Three, the Producer

As youngsters, many Threes remember being rewarded for their achievements. The grade on the test was more important to their parents than how the Three felt about the test. A scored touchdown or a concert well performed got more attention than the emotional ties and relationships within the team or orchestra. Performance and image were praised and rewarded; feelings or deep involvement with others were not.

Threes were loved for their achievements and were rewarded for winning and earning status and recognition, as well as for their leadership roles. Failure was to be avoided at all cost, because only achievers were worthy of love.

With their ability to adapt their energy and competitiveness to a variety of situations, Producers are compared to chameleons who take on the characteristics of whatever group they have chosen: the blue blazer and tan slacks of the businessman; the vested suit of the executive; the long hair, earrings, and scruffy jeans of the artist; the tweed jacket, patched elbows, and loafers of the professor. Image and success are top priorities, and Threes will adopt the image that fits the role needed to get the job done. They *become* that image, adapting chameleon-like to the setting. Car salespersons and politicians are the stereotypical models of the Three.

Threes are not vain about themselves; they are vain about what they do, and their self-esteem is derived from what they produce. When they are immersed in a task, they suspend their feelings so thoroughly that compliments or criticisms are perceived as directed to the product, not to them.

Take for example the Super Mom, with kids dressed perfectly, house immaculate, and a carefully structured calendar of events including school, sports, and social dates. In this case, the Producer Mom views the kids, the house, and the events as *products* of her efforts. When she receives a compliment, it is directed to her products—the kids, the house, the social calendar. She *is* what she produces.

In more intimate relationships, Threes again adopt the image of how one should look in an intimate setting, what they should do, what they should say. Rather than experiencing the feelings of their partner, they try to look and act empathically—they are playing the "intimate partner role" rather than actually sharing the feelings of the partner.

Type Three's Communication Style. Producers listen to comments about their products. Discussion of personal concerns such as feelings are uncomfortable because there isn't a tangible product involved. For example, Threes might express their feelings of love by conscientiously planning activities such as going to concerts, playing tennis, or taking trips. These activities are the *products* of love, and the quality of the products reflects the quality of the love. (Great dinner, wonderful concert equals great love.) A Three might not value "just visiting and hanging out for the day" because the product has no standards for evaluation.

In keeping with what we already know about Threes, it's not surprising that their lives are full of energy and busy with "getting things done." This focus on personal performance can lead to neglect of intrapersonal listening and self-reflection, and fits the Three's personality because self-esteem comes from the outside—from the product they've produced. Producers don't seek personal praise; they work for product praise.

Shane's Thoughts

Growing up, *what I did became who I was.* Of course, I didn't know that as a kid, but now I see it's true. When I was three or four, I found a big old box, about the size of a refrigerator, pulled it in the back yard on its side behind the bushes, cut a hole in the end for a door and one in the top for a window, put grass on the floor, and brought in some cans to use as dishes. Hurray! I'd made a house! I was proud.

When my older brother and my parents saw it they commented on what a great job I had done. Even aunts, uncles, and cousins admired it. I became Shane, the builder.

Later, in 5th grade, I won an essay contest, and became "Shane, the author." In high school I played basketball. I was pretty good—we won state my senior year, and I was high scorer—so it really pumped-up my image. (Shane the cool Jock!?)

I was recruited to play b-ball at seven universities and chose our state university—a top flight school with a renowned athletic program. I had a good freshman season; my grades were good (I was studying to be a mechanical engineer), and my image of student/athlete was glowing; I was PRODUCING.

Then something happened. Half-way into my sophomore season, the glow began to dim. The image wasn't pumping me anymore; BB wasn't fun. How could this be? I was scoring, rebounding, assisting, and we were winning. I had a "walk on water" image on campus, with my folks, with my girlfriend, but I felt empty.

I was taking a Speech-Communication class at the time, and the teacher was pretty down-to-earth and approachable (and also a big basketball fan). So after class, I asked him if I could come in and visit. That was okay with him. I clearly remember that conversation.

I told him I was everything I thought I'd ever want to be, but I was thinking of quitting the team.

"Why?"

"It's not, . . . well, . . . it's not fun, anymore."

"Fun?"

"Ya, all I feel is a lot of *pressure*. I come to practice, work hard, don't really know the other players outside of basketball. I'm there to perform—it's who I am."

"Pressure?"

"To keep up the image, you know. 'Shane J., 22 points; 11 rebounds; 8 assists; outstanding all-around player.'"

"Image?"

"Yes, as I just said, 'It's who I am.'"

"Maybe you're not who you think you are. Is there any more to you?"

"I hope so. Sure, has to be."

"There better be, because you're not happy with the image you have, do you think?"

"I guess."

"Sounds like you might want to quit that image."

"Hmm, we'll I didn't think about it that way."

"What's important to you?

"Well, what I can get done in life."

"What do you want to get done?

"Things that make people I care about proud of me."

"Okay, but what do *you* want to get done?"

"Me, ya, well. . . ."

"Sounds like you're feeling uncomfortable with basketball—if 'no fun' means uncomfortable. I mean 'fun' is sort of a feeling, and it isn't there for you with basketball, anyway. Also sounds like you've taken some time to listen to yourself and discovered you have feelings of your own—feelings not put on you by others, feelings that don't fit your image."

"I guess."

"You're a great player, and a lot of folks would sure miss you on the team. I love watching you play. But, all that aside, I think you've made a hell of a breakthrough in beginning to discover who you are. And I'd much rather see you knowing who you are than what others think you should be."

We ended the discussion with the prof. giving me a book on personality types—The Enneagram—and that started me on a trip of self-discovery that connected me to myself and ultimately to others.

I quit the team, and take my word for it, there were tons of pressure to "Finish what you started," "Get the job done," "Don't be a quitter." But staying on the team wouldn't have been fun; wouldn't have been me.

After that visit and my quitting the team, I was amazed at how little time it took for me to begin to listen to myself and others. I found it freeing and fulfilling.

Oh, not only did I brush off the image of star basketball player, but I also moved to another major. Today, I'm teaching high school French. I love who I am and what I'm doing. My parents and relatives are okay with it too.

Looking back on this personality game I played, here are some of the understandings about myself that I found.

First—and most helpful for me—I began to untangle my "image" feelings from my "real" feelings. This meant some intense internal listening to figure out which were really my feelings and which were the feelings I thought my "image" person should have. This was probably my hardest listening exercise, because I was so removed from who I was and so absorbed with who I thought I should be. I'd actually set aside a half-hour every morning to lie down, close my eyes, and meditate about what I was feeling.

After I was aware of my feelings, I came to realize that I had been bypassing my feelings, because my image of myself told me I had already "arrived." I was my image.

Finally, this intrapersonal listening made a huge change in my personal relationships. Before, I took on the feelings and emotions that went with my current image, now I could disclose *personal* issues, emotions, feelings, and listen with empathy and understanding.

Some author—I don't remember who—wrote, "We put on a mask to meet the world." I guess that's true, but it sure gets uncomfortable under that mask, and it feels good to take it off.

Personality Type Four, the Romantic: A person who is sensitive, introspective, and temperamental; feels special, gifted, and unique. Romantics explore their feelings and long to be understood while searching for the missing meanings of life.[9]

Also known as: the Artist, the Creator, the Individualist, the Mystic, the Melodramatic one.

The Romantic's view of the world: *My work is authentic and affects people; I don't fit the mold, my style is unique, deep and graceful. I often feel emptiness because something is missing.*

Self-description: "I am a sensitive artist, a poet of life. My art, however, leaves me feeling dark and melancholy—emotionally drained and vulnerable."

Positive characteristics: artistic, passionate, aesthetically sensitive, refined, authentic, unique, spiritual, accomplished.

Negative characteristics: moody, self-conscious, self-involved, contrary, self-deprecating, depressive, envious, melancholy, nostalgic.

Notable Fours: Marlon Brando, Jackson Browne, Mary Chapin Carpenter, Eric Clapton, Johnny Depp, Bob Dylan, Judy Garland, Michael Jackson, Jewel, Angelina Jolie, Prince, Meryl Streep, James Taylor, Virginia Woolf.[10] Paul Simon, Patrick Stewart, Miles Davis, J.D. Salinger, Tennessee Williams, Edgar Allan Poe.[11]

Overview: Type Four, the Romantic

As youngsters, many Fours report some degree of abandonment, whether from family members or other important people in their lives, and they harbor feelings of emptiness which become the backdrop for their approach to life. Reaching into personal feelings becomes Fours' obsession, and in a bitter-sweet way they revel in the drama of creating scenes where they are accepted and loved.

The earlier discussion of the Two personality, the Giver/Helper, noted that Twos tend to lose their sense of self and take the feelings of others as their own. The Romantic, however, runs in the opposite direction, tending to ignore others and bury themselves in their own feelings.

Since many Fours have experienced abandonment, they question their self-worth: "There must be some reason that caused them to leave me," "I had love, but now it's gone." Turning inward, they create scenes that could have corrected the situation: "If only I had. . . ." "I should have. . . ."

Romantics pursue life trying to fill this emptiness with love, while at the same time feeling an attraction to the dark, dramatic moods of their emptiness. Fours are attracted to their feelings of emptiness and longing, and experience "sweet regret" in these melancholy moods. Sometimes these moods reach states of depression, where Fours isolates themselves, focusing on past mistakes.

Perhaps to compensate for their feelings of unworthiness, Fours will pursue relationships that are unattainable or unavailable and reject those that are reachable. This behavior puts them in a no-win situation: "I want to have the depth of love that others have, but the person who could give me that depth is unavailable."

The rich imaginations of Fours create a picture of a splendid future, and these Romantics become angry and disappointed with mundane, day-to-day events. In their minds, they create relationships that always ride on a wave of "sweetness and light," but when faced with the reality of routine daily living, they become disenchanted. "He can't even clear the kitchen counter," "She doesn't have a clue about the poetry of Keats," "Can't he shut the lid?" "I had to take the bus into work." To protect this splendid dream-bubble from bursting, Fours will angrily push their partners away, but not totally out of the picture, since they still want the intimacy of their idealized world.

Type Four's Communication Style. Romantics find it difficult to listen in the present; their attention drifts to the past, to the future, the unattainable. They unconsciously listen for what is *missing*—the guest who didn't show up, the conversation that was interrupted. Instead of attending to the reality of the communication, Fours lose themselves by evaluating the message—focusing on what *should be* instead of what *is*. "Someday my prince or princess will come, but this one doesn't quite make it."

Fours feel anger from their sense of being abandoned, and this anger is often communicated as sarcasm. It is a way for Fours to get even for being so badly hurt. If there is no opportunity to vent to someone else, Fours will turn to self-criticism.

Romantics thrive on intense, dramatic communication—they can feel someone's grief and will help them evolve to a more comfortable emotional level. In a crisis—perhaps something dangerous or disturbing like a birth or a death—Fours are active, effective listeners.

Alison's Thoughts

In reading a book about The Enneagram, a simple descriptive sentence really hit home: "Fours are envious of the love they see in others, and they want something like that for themselves." Up to that time, I was just reading about personality types (a topic that I was mildly curious about), but that sentence summarized the theme of a letter I had written a couple months ago to an advice column that was carried in my local newspaper. Here's what I wrote:

Dear _____

I'm a 33 year old attractive (so I'm told) interior designer with a Master's degree and good income. I am usually pretty happy and sociable and have dated several men over the past six years. Our relationships usually start out well, but when things get close and intimate, I begin to notice flaws in my partner.

Sometimes these guys strike me as odd or inconsiderate. For example, one guy liked to put his bare feet on the coffee table while watching TV; one wouldn't shave before going on a date, saying it was the style to have a stubble beard; one would hit his fist on the table when the Steelers made a touchdown. Suffice it to say these "cracks" in character caused me to distance myself from them.

After I put some space between us, I'd begin to regret moving apart, and work toward renewing the relationship. But the closer we'd get, the more flaws I'd notice, and this yo-yoing farther and closer would eventually end the relationship altogether.

What I yearn for is a close, kind, understanding relationship with a nice guy, but it seems like the closer I get, the more I notice the negative aspects. Believe me, these guys aren't all negative by any means. Overall, they are fine people, but at close range, all I'm able to focus on are the flaws.

I see many of my friends with warm, hand-holding relationships, and I'm glad for them. Am I asking too much to have that for myself?

Alison, Waiting and Hoping in Indiana

Further reading and self-observation led me to know that I was a Four—a tragic romantic. What an eye opener *that* was, and how freeing to be able to accept the positive characteristics of my personality and work around the ones that were interfering with my relationships.

I'll probably never be able to have that perfect relationship, but I've been dating a fine guy for nearly two years, and we're getting married in May. I still stumble into my sense that maybe there's something out there that I'm missing, but now I'm able to go inside my mind and understand that this kind of thinking is just an escape from reality. Overall, I'm happy with where I am, and this is as good as it gets.

For the past two years I've been on this personality awareness trip, and here's what listening to myself has taught this Romantic:

I tended to believe that something was missing from my life, and was envious because my friends had what I was missing.

Because I longed for the perfect world—utopia—and the ideal lover, I was attracted to the distant and unavailable. After all, if my ideal world or lover was far off, I didn't have to face his imperfections.

Since my self-esteem was low, I would use my manners, moods, luxuries, and "classy taste" to raise my self-esteem.

I would enjoy wallowing in melancholy moods to experience my great (and admirable?) depth of feeling. I actually took pleasure in my dark moods.

I was bored and impatient with ordinary, everyday living. I wanted drama, loss, or sorrow, and I sometimes would escape the mundane through my imagination.

Finally, I found that I was sensitive to others' feelings, emotions, and pains, and I could allow them to unburden their pain and provide support for them.

Personality Type Five, the Observer: **A person who becomes aware (of things or events) through the senses; a bystander; a viewer.**[12]

Also known as: the Investigator, the Thinker, the Sage, the Wise One, the Philosopher, the Scholar, the Professor.

The observer's view of the world: *My deep commitment to gathering specialized knowledge makes me the undeniable expert in my field. I am thoughtful and wise.*

Self-description: "My mind is my best friend, and my thoughts can take on a life of their own, providing answers to complex questions."

Positive characteristics: thoughtful, objective, wise, knowledgeable, self-motivated, idea oriented, perceptive.

Negative characteristics: unapproachable, cold, aloof, detached, arrogant, "intellectual," nerdy.

Notable Fives: St. Thomas Aquinas, Isaac Asimov, Stephen Hawking, Samuel Beckett, The Buddha, Amelia Earhart, Albert Einstein, T.S. Eliot, Bill Gates, Alfred Hitchcock, Franz Kafka, Dean Koontz, George Lucas,[13] John Lennon, Lily Tomlin, Gary Larson, James Joyce, Susan Sontag, Emily Dickinson, Jane Goodall, Stephen King, Friedrich Nietzsche, Agatha Christie, Vincent Van Gogh.[14]

Overview: Type Five, the Observer

Fives report that they felt their territory was often invaded when they were children, and when their privacy was breeched, they defended themselves by withdrawing and turning their attention to the world of ideas. As adults, they remain reclusive, living almost hermit-like, at home, in their office, or at the library.

Observers avoid involvement—business and social interactions and obligations are viewed as coercive and competitive, and emotional connections are threatening. Safety and independence keep Fives from joining in. Intimate relationships are entered only when Fives know that their independence is assured, and they can comfortably withdraw when they want to.

Fives' isolation removes them from the world of human feelings and emotions, and they experience loneliness. Because of this desire for privacy, they haven't become practiced at human interaction, so building human companionship is difficult. To fill loneliness, Observers bury themselves in knowledge, the world of ideas, and fantasies.

Type Five's Communication Style. Observers shrink from human interaction. They have difficulty sharing their feelings with others, and use their private time to figure out how they really feel; they analyze and replay conversations they had during the day.

Being in the spotlight or the center of attention, for example, sales, or advertising, is uncomfortable for them. Observers feel that their intellectual gifts and cool objectivity put them above these pursuits, and they deserve to be sheltered from these professional competitors. They avoid group discussions, preferring to share their interests with friends in one-to-one settings, and many of these friends may not know each other.

When Fives do interact with others, they sometimes will "leave" the conversation and retreat into themselves, staring blankly at an object or above someone's head. When they do interact, they are reluctant to offer any personal information, since self-disclosure—especially of feelings— would expose too much of the private self.

Observers' need for independence is intense, and this intensity is communicated with expressed attitudes: "I don't need you"; "I can get along without you."

Dante's Thoughts

It's very difficult for me to write about myself, and I've been staring at the computer screen for over two hours without hitting a key. I've finally begun to understand who I am, and, importantly the design and mechanics of myself as a Five—Observer. It's comfortable for me to think about myself in the abstract, but writing my thoughts for others to read is very threatening to me. Anyway, here goes.

I grew up in a small house that afforded no privacy. Except for the one bathroom, there was no place to escape. My bedroom was a throughway from the front entry of the house to the bathroom, and the other bedroom shared the bathroom from the other side.

I'd never thought about this layout until I started reading about the Enneagram personality types, which made me realize that much of my adult behavior was shaped by my personality and the design of the house I grew up in. Kind of bizarre, but seems to be true.

Well, when I couldn't hide out in my bedroom, I'd go up to the attic, but it was often too hot or too cold. The next choice was the library, which was only three blocks away.

My dad was a chemist and mom an elementary school teacher. Education was important to them, and it naturally became important to me. I went to a good high school and majored in physics in college.

College became the ultimate "hide out" for me. I could work in the physic's lab, alone, until early morning, and during the day find solitude in the library. I could emerge from my social cocoons to interact with a few fellow physics majors and my professors, then remove myself to my private worlds to think things through and rehash the few conversations from the day.

This Observer lifestyle worked okay for college and for a while in my professional life (I work for a hydraulic pump manufacturer). But gradually I began to notice loneliness; my mind-world wasn't enough, and the few friends I had only shared ideas about our work and physics. So being the reclusive "mind gamer" that I was, I went about researching ideas about why I was feeling such emptiness in my life. Ironically, I thought dealing with loneliness could be solved by *thinking* about it—*working out a model of loneliness.*

Well, the research did, in fact (after three years of thinking) begin to produce some answers. I realized I was a Five, and quite literally had to come out of hiding to be less lonely. I know I'll always be an Observer, but at least now I can enjoy a much fuller life.

I've been married for a year-and-a-half, and I can share feelings with my understanding wife, and still, at times escape to my office (which is *not* connected to a bathroom) and close the door. She and I both know our personality types (she's a Two—a Helper/Giver), and we can use the knowledge of our types to work together. Our relationship is fun and fulfilling, and we really can connect and laugh sometimes about who we are.

I understand that part of this essay is supposed to be what I learned from exploring my personality type. Here's what this intrapersonal listening showed me, the Observer:

Almost everything I found out about myself came from turning inside myself and listening, and becoming *aware:*

- that I manipulated people by withholding and withdrawing. This was a power and control issue with me, "I'll finish the project or share my thoughts when I want to; not when you want me to."
- that I would replace my feelings and emotions with an analytic cover, and replace thoughts for actual experiences. For example, if I felt angry, I would push the anger aside and reconstruct the events that prompted the anger—what was done; what was said—and analyze the behaviors and words as a substitute for the feeling of anger.
- that feelings don't always have to hurt, they are just a part of who I am.
- that I wanted praise and recognition when I really hadn't done anything to earn anyone's attention.
- that I would leave those around me and retreat to my mind.
- of the three Ss relevant to us Fives—secrecy, superiority, and separateness.[15]
- of other peoples' feelings, needs and emotions.
- of withholding information about myself.
- that to be a whole person, I need to be involved emotionally, physically, and intellectually with people.

Personality Type Six, the Trouble Shooter: believes that the world is dangerous—Something to be feared; visualizes the problems or dangers for any situation.[16]

Also known as: the Skeptic, the Devil's Advocate, the Loyalist, the True Believer.

At the center of the Trouble Shooter's personality are phobias, which are defined as irrational, intense, persistent fears of certain situations, activities, things, or people.[17]

In dealing with these phobias, Sixes fall into two categories: *Phobic* and *Counterphobic.*

Phobic Sixes are paralyzed by their phobias and withdraw from threatening scenes.

Counterphobic Sixes confront their fears and advance into threatening scenes.

The Trouble Shooter's view of the world: Things go wrong; the world is dangerous; careful planning is necessary; things and people aren't always as they seem; I need dependable allies.

Self-description: "When I need to get something done or make a big decision, I seek the advise of people I trust; if no one's around, I'll postpone the decision and study all the aspects of the problem."

Positive characteristics: loyal, cautious, responsible, committed, witty, friendly, supportive, imaginative, self-sacrificing.

Negative characteristics: fearful, doubtful, paranoid, persecuted, suspicious, negative, accusatory, doubting, procrastinating.

Notable Sixes:

Phobic: Jason Alexander, Woody Allen, Kim Basinger, Rodney Dangerfield, Eminem, Jack Lemmon, Bob Newhart, Richard Nixon, Paul Reiser, Larry David.

Counterphobic: Harry Potter, George Carlin, Carrie Fisher, Mel Gibson, Gene Hackman, Dustin Hoffman, Tommy Lee Jones, Wynonna Judd, Spike Lee, David Letterman, Michael Moore, Paul Newman, Robert Redford, Julia Roberts, Meg Ryan, Jon Stewart, Ted Turner, Chuck Yeager.[18]

Overview, Type Six, the Trouble Shooter

As youngsters, many Sixes report losing trust and being powerless in interactions with authority figures: parents, relatives, teachers, pastors, neighbors, sitters, and so on. Often they felt powerless in determining how they should behave or even what they should believe. Growing into adulthood, these feelings of powerlessness led them to mistrust authority; consequently, Troubleshooters will either withdraw from or confront authority. In either case, when an authority does win the Six's trust, they will be loyal and supportive.

The last chapter develops the concept that external behavior is the product of internal dispositions, and since Sixes don't trust themselves, they have trouble trusting others and making confident decisions ("Should I?" "Maybe I should think more about it." "I'd better put this off 'til later.").

As discussed above, a core force of Sixes is *phobic*, which means *fear* driven. Sixes can either remain immobilized by fear or, through self-listening, face their fears, becoming *counterphobic* Sixes. For example, a young phobic Six might imagine there's a monster in her closet and she hides under the covers. A counterphobic Six imagines a monster in her closet, swallows her fear, and opens the closet door to check it out. The fear is there in both cases, but the reactions are different.

So we see that phobic self-doubt and lack of trust can immobilize Sixes to the point where they won't attempt anything but basic survival tasks. They look at what's involved in a project, and everything that could go wrong jumps out at them, stops them in their tracks, and they retreat into the safety of doing nothing.

However, Sixes who face their fears, counterphobic Sixes, can become effective Trouble Shooters; they are already acutely aware of problems so they become proactive and anticipate and prepare for problems ahead of time. These counterphobic Sixes use their imaginations to anticipate what and where problems might arise. With their knack for forecasting possible difficulties, they are well equipped for trouble-shooting and helping prepare for upcoming projects.

Type Sixes' Communication Style. Trouble Shooters listen with doubt: "Do I have all the facts?" "I know there's more to it than that; it can't be that simple." To overcome their fearful suspicions, they seek feedback from someone they trust about conclusions and decisions; moreover, they sometimes question whether they can trust this person at this time.

Sixes have trouble connecting with their feelings, but they love analyzing situations outside of themselves. At times, this focus on analysis leads to nonstop discussions about all the possible variables that might enter into a process.

Sixes want *clear* communication. They want to know others' thoughts on issues; they want agreement before moving forward on a project.

Nonverbally, Trouble Shooters watch for subtle messages. They will put exaggerated meanings into looks and gestures, and often these meanings are perceived as negative or threatening.

Helga's Thoughts

My life outlook has always had a negative cast to it. I remember being at a big wooded park with some friends when I was eight or so and being afraid of getting lost and not being able to get home. My friends assured me everything would be okay, and they knew the way out of there, but I could only settle down once we came to a familiar place.

Fear was always at the heart of my being, but I also wanted adventure, and fear and adventure had trouble mixing. For example, when I was in fourth grade we lived near a university campus that had what was known as "university cliff," a really steep, curvy hill that was probably three quarters of a mile long. Well, my friends would ride their bikes down it, entering it as fast as they could go, gaining speed all the way down. I really wanted to do that, but my fears would get in the way. I'd think stuff that no one else seemed to think about: what if a tire blew? What if a branch from last night's wind storm fell across the path and I hit it? What about my brakes? They could fail. What if someone walking or running up the hill couldn't get out of my way? What if last night's rain washed sand and gravel over the path and I'd lose traction and fall or hit another biker or a tree? And my imagination would go on and on and on.

But I wanted to go down that hill, so I'd prepare as best I could, try to shut off all my endless fear imaginations and go down the freaking hill, but only after a world of thought and procrastination.

Okay, plug this kind of behavior into almost everything in my life. Going to school, "What are my friends going to wear?" "Lunch, what should I take?" "Math is scary-hard." And, as usual, I'd extend my concerns on and on and on. I think if my parents and the law didn't make me go to school, I just would have stayed home. As it was, I procrastinated and stayed home "sick" as much as I could get away with.

Now that I'm on a roll I could extend my Troubleshooter behavior into so many parts of my life. Imagine my first real date; taking my driver's test; my first piano recital; getting a part in the play; leaving for college; my first cross country trip alone; getting married; the first kid. Believe me, none of these events went without worry, wailing, procrastinating, and the strong urge to run away and put my head under the blanket or just stay home and watch TV. Each event was overwhelming and my mind would almost reflexively snap into "Screw it; it's just too freaking much."

I'm a for-sure Six, and I wish I could have understood it earlier. The counterphobic part of me knows about my fear-driven self and kicks my ass to prepare and get on with it. But now that I can listen to my "Sixishness" I can move ahead with the knowledge that I'm typically well prepared for whatever I need to do (I still don't handle surprises well because I can't prepare for them). The old adage, "knowledge is power," really fits me here. Now that I'm aware of my personality traits as a Trouble Shooter, I can take advantage of them and not be paralyzed by them. **My routine is think, prepare, and DO IT.**

I replace procrastination with doing. This is really important for me because I can find any reason to put off doing even small, insignificant tasks, such as simply sending a birthday card to a friend.

I push myself to finish projects.

I seek situations where I can trust authority, so that I don't rebel against them or simply submit to them; rather, I work *with* them.

I modify my nonverbal listening, remembering that I tend to be suspicious and replace the suspiciousness with neutrality: "What's really being communicated?" Do a reality check.

I trouble shoot thoroughly but don't overkill preparation to the point that I'm immobilized.

At times I need to quit blathering about all the aspects of a problem and *listen* to others.

I remember to focus on positive outcomes rather than negative ones. (I tend to focus on worst-case outcomes—surprised?)

Finally, I accept change: it's usually okay, and it's inevitable anyway.

Personality Type Seven, the Enthusiast: Focuses on pleasure, adventure, and excitement; there is always something new and different ahead, lives for what tomorrow will bring.[19]

Also known as: the Visionary, the Planner, the Optimist, the Imagination Engineer, the Explorer, the Creator, the Quitter.

The Enthusiast's view of the world: *To explore what's over the next hill; to explore strange new worlds . . . to go boldly where no one has gone before.*

Self-description: "I love to have fun and be loose, and maybe my behavior is outrageous. I just move forward and don't look back."

Positive characteristics: approachable, pleasant, innovative, witty, enthusiastic, inspirational, optimistic.

Negative characteristics: overextended, irresponsible, scattered, shallow, distracted, hyperactive, undisciplined.

Notable Sevens: John F. Kennedy, Benjamin Franklin, Leonard Bernstein, Leonardo DiCaprio, Steven Spielberg, Robin Williams, Jim Carey, Elton John, Howard Stern,[20] George Clooney, Katie Couric, Tom Hanks, Goldie Hawn, Thomas Jefferson, Steve Jobs, Jack Nicholson, Brad Pitt, Barbra Streisand, Elizabeth Taylor, Billy Crystal, Dick Van Dyke, William Wordsworth.[21]

Overview, Type Seven, the Enthusiast

Fives, Sixes, and Sevens are fear-based personality types. The Fives deal with their fear by observing from a distance; Sixes cope with fear by either withdrawing or preparing for a feared event, and Sevens cope with fear by projecting their lives into the limitless possibilities of the future.

In some ways, Sevens remain children. Like Peter Pan, in Never-Never Land, Enthusiasts are happy-go-lucky folks who dream of flying (without an airplane), confronting pirates and crocodiles. They see themselves as valuable, and seek people and environments that affirm their unique worth.

Sevens report pleasant childhood memories. Even if someone were to judge Sevens' situations as undesirable, Sevens report little bitterness or blame, with an attitude of, "We just won't let that stuff drag us down." Sevens are in their own world of adventure, high spirits, and expectations, and become self-involved in their own excellence. This self-involvement can be so strong that they have difficulty accepting objective feedback and suggestions about where they're going with their lives.

Sevens cope with their fears by making plans to eliminate boredom and maximize fun, and they see their future options as limitless. There is always something to do, some place to go: "Right now, I'm committed to this path, but if it doesn't offer excitement and adventure, I have many other paths to take." This "go with the flow" approach keeps Sevens in an endless spin of possible options: if relationship *A* doesn't work out, there's always *B*; if the timing for *B* isn't quite right, *C* is usually a good choice.

Enthusiasts' strong optimism produces remarkably creative, unique, broad-based approaches to their problemsolving. For example, job option *A* might be flying a rescue helicopter for the Department of Transportation, but since that didn't work out at this time, the Seven turns to option *B*, washing dogs at a kennel, and later, option *C*, selling art supplies at a bookstore.

Type Seven's Communication Style. Enthusiasts communicate with positive, upbeat, charm. They listen with excitement and intensity. Nonverbally, they smile and appear attentive, using energetic, animated vocal and facial expressions and gestures.

Enthusiasts maintain emotional energy about all the activities and interesting things that are going on. Often their message content touches a variety of options which avoids focusing on and committing to a single course of action.

Confrontation is not comfortable for Sevens, and they are deft at sidestepping it by easing the conversation into new topics. When Sevens disagree, or think they know what is going to be said, or their abilities are being questioned, or they perceive that the content of a message is going to limit their choices and possibly push them into a commitment, they will stop listening or change the subject.

Lily's Thoughts

My parents always told me I could do anything I want; I just have to put my mind to it. "You're so good at so many things," they'd say, "you can go anywhere you want." I believed this, and also came to know that I was special. Multi-gifted. I really thought this was true.

What this belief in a magic multi-gifted approach did for me was open so many options that I couldn't settle on anything without always wondering what else was available. For example, I'd try ballet, but jazz looked intriguing, so I'd transfer to that—ballet was too much work anyway, and not nearly as cool. In high school, I wanted to be in drama; everyone thought I was a natural actor, so when I tried for a part (and didn't get it) I reasoned that I really didn't want to commit the time to it anyway because what I really wanted to do was mock trial and debate.

This jumping from interest to interest also affected my relationships. I'd date a guy for awhile, but when things smelled of "steady dating," I got a little frightened about being tied down and would ease my way out of the relationship—usually on good terms.

I always had great plans and could get people to join my team, but once the ball was rolling, I'd get kind of bored and want to begin another project. Just before I dropped out of college, I started a drama club with a bunch of friends. We selected a play, found a place to practice and stage it, but just when we were ready to mount the production, I turned the project over to my second-in-command because I got a chance to go to New Zealand with my cousin and his wife—it was just too good to pass up. Everyone understood, and there were no hard feelings as far as I could tell.

I was about twenty-three when money got tight and my jumping around lifestyle was most certainly providing me with excitement and adventure, but not with security. In fact, I was living in a dump with barely enough room to store my stuff. I had lots of friends, was always welcomed wherever I went, but couldn't pay the rent.

At this point, my life's circumstances pushed me to turn within myself to see what was going on. One of the many jobs that I jumped into was working in a bookstore, and it was here that I stumbled onto a book on the Enneagram. At first I thought it was just more popculture, psycho-babble crap like astrology, or *How to Succeed by Analyzing Yourself to Find the Real You in Ten Easy Steps*. True to form, I was ready to dump it and find something more exciting and interesting. But there was just enough intriguing information on personalities that I began to see where some of my friends fit into the types. As I paged my way through, I caught myself identifying with the Seven. "Hmmm, that's kind of like me," I thought.

With typical enthusiasm and energy, I immersed myself in Type Seven, and the more I read, the more I identified with it. Of course, my reflex was to jump away from it, since analyzing myself was totally foreign; my plan *B* was to grab another book to read, or plan *C*, go have a Coke with my friends. For some reason I opted out of those plans and stuck with the Enneagram book.

After about three months I began to get a better picture of who I was and what I was doing with my life. It was a great beginning and after almost two-and-a-half years, I'm still getting insights. Here's where I am:

At age twenty-seven I'm letting go of my preoccupation with youth and youthful adventure. I value maturing and committing to projects.

I'm listening to myself and realizing that my life has not always been such a bold adventure, and I'm talking through some of these issues with helpful people.

I'm looking at my behavior, and noticing that all my hectic over-scheduling, multi-tasking, and option hunting are just ways to run away from facing myself. The same with chasing superficial pleasure: it's just another way to escape, and leads to more and more running.

"Commitment" and "responsibility" are not dirty words (for me, they weren't even in my vocabulary), and first I had to commit and be responsible to myself—listen to my feelings and rationale for what I do—before I could commit responsibly to anything or anyone else. This was really hard.

Lastly, learning to stay in the here and now. This was huge, since *escape* was my reaction to almost everything. Escape through charm, pleasant stories, fantasy, adventure, excitement, new options. Now I say to myself, "Lily, what are you running from now?" If I listen to myself long enough, I can usually come up with the answer.

Personality Type Eight, the Boss: Makes decisions or exercises authority. Gives orders, especially in an arrogant or domineering manner.[22]

Also known as: the Top Dog, the Chief, The Leader, *The* Woman/Man, the Protector, the Power Broker, the Control Freak.

The Eight's view of the world: *I am in charge. I am competent, commanding; someone to be reckoned with who will right the world's wrongs.*

Self-description: "I'm a tough negotiator, and will dig deep to win. I'm a survivor who won't back down."

Positive characteristics: generous, inspirational, responsible, powerful, energetic, protective.

Negative characteristics: controlling, intimidating, confrontational, vengeful, punitive, exploitive.

Notable Eights: Charles Barkley, Muhammad Ali, Humphrey Bogart, Julius Caesar, Napoleon, Martin Luther King Jr.,[23] Rush Limbaugh, Sean Penn, Queen Latifah, Theodore Roosevelt, Frank Sinatra, Donald Trump, Denzel Washington, Pink, Franklin Roosevelt, Barbara Walters, John McCain.[24]

Overview: Type Eight, the Boss

Many Eights report growing up in combative homes where family members who maintained control were respected; those losing control were seen as weak and were not respected. Consequently, Eights are driven by power and control. Some degree of control is manifested in all personality types, but Bosses' focus on controlling is aggressive and direct; subtle diplomacy is not the approach to gain a grip on the situation.

In the Eight's mind, power equals control, so Bosses regularly check where they are in the power range. If they are in a subordinate position, they will push the rules to find out what penalties will be imposed on them. For example, in a social situation, Bosses may choose to smoke in a host's home, knowing that this might well be against the house rules. If they get away with it, they might look for new rules to test; however, if asked to smoke outside, the limit of power in this situation is clear. At this point, Bosses will seek out new limits to test.

In leadership positions, Eights will forgo diplomacy and use the massiveness of sheer power to build a secure empire. The empire may be the home, the workplace, the vacation cottage. In Eights' minds, fighting, rather than diplomatic alliance-building, is the path to intimacy, because in Eights' way of thinking, the true character of a person comes out in a fight. Consequently, Bosses will test the state of loyalty and trust of associates by aggressively pushing on sensitive issues— perhaps political or religious—to provoke a fight.

Eights will take a rigid position and defend it without listening to their own reasons for the position. They believe questioning themselves only weakens the strength of their argument: "I'm right, now let's build the facts and logic to back this up."

Eights strive for control in their lives, but when they achieve it, they become bored and start looking for trouble. They will take their extra energy and create turmoil by picking a fight, bothering neighbors, or making a big deal out of nothing: "Why is the toaster in *that* cabinet?"

Another way Bosses deal with boredom and unused energy is through extreme behavior. They might work all night, listen intensely to music, eat huge amounts of food, engage excessively in sex and/or liquor.

Type Eight's Communication Style. Eights listen with eyes and ears ready for conflict. Nonverbally, like poker players, they notice signs of weakness and vulnerability, watching for reactions and cues that signal defensiveness, uncertainty, ignorance, evasiveness, fear, insecurity.

Bosses listen for challenges to their assertions and aggressively push back whenever possible. They will defend their stand on an issue even when objective, outside observation proves they are wrong. However, when Eights are challenged, they will not readily admit defeat, but they will respect the challenger.

Eights perceive messages to be polarized—right or wrong; bad or good; strong or weak; fair or unfair, raw or burned. Middle of the road ideas don't often exist for them—Bosses talk and listen in "either/or" terms, and, in their view, they are *right*.

Etta's Thoughts

I guess the best way to get at this is to just write about myself and see where it goes. I'm forty-two years old, mother of three—two daughters, one son, undergraduate degree in electrical engineering from Marquette, law degree from Georgetown. Mainly work in patents, particularly where there are infringement disputes. I love heavy, confrontational cases, particularly involving big Fat Cats who think they can walk all over the little guy.

I've been married for fifteen years, and our tumultuous relationship is beginning to settle down and becoming more peaceful and easy, this corner being turned (starting about two years ago) by my very reluctant realization that I fit squarely into the Enneagram Eight—Boss—personality point. Believe me, squaring off and listening to myself was NOT natural and most certainly not easy for me. With me, admitting personal flaws means I LOSE. In fact, for me to admit flaws, faults, and cracks in my beliefs and stands on issues was a hell of a lot harder than college, law school, or raising kids. For some reason I still crumble and find it earth shaking to acknowledge to myself (and ultimately to someone else) that I was wrong. I despise being wrong (a loser) about anything—even tiny, totally inconsequential matters.

I'm the oldest of three, and our family is actually pretty caring and loving—at least I always thought so. As I look back, maybe not so much. Both my parents were very smart, bright people. Dad was upper management in a big manufacturing outfit; mom, mainly a homemaker. We all got along okay, but we were always playing a game of one-upsmanship. Reaching agreement was not a goal, but winning was. The tools used to win were anger, yelling, slamming doors, and sometimes with us kids, slugging it out. In spite of this win-at-all-costs culture, I'm the only one who is an Eight. My pilot brother is probably a Six, and Nancy, a Two.

I'll submit an example of how fixated on winning, winning, winning, I can get. A few years back, my brother (a pilot, two years younger than I) and I got into a discussion about the earth shattering concept of "clockwise" and "counter-clockwise." He was sitting across the table from me, and we were visiting about flying. In the course of the discussion, he mentioned that when you hand prop (stand facing the front of a small plane and turn the propeller to start it) you always spin the propeller, which is positioned diagonally from upper left to lower right as you face it, by grabbing the upper left end and pulling it downward which would turn it in a counter-clockwise motion. Sitting across from him, I authoritatively argued that that would be clockwise, from my point of view.

He agreed, and, had he been discussing this with another personality type, that would have ended the clockwise/counter-clockwise discussion. However, I, the Boss, had to expand my point of view to show his stupidity, and *win* the argument that I started and expanded.

Why wouldn't I just accept the fact that our positions at the table created a different point of view? Because "clockwise" and "counter-clockwise" didn't matter any more; it became more important that "little brother" wasn't right, because, "a person could, in fact, stand behind the plane and prop it clockwise."

"You could," he acknowledged, "but it would be almost impossible to stand the other way and do it."

"But you *could,* so you don't always turn it counter-clockwise," I pushed. "And you said you *always* prop counter-clockwise."

"Well, yeah," he admitted, "but you'd never do that."

"So," I kept pushing, "it's not always counter-clockwise, is it?"

"Given the way you're looking at it, I guess not," he resigned.

Although I don't say it out loud, I'm thinking, "I'm right; you're wrong—I WIN, you're a lousy pilot, Ha, Ha."

I hope all this gives the reader enough backdrop to see who I am, and was.

As I mentioned above, about two years ago an introduction to The Enneagram prompted me to start some self-observation. Here's where this intrapersonal listening has led me.

My obsession with power and control. As I look back, I can't believe I was so blind to this. P & C were literally the center of my life, and I used aggression and anger as the main tools to gain and hold P & C. As an attorney, this obsession, when linked with my concern for justice and protection for the downtrodden, armed me for success. I loved going after those S.O.B.s.

I discovered that I connected with friends and family by arguing and fighting. A good fight let me know where they stood on an issue, and, for me, (not necessarily for them, however) increased our intimacy.

I encountered health problems brought on by my excessive behaviors. When I'd get bored, I'd dig into a case I was arguing, sometimes not sleeping for a couple days, or I'd dig into booze or pizza. This bingeing to overcome boredom didn't begin to catch up to me 'til my late thirties. Here, again, this Eight behavior was chopping away at my health.

My legal profession was energized by my viewing the opposition as evil and my client as good, and I'd go after the opposition with all the passion of a priest exorcising the devil. This approach won many cases, but bringing this "either/or" approach into my personal relationships was not winning me much loyalty, love, or warmth.

I learned to use my Boss behavior when needed in my cases, and was sharply aware that I could turn it off when in personal settings. I found that there's a substantial difference in how I attend and listen to the enemy as opposed to friends and family. Life is much more comfortable now.

Personality Type Nine, the Mediator: Balanced viewpoint; sees the middle way and restores harmony; considers all aspects and the welfare of all involved; plays down personal concerns to build team spirit.[25]

Also known as: the Peace Maker, the Uniter, the Negotiator, the Accommodator, the Abdicator.

The Nine's view of the world: *If we just stay cool and calm, we can reach an agreeable conclusion.*

Self-description: "I try to understand where people are coming from, and accept them for who they are. Problems usually work themselves out if I'm patient and avoid criticism."

Positive characteristics: empathic, agreeable, easy going, down-to-earth, unpretentious, humble, welcoming.

Negative characteristics: lazy, resistant to change, indecisive, boring, stubborn, "spacey," apathetic.

Notable Nines: Tony Bennett, Matthew Broderick, Sandra Bullock, The Dalai Lama, Clint Eastwood, Dwight Eisenhower, Abraham Lincoln, Ronald Reagan, Carl Rogers, Ringo Starr, Renee Zellweger.[26] George Lucas,

Walt Disney, John Kennedy, Jr., Queen Elizabeth II, Sophia Loren, Geena Davis, Kevin Costner, Woody Harrelson, Ron Howard, Whoopi Goldberg, Janet Jackson, "Marge Simpson" (The Simpsons), Barack Obama.[27]

Overview: Type Nine, the Mediator

Nines report that while growing up they found themselves often overlooked. Their points of view were ignored, and the needs of others were given higher priority. Since most of the Mediator's ideas were paused or discounted, they drifted into the lives of others, putting their own priorities and feelings lower and lower until their own concerns and feelings nearly faded away.

Mediators have lost connection with personal views because they identify so completely with those of others. This lack of personal direction causes Nines to waste a good deal of time and energy, because with no internal focus, their thoughts drift from one unimportant diversion to another. Nines report missing deadlines because they will start noncritical tasks when they should be doing deadline sensitive projects. For example, spending half a day cleaning the garage when they have a crucial report deadline due the next day.

On the plus side, Nines' vague personal views make them natural mediators—they can enter a discussion with no personal bias and, consequently facilitate objective discussions which close with agreeable solutions for the parties involved. In addition, Mediators show remarkable understanding of personality types, and consequently, they can listen intently to understand others' points of view.

However, Nines' ability to get inside another's mind doesn't mean they are personally committed. They can stay with a situation for a long time—feeling it, drifting along with it—without buying into it. Mediators will stubbornly decide not to decide, since they actually do not know what they want. If pushed by someone to make a commitment, they will put the matter out of mind, hoping it will eventually go away.

Type Nine's Communication Style. Mediators will agree without committing: nonverbally and verbally, they will communicate their understanding and agreement with head nods and affirming words. "Sure," "I understand," "Yes," "Certainly," "I see" "UhHum"—but these encouraging and positive symbols do not signal that Nines have made a commitment to anything that's been discussed. Listeners need to understand that when Nines communicate *agreement*, they are not necessarily *committing*.

Mediators have a hard time saying "No." They have listened to all the feelings and points of view of others, and don't want to disappoint them by turning them down. So to keep the peace Nines will signal understanding of an issue, but, in fact, they might be a long way from agreement and commitment.

Communication that pressures Nines to make a decision will likely be met with significant stubbornness, and Nines can be the most stubborn of all personality types, especially when someone is pushing for a decision or trying to get them to move away from a previously-made decision.

Templeton's Thoughts

It took me almost two weeks to agree to write this essay detailing my journey from my pre-Nine life, through my discovery of my Mediator personality type, to where my life is now. Let's get started.

I'm thirty-three and gay. It's important to know this because any kind of decision for us Nines comes glacially slow, and my excruciating decision to come out as gay is, I think, a classic study in how we Mediators communicate with ourselves.

It's not so much that I'm a procrastinator, I just get so into other peoples' mind streams that I forget my point of view or don't even seem to have a position on a subject. Landing on a decision is a big deal for me, so I just keep jumping into others' heads and sort of "feel along with them," as my personal feelings and opinions fade away. It's easier to latch on to someone else's thoughts than my own. I think I'm afraid to offer my own thoughts because as a kid, they were brushed aside or ignored.

So here's the picture. I'm a Mediator facing a monumental decision to come out as gay. I have to emphasize that my goal in this writing is to profile the process of intrapersonal communication in my Mediator's mind when making decisions. It just happens that this process centers on my sexual orientation.

Having thoroughly studied The Enneagram, I'm abundantly aware of the nine personality types. I'm good at seeing how people fit into each type, and at one time in my life, if I could have wished myself into another type, it would have been anything but a Nine. As things turned out, though, being a Nine worked out fine.

Remember, as a Nine, I lose myself to the thoughts of others, so when discussing sexual preference, I would identify (lose myself) to views that ranged from general acceptance: sexual orientation is just a part of who a person is, to rejection: sexual orientation is a moral flaw that needs to be repaired.

Please try to get the picture of the fact that with my personality, intrapersonal listening was virtually shut off while I grabbed on to all the outside ideas coming at me. Can you see how paralyzing to decision-making this is? I would identify with all other views but my own.

Since I was afraid of being put down for expressing my own ideas and preferences, I wouldn't say anything and would act as if my beliefs, feelings and opinions didn't exist. As I thought about how I was thinking, I realized I was putting everyone's views above my own. I was ignoring myself and that made me mad at myself and at others because I blamed them, perhaps unreasonably, for not letting my views come out.

I would listen to all the pros and cons, the rights and wrongs, the ups and downs of gay vs. straight. And with every discussion, I would move with the discussants in a kind of fluid path like using stepping stones in a garden. I would mentally step from one to the other idea remaining neutral, and unaware that I was hoping to make a decision about *my* life. I was so tuned-in to everyone else that *I* was not in the picture. I had to keep plugging in the fact that I am gay and a Mediator, and bring my thinking back to my own needs. This wasn't easy, but I did it.

After pondering and procrastinating for almost three years (I was twenty-four at the time) I finally determined to "come out." I did it stubbornly and angrily: "By God, I'm gay; take it or leave it!" I told them; that's it. It's behind me.

Coming out was a significant turn in my life, but the intrapersonal processes I learned have changed *all* aspects of my life, and that's the major point of this narrative.

Here are some personal reactions I now listen for and some strategies that keep me on track:

- Losing my own point of view and becoming dependent on the ideas of others. Correct by separating *me* from *them*. Understand their view and compare with mine.
- Blaming others for failures. Correct by including personal input in decision-making and accept responsibility for the outcome. Voice my opinions.
- Stopping listening; getting stubborn. Correct by reopening discussion. Become willing to listen.
- Spacing out. Correct by reentering the outer world. Consciously attend to those around me. Again, voice an opinion.
- Confusing priorities. Correct by asking myself if what I'm doing is *most* important.
- Fearing change. Correct by reminding myself that change will happen and that having a voice in it can have a positive effect.

Summary

Chapter 6, Listening to Ourselves, explained the relationship between internal and external listening behavior, concluding that internal awareness of personal needs directly affects how we respond to those around us. This chapter expands the range of internal awareness beyond personal needs by introducing nine personality types (as identified in the Enneagram) that can also predispose us to certain patterns of listening responsiveness. The idea is that the more clearly we can identify our personality traits, the better we can work with and around them to improve our listening effectiveness.

The nine personality types as identified in the Enneagram are: 1) the Perfectionist, 2) the Helper, 3) the Producer, 4) the Romantic, 5) the Observer, 6) the Trouble Shooter, 7) the Optimist, 8) the Boss, and 9) the Mediator.

Notes

1. For further reading, see:

    Helen Palmer, Ph.D., *The Enneagram: The Definitive Guide to the Ancient System for Understanding Yourself and the Others in Your Life* (San Francisco: Harper and Row, Publishers, 1975).

    Ginger Lapid-Bogda, Ph.D., *How to use the Enneagram System for Success* (New York: McGraw-Hill, 2004).

    Michael J. Goldberg, LLD, *The 9 Ways of Working* (New York: Marlowe & Company, 1999).

    Don Richard Riso, *Understanding the Enneagram: the Practical Guide to Personality Types* (Boston: Houghton Mifflin Company, 1990).

2. http://www.thefreedictionary.com/perfectionist
3. http://www.enneagram.net/type1.html
4. http://www.enneagraminstitute.com/TypeOne.asp
5. http://www.thefreedictionary.com/giver
6. http://www.enneagraminstitute.com/TypeTwo.asp
7. http://www.thefreedictionary.com/doer
8. http://www.enneagram.net/type3.html
9. http://www.lessons4living.com/enneagram4.htm
10. http://www.enneagram.net/type4.html
11. http://www.enneagraminstitute.com/TypeFour.asp
12. http://www.thefreedictionary.com/observer
13. http://www.enneagram.net/type5.html
14. http://www.enneagraminstitute.com/TypeFive.asp
15. Palmer, p. 234
16. http://www.9points.com/types.htm#p6
17. http://en.wikipedia.org/wiki/Phobia
18. http://www.enneagram.net/type6.html
19. http://www.eclecticenergies.com/enneagram/type7.php
20. http://www.enneagraminstitute.com/TypeSeven.asp
21. http://www.enneagram.net/type7.html
22. http://www.thefreedictionary.com/boss
23. http://www.enneagraminstitute.com/TypeEight.asp
24. http://www.enneagram.net/type8.html
25. http://www.wellpathresources.com/enn/en9.php
26. http://www.enneagram.net/type9.html
27. http://www.enneagraminstitute.com/TypeNine.asp

Chapter Seven
Awareness Exercises

Name_____ ID#_____

1. What personality type fits you?

2. List two traits that put you in that type. (Example: *fear, artistic*)
   a.

   b.

3. List three behaviors that fit that type. (Example: *argue, "space out"*)
   a.

   b.

   c.

4. Describe the traits of someone you know who is a One.

5. Describe the traits of someone you know who is a Two.

6. Describe the traits of someone you know who is a Three.

7. Describe the traits of someone you know who is a Four.

8. Describe the traits of someone you know who is a Five.

9. Describe the traits of someone you know who is a Six.

10. Describe the traits of someone you know who is a Seven.

11. Describe the traits of someone you know who is an Eight.

12. Describe the traits of someone you know who is a Nine.

Chapter Seven
Awareness Database

Name_____   ID#_____

1. I'm assertive and self-confident.

   A.   B.   C.   D.   E.
   seldom   frequently

2. I am a true friend, and I let people know how much I care for them.

   A.   B.   C.   D.   E.
   seldom   frequently

3. I hate to see people going over the speed limit and not getting caught.

   A.   B.   C.   D.   E.
   seldom   frequently

4. I work to build the appropriate image for the situation.

   A.   B.   C.   D.   E.
   seldom   frequently

5. I have the capacity for deep thinking and original thoughts.

   A.   B.   C.   D.   E.
   seldom   frequently

6. I usually need to oversee projects to be sure they are completed properly.

   A.   B.   C.   D.   E.
   seldom   frequently

7. I hate being inactive, so I keep on the go as much as possible.

   A.   B.   C.   D.   E.
   seldom   frequently

8. I believe in the saying, "Be true to yourself," and I try to act authentically.

   A.   B.   C.   D.   E.
   seldom   frequently

9. I see little reason to worry; most things work out just fine.

   A.   B.   C.   D.   E.
   seldom   frequently

10. I am usually at one extreme or the other: it's all-or-nothing. Of course I prefer the "all."

   A.   B.   C.   D.   E.
   seldom   frequently

11. I get picky and obsess about some things, but they're done right.

    A.   B.   C.   D.   E.
    seldom   frequently

12. I have trouble expressing my complex ideas, and people don't understand where I'm coming from.

    A.   B.   C.   D.   E.
    seldom   frequently

13. I don't usually think about myself very much; there's little value in that, so why worry?

    A.   B.   C.   D.   E.
    seldom   frequently

14. When I'm having problems getting something done, I change my approach and do anything it takes to get it done.

    A.   B.   C.   D.   E.
    seldom   frequently

15. I'm thoughtful and generous, and I've enriched the lives of those around me.

    A.   B.   C.   D.   E.
    seldom   frequently

16. My life has been sad and painful; I've experienced many losses.

    A.   B.   C.   D.   E.
    seldom   frequently

17. I love to bargain and make deals; most of the time I come out on top.

    A.   B.   C.   D.   E.
    seldom   frequently

18. I am very helpful at planning. I know what supplies to get and can predict what problems will arise.

    A.   B.   C.   D.   E.
    seldom   frequently

Chapter Eight

Listening and Stress

Intrapersonal and interpersonal listening are highly correlated: as the thoroughness and quality of intrapersonal listening increases or decreases, the effectiveness of interpersonal listening increases or decreases. Because of this relationship between listening to ourselves and listening to others, three chapters—6, 7 and 8—are devoted to intrapersonal listening as preparation for listening to others.

Chapter 6 introduced the idea that intrapersonal listening to our need satisfaction and level of self-esteem is the *starting point* for interpersonal listening. Chapter 7 expanded the intrapersonal discussion by identifying personality traits which play a role in our listening behavior. This chapter examines how stress affects listening.

Stress alters our psychological and physical health, and certainly interacts with our listening. Stress is a part of living; it can motivate us or hold us back. It can push us to accomplish goals, or it can be a potent source of noise in the communication process, affecting our ability to listen to ourselves and others.

In this chapter we will first define stress; second, discuss the effects of stress on health; third, look at how stress supports or diminishes listening effectiveness; fourth, examine common reactions to stress; fifth, define and discuss stressors; and sixth, explore stress-management techniques to improve listening effectiveness.

Defining Stress

Much has been written about stress. In materials science, stress is studied as the amount of force and repeated bending that will fatigue a specified material to the point of weakening or destroying the material. In this context, stress is viewed as a negative physical disturbance to a physical property. However, repeated stress in the form of flexing and bending can also have positive results, since for some materials stress helps maintain their supple, vibrant, flexible, and responsive qualities. For example, wooden airplane wings need to be flown to retain resiliency and not become brittle and rigid. Tires also need to be driven and stressed to maintain their usefulness.

Just as materials are stressed by a change of circumstances—an outside force—we humans are also stressed by outside forces, and if we perceive the stress as extremely threatening, although we do not bend or break, we will experience anxiety and anger when we listen intrapersonally. Eliminating all stress in our lives is impossible, and even if we could, removal of all stress would make us inflexible and nonresponsive, since a certain amount of anxiety and even anger can motivate us toward productive behavior.

So stress can be both good and bad: it can motivate us or cause problems when we have too much or too little in our lives. Our task, then, is to listen to our stress level and make a judgement—is it enough to motivate me? Or, is it so much it paralyzes me? Too much stress can short-circuit thinking and shut down our ability to

listen actively: "I was so angry I couldn't think!" "I felt so anxious and upset that I couldn't hear a word the doctor was saying." "When that twin-engine plane cut me off, I totally missed the radio call." Too little stress also diminishes the quality of our listening: "I sat there while he droned on and on, waiting for the hour to be up." "What did this stuff have to do with me?" "Nobody cares if I understand this information or not."

Human stress is generated by life's events, and people experiencing the same event will react differently. For example, reactions in a stalled elevator might range from panic to catnapping. Stress, then, produces a *personal, individual* reaction to a situation. *Personal and individual* because the same situation might produce a high level of stress in one person, and little or none in another. Different reactions come from the unique backgrounds of each individual.

Moreover, as situations produce stress, these individual reactions can change behavior in a couple of ways. The first way that sources of stress (called stressors) change behavior occurs *during* events. For example, imagine two hikers climbing a trail with a sheer cliff on one side. One of the hikers listens to his fear and stops or turns back; however, the other hiker feels no anxiety at all and casually hikes up the path. In addition to the anxiety that is expressed during the hiking situation, another reaction to the stress could be *avoidance behavior,* where a person senses a real or imagined threat and consciously or unconsciously *avoids* the situation by turning down the invitation to go hiking.

In addition to anxiety, life events might provoke anger, which is a source of negative stress. For example, the event might be something as common as reading a music concert review in the local newspaper. A negative newspaper review of a concert performed by a group called *Mannheim Steamroller* prompted this remarkably angry and stressful letter from someone who obviously disagreed with the reviewer's comments:

> Why don't you pick on me? I'm in the phone book and easy to find here in Windsor Heights. Pray you and I never come face to face. We'll find out what you are made of for sure. When I was a lad we used to hire a man to "cull" the chickens, you know, get rid of the ones who weren't worth keeping. If the *Register* would do that, you would be the first one to go. You couldn't chew on Chip Davis's [*Mannheim Steamroller's* leader] tennis shoes. When you die, be sure they cremate you and scatter your worthless ashes on top of the land because if they try to bury you, the earth will reject your miserable carcass.[1]

Stress coming from anger does not always end on the written page. Sometimes it ends in thoughtless tragedy, as this example of road rage shows:

> Dateline: December 4, 2002. Orange County, California. A 29-year-old man was shot to death, an apparent victim of road rage. According to newspaper accounts, he had a reputation for never backing down from a fight.

> The man and his half brother were heading home from a plumbing job when the trouble began. Apparently, three men in another car zoomed in front of their car. These men started hurling profanities and flashing obscene gestures at the brothers, who returned the insults.

Things escalated until a gun was pulled. Rather than backing down, the man got out of his car and began walking toward the gunman. Two shots rang out, missing the man, who then continued to walk toward the gunman until he was shot and killed.[2]

From this discussion of aspects of stress, we can now offer a definition: *Stress: A personal reaction of anxiety and/or anger resulting from a perceived threat.*

The Effects of Stress on Health

As we have discussed, stress carries positive and negative effects, and to operate effectively, we listen intrapersonally to gauge our levels. Stress can produce a response that supports and protects us, and it can help us adapt to situations. When we are threatened, stress gives us extra alertness and energy—sometimes called the "fight or flight" response (which in a primitive situation is a necessity for survival). When a situation threatens us, those old caveman hormones kick in, enabling us to think quicker, run faster, hit harder, and see and hear better.

However, stress narrows our focus to the immediate threat, and can limit other options that might get us out of the situation, or into a worse situation. For example, if a deer trots onto the road, we might listen visually to the deer only and miss an option to turn onto the shoulder of the road, or, tragically swerve into the lane of oncoming traffic. Heart rate increases, breathing is faster, and blood pressure goes up. These reactions are positive and necessary for high-demand situations, where energy and alertness are crucial.

We are all aware of people—maybe ourselves—who have experienced stress to succeed. Imagine the anxiety of Charles Lindbergh in preparing for his solo flight across the Atlantic, knowing the necessity to stay alert and oriented during the flight, or the anxiety of Lisa Vetterlein as she prepared to capture the women's bicycle speed record, squeezing into a fifty-five pound recumbent bike on a flat Nevada desert road and pedaling almost 69 miles an hour.[3] Consider the anger and anxiety created by a crippling disease that motivated Dr. Salk to work ceaselessly to find a cure for polio, or the anxiety and anger which pushed an attorney to build a case that saved an individual she believed innocent from the electric chair. Imagine also the exhausted athlete, employee, or student who "psyches herself up" to play the game, or understand the lecture. These examples show the positive results of stress on human performance.

However, when stress intensifies beyond healthy motivation and goal achievement, it becomes noise in the system, and can cause serious physical, psychological, and social problems, and can interfere with our ability to be responsive to others. A number of studies conclude that negative stress contributes to health problems. One general study that looked at the effects of excessive stress on health analyzed the medical costs of 46,000 employees working at six U.S. companies. Those workers who were found to be at high stress levels had medical bills (usually related to risk factors for heart disease) that were three times higher than those within the normal stress range.[4]

Stress increases the odds of getting sick. When we experience stressful negative events, such as the death of a friend or family member, financial losses, moving to a different part of the country, personal injury, or divorce, the susceptibility to illness increases. Positive events—like family togetherness, financial stability, success in a class or sport, or friendship development—lower stress, and the frequency of illness.

A number of studies link stress, experienced as anxiety, with illness. In one, researchers surveyed 364 girls ages twelve to sixteen. The girls were surveyed at the beginning of the school year, in the fall, and at the end in spring. The girls reported their positive and negative life events for the previous and current school year, as well as their illnesses during these times.

Researchers found that girls who had more negative life experiences were ill significantly more often than those with fewer negative experiences. Not surprisingly, those whose negative events were close to or equal in number with their positive life events had fewer reported illnesses. The majority of illnesses were upper respiratory infections like colds, sore throats, or headaches.[5] Of course, the relationship between stress and upper respiratory infections is not limited to females; other studies including both sexes reached the same conclusions.[6]

Stress expressed as anger, which includes hostility, arguing, and road rage, also makes us more vulnerable to illness. One study found that respiratory illnesses such as asthma, internal diseases such as those found in the liver, and rheumatic arthritis are related to anger and hostility. The study found that men who were highly resentful, suspicious, and aggressive were significantly more susceptible to these illnesses.[7]

Excessive stress may be linked to illness because of its effects on our immune systems, increasing vulnerability to illness. A number of studies support this linkage; we will touch on three of them: stress in a care-giving setting, stress during college exams, and stress on newlyweds.

Stress-induced changes in immunity were studied in a sample of caregivers for Alzheimer's disease patients. The caregivers had worked with their patients for an average of five years, eight hours a day, and showed lowered immune function when compared to a similar group of non-caregivers. Moreover, the caregivers missed more days of work because of sickness, were sick for longer amounts of time, and went to the doctor more often. Again, the main difficulty was upper respiratory illness.[8]

College exams also generate stress and affect immunity. To measure the stress caused by exams, medical students were monitored before and during course exams, and immune function was found to be lower during exam time than it was before the exams began. The study does not report illnesses resulting from the lowered immunity, perhaps because the exam period is relatively short, and the students could quickly recover from the situational stress of exams.[9]

Anger and anxiety both seem to lower immune functioning. An interesting study that explored anger and immune function involved ninety newly married couples who had gotten their marriage licenses four to six months before the study.[10] The couples were all healthy and happily married. Before the study began, the newlyweds were admitted to a Research Center for a day so that their diet could be controlled. (Caffeine, alcohol, sugar, and other foods could affect their behavior.)

In individual rooms, while being videotaped, the couples were asked to discuss two or three marital problems. They had thirty minutes to complete these discussion. When all the discussions were completed, the videos were viewed by a team of coders who were trained in holistic listening to understand behaviors and language that indicate anger. After listening to the videos, the coders divided the couples into high- or low-anger categories.

Next, the researchers measured the immune functions of the couples and compared the high-anger couples and the low-anger couples. Consistent with other studies, the immune levels of the high-anger couples were lower than the levels of the low-anger couples.

One final experiment focused on stress and healing. This creative (and somewhat bizarre) study involved eleven volunteer dental students. The experimenters hypothesized that high stress would slow healing, and low stress would hasten healing. They reasoned that stress would be higher during final exams and lower during summer vacation. So, here is what they did: they made small scalpel cuts on the hard palates (roof of the mouth) of the students during summer vacation and again during final exam time. They measured the size of the wounds from the time of the cut to the final healing to determine how fast they healed, and found that the rate of healing was 40 percent slower during final exam time (high stress) than summer vacation (low stress).[11]

From these studies, we see that excessive stress can increase frequency of illness, lower immune system function, and slow healing. Additional studies conclude that stress produces lower tolerance to pain, raises cholesterol levels, and increases cardiovascular disease. Clearly, excessive stress affects us physically and limits our ability to perform effectively.

Stress and Listening

As we have seen, excessive stress—anxiety and anger—is hazardous to our health. Beyond the physical and psychological effects, what does stress do to our relational behavior? How does it affect our communication and our ability to listen?

First, excessive anger and anxiety keep us from focusing on others around us. Because our nervous systems become overloaded, we might literally run out of mental and emotional space for anything other than the threat we are experiencing. By definition, threats are outside our normal experiences, and we are not prepared for them. Consequently, this system overload numbs our responsiveness and involvement with those around us, and listening ability is diminished.

Stress is part of life. We have all been in situations that cause stress. Think of how overwhelmed we felt when learning to drive. The perceived threats were multilayered: the mechanical aspects of the car—steering, braking, shifting, using the mirrors—traffic, pedestrians, stop lights, parallel parking, highway driving, road conditions, and so on. Try to remember the anxiety of those times and how difficult it was to listen to anyone, even the instructor. Our whole world was focused on driving the car, and our thought system was barraged with so many new threats that there was little room for talking and listening.

Fortunately, the human system is adaptable. If we practice something enough, we can lower the stress level and function effectively. As we logged more time driving, the intensity of the threats lowered, and we could begin to focus on people around us. I went through this "high threat moving to low threat" process when I was learning to fly a glider while it was being towed by another airplane. Basically, glider towing involves formation flying; that is, being pulled by a 200-foot rope hooked to a single engine plane. This was a high-stress situation for me. It not only involved remembering the flying concepts of roll, pitch, and yaw, but also aligning the glider with the tow plane and the horizon. Since I had little flying time, the anxiety overwhelmed me, and I was so intent on controlling the aircraft that the idea of conversing was not an option. My mental and psychological system was full. After more time on tow, I clearly recall the first time I was able to talk while towing. It was a significant breakthrough at the time.

But we need to remember that some degree of stress is beneficial; without it, we lack the alertness, awareness, and motivation to be responsive to people and situations. We need positive stress to help us be alert to the significance of what is involved in driving, or flying, because when stressors become too routine or familiar, performance drops. We need only read car or airplane accident reports to understand that a high percentage of accidents occur because of a lack of positive stress: The cause being listed as "driver or pilot error." It would be valuable to

catalog listening error reports, to get a picture of how many listening errors result from lack of positive stress that would help the listener be aware, alert, and motivated to understand the message.

It is this process of attending to our negative and positive stressors that helps us manage listening effectiveness. We will periodically be faced with stressful situations that impair our listening. To cope with the effect of the stress and improve listening, we need first to listen intrapersonally to being over- or understressed and then identify the stressors. Once aware of the feelings and causes of stress, we can begin to manage it.

Reactions to Stress

Logically, before we can begin to look for causes of stress (stressors), we need to know if we are reacting to stress. This awareness comes from recognizing the symptoms of stress. Recognizing general stress reactions can help us gain a personal understanding of situations that are stressful. Here are some common symptoms that could be stress related:

Physical Symptoms

- sleep disturbances
- back, shoulder, or neck pain
- tension or migraine headaches
- upset or acid stomach, cramps, heartburn, gas, irritable bowel syndrome
- constipation, diarrhea
- weight gain or loss, eating disorders
- hair loss
- muscle tension
- fatigue
- high blood pressure
- irregular heartbeat, palpitations
- asthma or shortness of breath
- chest pain
- sweaty palms or hands
- cold hands or feet
- skin problems (hives, eczema, psoriasis, tics, itching)
- periodontal disease, jaw pain
- reproductive problems
- immune system suppression: more colds, flu, infections
- growth inhibition

Emotional Symptoms

- nervousness, anxiety
- depression, moodiness
- "butterflies"
- irritability, frustration
- memory problems—misplacing items
- lack of concentration
- trouble thinking clearly
- feeling out of control
- substance abuse
- phobias
- overreactions

Relational Symptoms

- increased arguments
- isolation from social activities
- conflict with co-workers or employers
- frequent job changes
- road rage
- domestic or workplace violence
- overreactions[12]

As we scroll through this list, we may become aware that we have some of these symptoms, and acknowledge that some undoubtedly are stress related. After we are aware that we have stress symptoms, we can begin the process of identifying the stressors that are responsible. For example, we might experience the symptom of road rage when we are under time pressure or anxious about a speech we will be giving. Or we might overreact to a relatively neutral situation because we are stressed by the fact that one of our parents is gravely ill. In either case, stressors are having an effect and are clouding the way we listen and react to the world around us.

Stressors

Once we identify that we are not listening well because of stress, we can begin a systematic internal investigation into the stressors in our lives. What we say to ourselves is, "I'm having a hard time listening. I wonder what's stressing me?" and we begin the process of reviewing possible sources of stress. Once we identify the negative stressors, we can minimize their effect with a program for reducing stress.

Stressors are external situations, people, events, environments, or behaviors that threaten us and provoke individual responses of anxiety and/or anger. For example, a professional acoustical musician whose life is centered on subtle nuances of sound might be stressed about what she considers to be a noisy rush of air in the ventilation system in an auditorium. The rushing sound triggers stress and discomfort for her, making it difficult to listen to the music. However, a person with no background in acoustics might be completely unaware of the ventilation sounds, and thoroughly comfortable with the situation. So with the diversity of human life comes a diversity of potential stressors, and to be effective listeners we need to be aware of our own unique reactions. "What needs aren't being met? What personality traits are increasing my stress levels?"

To help clarify the idea of stressors, we will first take a look at some of life's common stressors. Then we will discuss how two of these stressors—death of a close family member and interpersonal relationships—affect listening.

Stressors (Listed from High to Low Stress)[13]

1. Death of spouse/partner
2. Going to prison
3. Death of close family member
4. Major personal illness/injury
5. Interpersonal relationships (divorce, separation, getting married, dating, reconciliation, arguments, sexual difficulties)
6. Being fired (dropped from school)
7. Retirement from work
8. Major illness of family member
9. Pregnancy
10. New family member arriving (birth, parent coming to stay indefinitely, adoption)
11. Major work adjustment of any sort
12. Major change in financial status (up or down)
13. Close friend dies
14. Career change
15. Taking out a mortgage/heavy loan
16. Difficulty with mortgage repayments
17. Major change in work situation
18. Child leaving home
19. Trouble with in-laws
20. Outstanding personal success
21. Spouse/partner starting/leaving work
22. Starting or stopping formal education
23. Major change in living conditions
24. Change in personal routines
25. Trouble with the boss
26. Major change in work conditions
27. Moving to a different house
28. Changing to a new school
29. Major change in leisure habits
30. Major change in community activities

31. Major change in social activities
32. Taking out a small mortgage/loan
33. Major change in sleeping habits
34. Major change in eating habits

35. Christmas
36. Minor law violations (involving fines, etc.)
37. Demanding schedules

To control stress, then, we need first to become aware of the stress and that we are reacting to it. Next, we search for events in our lives that could be stressors and analyze how the stressor affected us. To help us along with this process, we will analyze three narratives that detail two stressors: the first narrative deals with death of a close family member, and the next two relate to interpersonal relationships. These narratives offer accounts of how stress affected listening and how coping strategies were applied to lower the stress.

Stress Reaction and Analysis to Stressor #3: Death of a Close Family Member *and Effect on Listening*

My brother died shortly after his 65th birthday. For the last few years, we had been quite close, but I at first didn't really realize how much I missed him. We went to the funeral; I gave a eulogy at the church; we visited with the relatives, and we went back to our home state. But I found myself to be irritable and short tempered. I couldn't focus and had trouble listening accurately. I had trouble fully understanding what was being said and found myself impatient and angry at others. It wasn't that others were being thoughtless or uncaring; I was just not ready to listen calmly to what they had to say. One time, after what was in reality an unimportant disagreement, I left the room slamming the door behind me. It was later that my wife pointed out to me that perhaps my behavior was a reaction to my brother's death and the mourning I was going through. Now I see she was right.

A Personal Listening Analysis of How His Brother's Death Affected Him

As I look back at the stress that my brother's death brought into my life, I now realize how angry and empty I felt. He was my closest relative, and I was in a state of disbelief.

A minor incident that normally wouldn't have bothered me at all found me overreacting and releasing all this anger on someone who didn't deserve it. I was simply unaware that his death was churning up so much anger and resentment in me, and it came out. My behavior was totally unjustified.

At the time, if I had processed what I was going through and had become *aware* that I was obviously under stress, I could have looked for the stressor causing the anger. Then facing the fact that my brother's death was creating anger in me, I could have *faced that fact* and understood what *it was doing to me*. I'm pretty sure facing this stressor and *thinking about what it was doing to me* would have kept me from dumping this pent-up anger on an undeserving person who caught me at the wrong time.

Stress Reaction and Analysis Related to Stressor #5: Interpersonal Relationship *and Its Effect on Listening*

Dear Carolyn:

I am 29 with (too) many responsibilities. I am not lacking in relationship experience. This is why my behavior is so strange. When someone truly impresses me, beyond mere physical attraction, I become an adolescent all over again. I'm an excellent conversationalist, yet when I'm facing this particular woman who works in my grocery, all of that becomes useless. She's given signals she might be interested. I tell myself to just talk to her, but then this mental wall builds, and I become *dumb and clumsy*. Is there something psychologically wrong when I can't even make myself get to know her? If I could "just do it," I wouldn't be writing you.
—Somber Admirer in Indiana

Carolyn's response:

> Dear Somber Admirer:
>
> Buy groceries and just nod. Or smile. Or, in a devil-may-care-moment, say hi. Do this until seeing her becomes so *routine* that your *faculties start to return.* Or forget cool. "When I try to talk to you, it comes out dumb and clumsy." Striking up conversation, cold, with someone attractive is the hardest thing in socialdom; adrenaline is normal and tough to shrug off. *Familiarity* takes care of both problems. [Italics mine][14]

Analysis of Somber Admirer

Somber admirer is definitely stressed; he needs to listen internally to his feelings and stress levels (". . . (too) many responsibilities"), and he is puzzled by the effect that this attractive woman—stressor—has on his normally competent communication behavior. The stress seems to be heightened (". . . this mental wall builds, . . .") by his observation that she also might be interested in him, and his attempts to interact with her become "dumb and clumsy."

Carolyn's advice is wise and helpful. She emphasizes the idea that stress reduction comes with facing the stressor even in a distant way ("just nod") and eventually build up to a "hi." Central to her advice is the idea of making the encounters with the woman routine and familiar. Somber is stressed by fear of the unknown, so by gradually exchanging greetings and disclosures with this woman, familiarity and comfort will lower his stress and improve their communication.

Stress Reaction and Analysis Related to Stressor #5: Interpersonal Relationships *and Effect on Listening* (Excerpt from the Novel Crow Lake)

This narrative discloses the thoughts of the main character from this novel, twenty-six-year-old Kate Morrison. The stressors come from several interpersonal sources. Kate has returned with her fiancé to the small rural community of her youth to celebrate the birthday of her nephew—her brother Matt's boy. As a young girl, Kate worshiped Matt, whose passion for nature motivated her to earn a Ph.D. in biology. Now, however, she feels distant from Matt who was her childhood mentor and hero, and she carries resentment toward Matt's wife, Marie, because Kate believes that Marie's pregnancy kept Matt from pursuing his educational goals.

Additionally, memories of growing up in this community—the death of her parents, the sometimes rocky relationship between her brothers, the sacrifices made for her and her sister Bo, the fights, the hardships, the crimes, as well as the kindnesses, and warmth of those who helped them and loved them—evoke anxiety and some anger in Kate because the lives of the people she was close to did not turn out as she hoped they would.

This whole mix of memories and emotions collapses on Kate when she comes home for the birthday party, and the stress is intensified by the presence of her fiancé, Daniel, as he is introduced to these people from her past. Daniel comes from a family of professors, and Kate's background is rural, farming. These cultural differences between her and Daniel also increase her stress level. Kate shares her thinking:

> The world kept on turning. Marie organized us, after a fashion. I was given the job of washing glasses. As far as I could see they were already perfectly clean, but I was glad to do it; it meant I could stand at the kitchen sink *with my back to the room.* I washed them meticulously, one at a time, and dried them carefully, and placed them on trays for the men to take out to the tables. Daniel appeared beside me and said, "Like a dryer?" but I shook my head, and after hovering uncertainly for a moment or two he moved away. When I finished the glasses I washed the bowls Marie had been using, and the cutlery, and the cake tins, and the baking trays. Behind me Bo and Marie were putting the finishing touches to the food and the men were standing about, talking and laughing and getting in the way. Daniel was there somewhere. I could feel his eyes on me. Marie's also. Several times she thanked me, and said, tentatively, that I'd done more than my share, wouldn't I like a coffee, but I

smiled quickly in her general direction and said that I was fine. *I was relieved to find that I was capable of speech and that my voice sounded normal.*

I wondered if I could stay there all day, washing dishes until the party was over, and then *say that I had a headache and go up to bed.* But I knew that wasn't possible. There are certain occasions that *nothing short of death excuses you from, and this was one of them. I didn't know how I was going to get through it though. There was such turmoil inside my head.* Still simmering under everything was my *anger* with Daniel, but on top of that my brain kept delivering *snapshots from the past:* Matt, sitting beside me on the sofa in the living room after Aunt Annie had broken the news that the family would be split up, trying to point out New Richmond on the map, trying to convince me that we would still be able to see each other. *I could see my child-self,* sitting beside him, *my mind possessed by a whirlwind of despair.* [Italics mine][15]

Analysis of Kate Morrison's Stress

In this narrative, Kate is aware that she is experiencing a dizzy feeling of stress ("The world kept on turning"), and she tries to cope with her anxiety and anger by avoiding those around her. She is also concerned that her anger will explode irrationally, so she continues to buy time by keeping busy with thoughtless chores, in this case washing dishes ("I was glad to do it; it meant I could stand at the kitchen sink with my back to the room.") The burden of the stress also shuts out communication with her fiancé, whom she dismisses when he offers to help dry the dishes.

Kate's avoidance of those around her allows her to think through the anxiety and anger. By going over the situation in her mind, she is gratefully able to gain some ability to communicate because she becomes familiar and comfortable with the situation. ("I was relieved to find that I was capable of speech and that my voice sounded normal.")

The pressing urgency to get away, to think, to puzzle all these anxious, angry feelings out is almost overwhelming for Kate. She wonders if she could stay at the sink all day doing dishes or feign a headache and go up to bed. But her sense of social requirements make these options impossible. ("There are certain occasions that nothing short of death excuses you from, and this was one of them. I didn't know how I was going to get through it though. There was such turmoil inside my head.")

Clearly, Kate is fumbling through a vague program to cope with her stress: she is facing her feelings of anger and anxiety (". . . a whirlwind of despair"), and buying time to process them with hope of reconnecting with those people she cares about at the birthday party. Had she chosen to avoid totally the situation (going to bed with a headache), she would have given up a chance to become familiar and comfortable with the situation, and effective listening and interacting would not have had a chance to happen.

In all three cases—Brother's death, Dear Carolyn, and Kate Morrison—stress causes listening problems. Moreover, each of these examples shares common problems and solutions. In the next part of this chapter, we will examine these problems and solutions and develop a process for coping with stress and improving listening effectiveness.

A Program to Regulate Stress and Improve Listening

The previous two chapters show that listening effectively to others happens only after we listen to ourselves and are comfortable and relaxed. This process of listening to ourselves applies as well to minimizing stress, and it follows three steps: (1) listening for internal stress, (2) identifying the stressor, and (3) imagining and analyzing the stressor to become familiar and comfortable with it.

Listening for Stress

By definition, stress is *anxiety and/or anger resulting from a threat,* and as we have seen, anxiety and anger cause physical reactions ranging from muscle tension to severe illness. So at its onset, stress often results in physical tension, and recognizing this tension is the first step in controlling stress.

Being aware of muscular tension is simple, but it takes some practice to get good at it. Tension awareness involves comparing relaxed muscles with tense muscles by systematically tensing and relaxing specific muscles. For example, you make a tight fist and hold it for fifteen seconds and then release, or you curl your toes tightly, imagining that they are grabbing a marble, and hold that toe-fist for fifteen seconds; then relax. After letting go, you notice a significant difference between tension and relaxation. Next, you tense your legs by bending your ankles to point your toes at your knees; then relax and compare the tension with the relaxation. This tensing and relaxing should proceed through various muscle groups (knees, thighs, stomach, buttocks, chest, shoulders, hands, jaw, forehead) so you can be aware of the difference between tensed and relaxed muscles. (This process of stress management is often done with a workshop trainer; however, you can become aware of tension and relaxation by following these steps.)

The purpose of this tensing and relaxing is to know your particular responses to stress. When you encounter a stressor, there will be tension somewhere in your body, and you need to recognize it when it is there. These muscle reactions to stress will vary with individuals, and they can occur in any set of muscles. Some may experience tension in their legs, others in their shoulders, others in their chest, and so on. After determining that you are experiencing stress by noticing muscle tension, the next step is to figure out what stressors are responsible for the tension.

Identify the Stressors

Once muscle tension tells you that you are experiencing stress, you can set some intrapersonal listening time aside to scroll through possible stressors. "Is there a relationship I'm anxious about?" "Am I anxious about my driver's ed lesson?" "Am I angry about a performance or job assignment?" "Am I worried about a child that is sick?" "Do I have an important presentation that is hanging over me?"

There might be some stressors that are difficult to find, since a stressful event from childhood could be triggered by a recent event. Coming to terms with these deeply rooted stressors may require professional counseling or psychotherapy, and that process is well beyond the scope of this book; however, most day-to-day stressors can be identified and their disruptive impact on listening can be minimized.

Your muscles tell you that you have stress, and you have found the stressor. The next step is to use imaging to familiarize yourself with specific stressors so that they become comfortable and routine parts of your life. No matter what the stressor, it is encouraging to know that you can reduce its influence by imaging it, since imaging will produce the same muscular tension you would experience with the actual stressor. By repeated diaphragmatic breathing and imaging of the stressor, the stress-related tension will diminish, just at it would with repeated listening driving or flying. The advantage here is that you can prepare for the stressor in your private listening moments.[16]

Image the Stressors

Imaging is a simple process. After identifying the stressors, you can begin to make them familiar uand routine by diaphragmatic—breathing from your stomach—breathing and picturing them in your mind. You settle down in a quiet place and imagine stressors that are causing muscle tension until you are comfortable with them, and the tension is gone. When your imaging reaches this level of comfort, the comfort will remain when you are experiencing the real-life stressor.

For example, you have had an argument with your husband and are now driving to work. Your stress is at its upper limit; you can feel the tension in your neck and shoulders, and you make a conscious effort to relax, knowing that you will be working out a solution with him later in the day. Right now there is little you can do about those differences, so you put the argument aside and focus on your work schedule. First item on your agenda is an important meeting with your boss and three co-workers. The meeting will address sales approaches for a new product, and there will be intense feelings about the types of publicity and advertising to be used.

Remembering that you have this morning meeting (stressor) brings back the tense muscles in your neck and shoulders, so when you get to your office, you shut out all interruptions. Closing your eyes in the privacy of your office, you begin your belly breathing and visualize the meeting room: the desks and chairs and their location, the lights, the smells, the temperature, the wall clock, the computer, and every detail that will put your mind in the meeting room. Then you image the participants: the boss and the co-workers, their faces and mannerisms, their clothing, their voices, their cologne, the ideas they might offer. You imagine the meeting until it becomes a familiar, routine event—it is not a stressor anymore; it its simply a meeting. Naturally, there is a certain amount of stress, but it is positive and energizing; it has made you alert and ready to interact. The neck and shoulders are relaxed, and the negative tension energy can be directed away from yourself, and you can listen actively to the boss and co-workers at the actual meeting.

Now you are the husband who argued with your wife this morning. You are traveling to your office at the hospital where you work as a counselor. Like your wife, you are experiencing anxiety and anger at the way things went this morning. As you monitor your body, you become aware of tight stomach muscles and a vice-like grip on the steering wheel. You know you have clients scheduled and need to prepare yourself to listen as a therapist to their concerns. Realizing that this tension, if not relieved, will interfere with the therapy sessions, you move your thoughts from the argument, knowing that you will have time to settle the issues at home in the evening.

When you arrive at the clinic, you read through the schedule of clients and take a few moments to image them. You also belly breathe and imagine their appearance, mannerisms, and if they are clients you have seen before, their concerns. Some of the clients are particularly difficult to work with, and their images cause some stress that you notice in your stomach and hands. You make a point to image these clients until they are familiar and your muscles are relaxed. Now you are ready to do your job as a therapeutic listener.

The husband and wife are both coming home from work. The day was busy and productive. Her meeting went well; many of his clients were making progress. The argument from this morning has faded, and they are both recalling where they were in the disagreement when they left for their jobs. As they recall the morning's anger they begin to notice tension—his in the stomach and hands; hers in the neck and shoulders.

Time to breathe and use the imagination. She images him in the den where they will continue the discussion; he is imaging her in the den also. They know each other well, and the imaging is detailed. As they drive, it does not take long to relax the muscular tension and be of a mind to listen to each other. As they discuss the matter, they may not agree on all the points of concern, but their minds will be clear and they will listen and understand each other's viewpoints.

Summary

Stress is part of life, and how we manage it affects our listening effectiveness. We defined stress as a *personal reaction of anxiety and/or anger resulting from a perceived threat,* and noted that positive stress motivates us to reach goals by keeping us alert and responsive, while negative stress becomes noise that downgrades productivity and health resulting in lowered listening responsiveness.

Managing stress starts with becoming aware of symptoms that can be physical, emotional, and relational, and then identifying the source of the stress, the stressor. Once the reaction to stress and the stressor are known, we can engage a stress-reduction program that uses breathing, imaging and muscle relaxation.

Notes

1. Rob Borsellino, "Exclamation marks served on bed of capital letters," *The Des Moines Register* (December 21, 2005), pp 1B–2B.

2. Tony Fiore, "Anger and your driving," http://1stholistic.com/Reading/health/A2004/health anger-and-your-driving.htm

3. http://www.kendausa.com/bicycle/news/bicycle_news_513.html

4. R. Goetzel, D. Anderson, R. Whitmer, R. Oziminkowski, R. Dunn, and J. Wasserman, "The Relationship Between Modifiable Health Risks and Health Care Expenditures. An Analysis of the Multi-Employer HERO Health Risk and Cost Database." The Health Enhancement Research Organization (HERO) Research Committee, *Journal of Occupational and Environmental Medicine*, vol. 40 (1998), pp. 843–854.

5. J. Seigel and J. Brown, "A Prospective Study of Stressful Circumstances, Illness Symptoms, and Depressed Mood Among Adolescents," *Developmental Psychology*, 24 (1988), pp. 715–721.

6. J. Kiecolt-Glaser, J. Dura, C. Speicher, O. Trask, and R. Glaser, "Spousal Caregivers of Dementia Victims: Longitudinal Changes in Immunity and Health," *Psychosomatic Medicine*, 53 (1991), pp. 345–362.

7. A. Ranchor, R. Sanderman, J. Bouma, B. Buunk, and W. van den Heuvel, "An Exploration of the Relation Between Hostility and Disease," *Journal of Behavioral Medicine*, 20 (1997), pp. 223–240.

8. Kiecolt-Glaser, et al., 1991.

9. J. Kiecolt-Glaser, R. Glaser, E. Strain, J. Stout, K. Tarr, J. Holliday, and C. Speicher, "Modulation of Cellular Immunity in Medical Students," *Journal of Behavioral Medicine*, 9 (1986), pp. 5–21.

10. J. Kiecolt-Glaser, W. Malarkey, M. Chee, M. Newton, T. Cacioppo, H. Mao, and R. Glaser, "Negative Behavior During Marital Conflict Is Associated with Immunological Down-Regulation," Psychosomatic Medicine, 55 (1993), pp. 395–409.

11. P. Marucha, J. Kiecolt-Glaser, and M. Favagehi, "Mucosal Wound Healing Is Impaired by Examination Stress," *Psychosomatic Medicine*, 60 (1998), pp. 362–365.

12. *Helpguide: Expert, Non-Commercial Information on Mental Health & Lifelong Wellness*, http://www.helpguide.org/mental/stress_signs.htm

13. http://www.intelihealth.com/IH/ihtIH/WSIHW000/9105/28956/288782.html?d=dmtContent

14. Carolyn Hax, "Tell Me About It," *The Des Moines Register* (October 26, 2005), p. 5E.

15. Mary Lawson, *Crow Lake*, Canada: Vintage Canada, 2003, pp. 284–285.

16. T. Kontogiannis, "Training Effective Human Performance in the Management of Stressful Emergencies," *Cognition, Technology & Work* (London: Springer-Verlag London Ltd, 1999), pp. 7–24; and Erica L. Johnsen, M.A., and Susan K. Lutgendorf, Ph.D., "Contributions of Imagery Ability to Stress and Relaxation," *Abstract, Annals of Behavioral Medicine*, vol. 23, no. 4 (2001), pp. 273–281.

Chapter Eight
Awareness Exercises

Name_____ ID#_____

Before completing these exercises, take a few moments to concentrate on the definition of stress: *A personal reaction of anxiety and/or anger resulting from a perceived threat.*

    Exercises 1–8 ask for personal information; responses 9–14 can be based on personal and/or someone else's experiences.

1. List and briefly describe two specific threatening situations that make you anxious.

    A.

    B.

2. Describe one of these anxiety situations in greater detail.

3. List and briefly describe two threatening situations that make you angry.

    A.

    B.

4. Describe one of these angry situations in greater detail.

5. Describe how you react to anxiety-producing stress.

6. Describe how you react to anger-producing stress.

7. In what part(s) of your body do you notice stress?

8. List three of your personal stressors.

   A.

   B.

   C.

9. List two examples of stress-related physical symptoms (your own and/or someone else's).

   A.

   B.

10. List two examples of stress-related emotional symptoms (your own and/or someone else's).

    A.

    B.

11. List two examples of stress-related relational symptoms (your own and/or someone else's).

    A.

    B.

12. Describe an example of a possible stress-related illness (your own or someone else's).

13. List and briefly describe two stressful situations that resulted in ineffective listening (your own and/or someone else's).

    A.

    B.

14. List and describe two stressful situations where stress management increased listening effectiveness (your own and/or someone else's).

    A.

    B.

Chapter Eight
Awareness Database

Name_____ ID#_____

1. I experience stress _____ times per day.

   A. 0   B. 1–3   C. 4–6   D. 7–9   E. 10 or more

2. I am aware of my stress _____ of the time.

   A. Less than 30%   B. 30%–40%   C. 50%–60%   D. 70%–80%   E. 90% or more

For exercises 3 to 12, use this scale:

A.	B.	C.	D.	E.
often				seldom

3. I am calm.

   A.   B.   C.   D.   E.

4. I can cope with stress.

   A.   B.   C.   D.   E.

5. Stress lowers my listening effectiveness.

   A.   B.   C.   D.   E.

6. I take definitive steps to lower my stress.

   A.   B.   C.   D.   E.

7. I am aware of stressors in my life.

   A.   B.   C.   D.   E.

8. I have experienced stress-related illness.

   A.   B.   C.   D.   E.

9. I have experienced stress-related physical symptoms.

   A.   B.   C.   D.   E.

10. I have experienced stress-related emotional symptoms.

   A.   B.   C.   D.   E.

11. I have experienced stress-related relational symptoms.

    A.   B.   C.   D.   E.

12. I can effectively cope with stress and listen effectively.

    A.   B.   C.   D.   E.

Part Two

Practicing Sensible Listening

Chapter Nine

Listening Comprehensively

Listening Roles and Relationships

The overall goal of this text is to prepare the reader to listen effectively. Part One explores general topics that operate in every listening situation. The first chapter reminds us that listening affects the quality of family, social, and business operations. The remaining chapters identify and explore: a communication model which defines variables that operate in every face-to-face listening setting, holistic listening and media, listening to movement, and intra-personal listening to our needs, personalities, and stresses. With the background information from Part One, we can now prepare for specific listening roles and relationships.

Part 2 introduces listening roles and relationships where specific rules apply. Chapter 9 focuses on the comprehensive listening role; Chapters 10, 11, 12, and 13 discuss the therapeutic, critical, consumer, and appreciative listening roles. Chapters 14 and 15 apply listening principals to partnerships and cross-cultural relationships. This chapter elaborates on six aspects of comprehensive listening: information, vocabulary, concentration, memory, note taking, questioning, and listening to detect and identify. It finishes with some guidelines to help understand and retain more information.

The Comprehensive Listening Role

In the comprehensive listening role we listen to understand and remember information from briefings, reports, seminars, conferences, oral papers, and other presentations. In the comprehensive role, we are focused on what we can take from the sender; we are being productively selfish. We have succeeded if the message we have created in our mind is the same as the message that was intended by the sender, which might be anything from directions, to a list of tasks.

However, when listening to a ten-minute message, most receivers untrained in listening practices are functioning at 25 percent efficiency; consequently, 75 percent of the message is lost. Moreover, after more time goes by, even less is remembered or comprehended.[1] So, after a couple hours, maybe only 5 or 10 percent of a message is remembered.

Information

Information is found primarily in three parts of the message: (1) the main points, (2) supporting material that explains or proves the main point, and (3) inferences.

Main Points

Main points might be obviously stated: "My first point is . . .," or the main point might be indirectly presented: ". . . the answer to the question is . . ."; "There are two approaches to this problem . . ."; "The topic this morning is . . ."; "In summary, keep in mind . . ."; "So we can conclude that. . . ."

The main points may be indicated by transitions, which are sentences or phrases that connect one main point to another. Examples of transitions are, "Now that we've discussed the importance of factor A, let's turn to factor B."; "An additional cause must also be considered."

Supporting Material

Supporting material proves or clarifies the main points. Examples are illustrations, statistics, stories, analogies, visuals, or quoted material. Phrases that indicate supporting material are: "For example . . ."; "To illustrate this idea . . ."; "Looking at the compared data . . ."; and "Here's a story that might illustrate this idea. . . ."

Inferences

An inference is an unstated or implied conclusion. Sometimes a sender might infer a point that is important but not directly stated. In addition to the words, the sender's tone of voice, looks, and movements might offer clues to inferred or implied messages. The sender might say, "Wouldn't you really rather have freedom of choice on this matter?" The inferred answer might be, "Yes, of course I would." Or the sender might ask, "Do we want economic growth or a stagnant economy?" As a listener, you listen to the words and tone of voice and infer the point the sender is trying to make.

We must be sure the inferences drawn are legitimate, and that they are intended by the sender. We need not *agree* with the intended inference, because *as comprehensive listeners our goal is to understand the intended message and not evaluate it.*

To help clarify listening for main points, supporting material, and inferences, this speech titled "The Light Side of Listening" is presented with comments.

> I chose the title, *The Light Side of Listening*, because when discussing listening I usually focus on the dramatic effects of listening errors and the crucial nature of listening in business. But this evening, as we approach the holiday season, I've shifted my focus to some of the more fun aspects of listening, and I'm glad I did, because the lighter side of listening is something that I haven't often focused on.
>
> [*Before going into the body of the message, the speaker previews the four main points to be discussed, and the comprehensive listener should attend to these points.*]
>
> This evening, I first want to give you my definition of listening; second, I'll discuss the idea that listening can be fun and rewarding; third, a lot of humor comes from listening mix-ups; and finally, listening inspires our imaginations. First, let's take a look at my definition of listening: Listening is using all of our senses to gather information and then give meaning to that sense input. [*The speaker has stated the first point—the definition of listening—and now offers supporting material to help the listeners understand the definition.*]
>
> This definition tells us that we listen with more than our ears. A deaf person can listen. In fact, we listen with our eyes and our noses. We listen to touch and to taste, also.
>
> [*Now, the speaker transitions to the next main point. He alerts the listener that he is finished with the first point, and he previews point number two.*]
>
> Now that we've an understanding of the nature of listening, let's look at how listening can be fun and rewarding.
>
> Everyday listening can be fun and give us personal rewards. [*The speaker supports this point by giving examples and illustrations.*] Many of us enjoy the outdoors—hunting, fishing, or taking pictures. [*In the next four examples, the speaker through words and tone of voice, infers the fun aspect of listening.*] Imagine yourself standing in a quiet spot listening to a beautiful autumn scene. Imagine listening to carolers on a clear, frosty, winter evening. The crunch of snow under your shoes. Listening to little kids *actually* getting along. [*The speaker finishes point two and transitions to point three.*]

"The Light Side of Listening," by Paul Kaufmann, for the Army Aviation Support Facility, Boone, Iowa, April 7, 1997.

So the lighter side of listening is fun and rewarding. Next, let's look at some of the humor that comes from listening.

A good deal of humor comes from listening mix-ups. [*The speaker offers three examples as supporting material for this assertion.*] Humor comes when someone *thinks* he's listening and assigning the correct meaning, and he's not. Humor comes when someone listens and is unable to assign accurate meaning. Humor comes when someone listens and assigns the wrong meaning because of stereotyped thinking.

[*The speaker transitions to his fourth and final point by summarizing points one, two, and three and previewing point four.*] We've discussed a definition of listening, talked about the idea that listening is fun, and adds humor, now let's look at the final point. Listening inspires our imaginations.

[*The speaker concludes the message by summarizing the main points.*] My goal this evening was to provide a little diversion from the important discussions and decisions you are involved with and also help us prepare for a holiday season that will be full of opportunities for listening. I also hope we leave with a higher awareness that listening is hard work because it involves all of our senses, and that there is a light side of listening: it can be fun and rewarding; a lot of humor can come from listening, and listening can inspire our imaginations.

In addition to listening for main points, supporting material, and inferences, we listen to *specific* vocabulary for information.

Vocabulary

The comprehensive listening role is focused primarily on the words of the sender, and it is important to be aware of the impact of words on understanding the message.

We have four vocabularies, listed here in order of size:

1. Reading vocabulary

2. Listening vocabulary

3. Writing vocabulary

4. Speaking vocabulary.[2]

As adults, on the average, we possess reading vocabularies of 20,000 word families, out of the possible 800,000 to one million words in the English language. However, our listening vocabularies average only 12,000 to 15,000 words.[3] The problem in comprehensive listening is that we do not all know the same 15,000 words, so there is a possibility of assigning an incorrect meaning or no meaning at all to the words being sent.

It seems reasonable, then, the larger the vocabulary we have, the better the chance of comprehending and attaching accurate meanings to the words. One way to increase the probability of accuracy is to develop an interest in words. We can note words and word combinations that are new to us, look them up in a dictionary and use them, so that they become part of our listening vocabulary, realizing that the more words we understand, the better the chance of assigning accurate meaning when listening.

Concentration

To comprehend we must concentrate, and concentration is hard work. Research ranks *inattentiveness*—lack of concentration—as one of the most important listening barriers,[4] and concentration is substantially affected by time and internal and external noise.

Time

One of the most significant sources of noise affecting comprehensive listening in our culture is time. While on the phone, we might be splitting our concentration time by writing a note or reading a short article or using the computer. While listening to a lecture or a report, we might be giving time to that overdue project, reading a newspaper, text messaging, or visiting with the people around us.

Our culture puts a premium on time, and often we feel that we cannot give our total time to one message, so we focus on several different messages at the same time. The main message becomes like a camera out of focus—we get some of it, but lose the subtle fine points that can be significant to our understanding of the information.

Time pulls our attention away from effective, focused comprehensive listening and so does weak concentration on the central message being sent. We lose our concentration because of internal and external distractions.

Internal Noise

Internal reasons for weak concentration might come from our own unmet needs, self-esteem, personalities, or stress. Intrapersonal communication sets the stage for listening and all other interpersonal communication, and it is smart to remind ourselves that all communication begins with the self. If we are focusing on our own behavior or self-esteem while trying to listen to someone else, we will be comprehending only a portion of the external message.

We might be attending to internal noise: the headache we have, our hunger, or what we are going to say next. We might be thinking, "I know what he's going to say; I've heard this before; It's the same old stuff."

External Noise

External noise that interferes with our concentration might be a siren, the ringing of a cell phone, a hot room, or the person next to us. We may also be focusing on the sender rather than the message, but the sender's tone of voice, clothing, and mannerisms are our concern only insofar as they enhance the information in the primary message.

When in the role of comprehensive listener, we need to realize that the average human mind can process about 500 words per minute, but the average speaker talks at only 140 words per minute. Therefore, a 360-word-per-minute concentration slippage exists in the listening/speaking system; that is, our minds could process 360 more words per minute than are being spoken. Because of this thought-speech differential, we can take mind trips while the sender is speaking. If these mental trips get longer and longer, the listener may not come back and will lose a substantial portion of the message.[5]

A way to remedy these mental trips is to focus on every word being said until we become reengaged in the listening process. In addition, the listener might spend the extra processing time to create mental examples and illustrations based on the content of the message.[6]

Memory

The effectiveness of comprehensive listening is measured by recall and understanding. If one could recall and understand 100 percent of a message, that would indicate perfect comprehensive listening.

Certainly comprehending information without remembering it is not effective listening. One program designed to help us remember suggests four steps: (1) consciously make the choice to remember, (2) create a visual picture of the message you want to remember, (3) associate the message with something familiar to you, and (4) repeat and discuss the message to yourself or others.[7]

1. *Choose to remember.* You might be listening to a presentation about the function of control surfaces on airplanes. You want to remember this information, so you tell yourself, "I want to remember this; it is important."

2. *Create a picture.* As the sender talks about the effect of the *elevator* and the *pitch* of the airplane; the *ailerons* and the *roll*; and the *rudder* and the *yaw*, you visualize these maneuvers.

3. *Associate with familiar.* Now you connect these control surface functions to something you have experienced like riding a bicycle or steering a boat. Or you can make other creative connections. You might think of an elevator, which goes up and down, and connect it to the idea of *pitch*, which raises or lowers the nose of the plane; you could connect the fifth and sixth letters in *ailerons* as the first letters in *roll*; and you might change the spelling of *rudder* to *yudder* to remember *yaw*.

4. *Repeat and discuss.* Finally, you repeat and discuss the ideas: elevator/pitch; ailerons/roll; rudder/yaw, until they become familiar. If you diligently keep these listening exercises active, you will remember the information.

A number of mental devices can help us remember and understand information. One is called a *mnemonic* device, which is frequently used to make acronyms. (An acronym uses the first letter of a list of words, to make a name.) For example the acronym HOMES can be a key to remember the Great Lakes—Huron, Ontario, Michigan, Erie, and Superior. While listening, we can make mnemonic associations that are simple, yet help us remember names or dates. The mnemonics might be silly and outrageous, but nonetheless help us remember.

Another memory helper is the *link* system where the listener links or associates vivid images to the information being sent.[8] Again, the link can be as ridiculous as it needs to be to remember it. For example, imagine being at a meeting, and being introduced to Harry Jackson, a car salesman. To remember his name and what he does, you link his name to a car with hair (Harry) growing all over it; the trunk open, exposing the spare tire and the jack (Jackson). Sitting in the car is the man you just met. The next time you need to communicate with him, there is a good probability that you will remember his name and what he does. Or you are listening to a talk about the workings of the human eye, and the sender notes that the rods sense the lightness and darkness, and the cones sense color. You link rods and light with lightning rods, and the letter "C" (Cones) with the "C" in color and remember the information for future reference.

Additionally, when we listen we can link in with numbers. For example, the telephone number, 322-7743 has a natural link with the number seven. The obvious link is with the two sevens, but there are two other links—322 adds up to seven and so does 4 and 3. Linking can become an effective way to help comprehensive listening and remembering.

As a final thought, researchers in memory indicate two ways to improve memory that will help in preparing for the comprehensive listening role:

1. Be motivated. Have a strong desire to remember. Ask yourself, "What's in it for me?"

2. Focus your concentration on remembering.[9]

Note Taking

Research has found that note takers recall messages in more detail than non-notetakers.[10] Taking notes increases involvement in the listening process, and it can help in understanding and remembering messages in at least three ways.

First, studies have found that note taking helps us focus our concentration by increasing our sense involvement and our attention to the message. Note taking is a form of holistic listening since we use our ears, eyes, and hands (touch) to process the message. This heightened attention and involvement increase the chances of recalling the message at a later time.[11]

Second, note taking raises our awareness of the structure of the message. Note taking helps us visualize the flow of the message. We can see how the main points develop the thesis of the presentation, how the supporting material clarifies our understanding of these main points, and how the sender transitions from point to point.

The third value of note taking is that we have a "hard copy" of the message to review and study, after the message is completed. When we need to review, we can look over the notes which will help us remember. As soon as possible after the presentation—while the information is still fresh—the listener should read the notes and make any changes for clarity and completeness, highlighting any misunderstandings and clarifying them by asking questions or researching for answers. Developing a reliable and accurate system of note taking will result in fuller understanding and retention of information, greatly increasing our effectiveness as comprehensive listeners.

Questioning

Questioning is a part of active listening because it can help ensure accuracy of meaning and help us remember messages. Questions not only help the listener clarify messages, but they also give the sender a chance to correct unintended or confusing information. Necessarily, questions should be relevant to the message being sent. We need to keep in mind that our purpose in questioning is to help clarify and retain the message. Off-topic questions or questions that go beyond the sender's intended goal can disrupt the communication and ultimately lessen the amount of information exchanged. Questions should be thoughtful and to the point. They should be an attempt to clarify the sender's message and not become a forum for the listener to express personal views.

Listening to Detect

The main focus of this text is listening to people in face-to-face settings. However, an important part of the comprehensive listening role sometimes involves listening to inanimate objects and artifacts. In this category of comprehensive we become detectives focusing on detecting and identifying sounds, smells, visual inputs, tastes, or touches. This is holistic listening applied to things, and was introduced in Chapter 3 in the discussion about identifying smells and tastes. The sole goal of listening to detect is to do just that—detect and identify the source of the message without evaluation.

We listen to detect every day. When crossing the street, we listen to identify traffic—its speed and distance from us. We see a puff of smoke coming from the car—is it burning oil, is the gas mixture too rich, or is it water vapor? We open the refrigerator and ask ourselves, "What is that smell?" We notice an unusual taste and try to identify it. We feel a sting in our arm and explore to identify the source.

A number of detective novels, TV programs, and movies are built around listening to detect. Crime scene investigators use elaborate sampling and analytical tools to identify types of blood, other fluids, fabrics, materials, residual powders, and chemicals. Even well before the use of high-tech analysis, detectives were skillfully using holistic listening to identify clues that might play a part in solving a crime. Of course successful detectives have always spent their professional lives fine-tuning these listening skills, and frequently we are all detectives listening to identify the things that affect our lives.

Arthur Conan Doyle, the author of the Sherlock Holmes detective stories, was a physician who made listening to detect Sherlock's most powerful crime-solving trait— ". . . go everywhere, see everything, overhear everyone," Holmes advises as he works through an investigation. In fact, four valuable guidelines for listening to detect come from Holmes:[12]

1. *Observe intensely and remain objective.*

Here, the great detective reminds us to keep personal biases and preconceived notions out of the detection process—listen to reality and identify.

Holmes: "It is a capital mistake to theorize before one has data. Insensibly one begins to twist facts to suit theories, instead of theories to suit facts."

Watson: "Holmes, you see everything."

Holmes: "I see no more than you, but I have trained myself to notice what I see."

(From *The Adventure of the Blanched Soldier*)

Sherlock Holmes and his partner, Dr. Watson decided to take a vacation from detective work and went camping. They had turned in for the night and were lying there and looking up at the sky.

Holmes: "Watson, look up. What do you see?"

Watson: "Well, I see thousands of stars."

Holmes: "And what does that mean to you?"

Watson: "Well, I suppose it means that of all the planets and suns and moons in the universe, that we are truly the one most blessed with the reason to deduce theorems to make our way in this world of criminal enterprises and blind greed. It means that we are truly small in the eyes of God but struggle each day to be worthy of the senses and spirit we have been blessed with. And, I suppose, at the very least, in the meteorological sense, it means that it is most likely that we will have another nice day tomorrow. What does it mean to you, Holmes?"

Holmes: "To me, it means someone has stolen our tent."

2. *Put the pieces together.*

Here, Holmes advises the listener to remember previous facts and information and then determine how they all fit together to form a complete sense of the situation.

Holmes: "Each fact is suggestive in itself. Together they have a cumulative force."

(From *The Adventure of the Bruce-Partington Plans*)

3. *Be energized and relentless in your search for information.*

Description of Holmes searching for clues: "He was out on the lawn, in through the window, round the room, and up into the bedroom, for all the world like a dashing foxhound drawing a cover."

(From *The Devil's Foot*)

4. *Use your right brain try to imagine what this information might mean.*

Once information has been identified, you can create a plausible set of circumstances and behaviors (investigators would call this a "Mode of Operation") that explain the information you have gotten. This guess, or hypothesis, of what happened can be tested with further listening to determine if, in fact, that is what happened. If facts are consistent, the hypothesis is close to reality; if further listening turns up information that is inconsistent, you create a new hypothesis that could be consistent with the new findings.

Here, Dr. Watson has listened for some facts and tests a hypothesis:

Watson: "I am able to say that you were greatly preoccupied when you got up this morning."

Holmes: "Excellent! How could you possibly know that?"

Watson: "Because you are usually a very tidy man and yet you have forgotten to shave."

Holmes: "Dear me! How very clever! I had no idea, Watson, that you were so apt a pupil. Has your eagle eye detected anything more?"

Watson: "Yes, Holmes. You have a client named Barlow, and you have not been successful in his case."

Holmes: "Dear me, how could you know that?"

Watson: "I saw the name outside this envelope. When you opened it you gave a groan and thrust it into your pocket with a frown on your face. . . . ."

Holmes : "Just a little [inaccurate], I fear. Let us take the points in their order: I did not shave because I have sent my razor to be sharpened. I put on my coat because I have, worst luck, an early meeting with my dentist. His name is Barlow, and the letter was to confirm the appointment. . . . But go on, Watson, go on! It's a very superficial trick, and no doubt you will soon acquire it.[13]

Listening Guides

Over the years, Dr. Ralph Nichols—who is considered the first in-depth investigator of listening—compiled a list of techniques that are used by effective listeners. The techniques apply to all listening roles but are especially useful for the comprehensive role where listeners will sometimes find themselves dealing with topics that they would not normally choose. For example, an artist might find a lecture on the composition of sixteenth-century painting canvasses highly stimulating; however, a mechanical engineer might (but not necessarily) find it a less attractive subject. Nonetheless, both listeners are responsible for coming away from the talk with as much information as possible. So, there are times when we want to listen comprehensively, and times we would rather be elsewhere. In either situation, we still need to listen actively for understanding and retention of the message.

Here are ten guidelines adapted from Dr. Nichols' observations that we can bring into play to support us in these listening situations:[14]

1. Find positive aspects about the subject. While preparing to listen to the presentation, think about aspects of the topic that might be interesting. Work to form the attitude that this subject will be interesting.

2. Focus on the content of the message and avoid critiquing the speaker or the delivery.

3. Stay relaxed and calm. Sense your stress and belly breathe. If the topic is one that is stimulating to you—for example, one that is exciting or anger producing—keep cool. Cool heads can think and process better than those that are overstimulated.

4. Listen for more than the facts. The facts are important, but keep the big picture in mind. Ask yourself, "What main point are these facts supporting?"

5. Listen for larger meanings—the major points—and avoid trying to take notes on every fact or detail. If you can note the main ideas, many of the supporting facts will come to mind as you review your notes.

6. Make your attending behavior genuine. Avoid giving the outward signs of attending—eye contact, head nodding, note taking—while internally, you are not focusing on the message at all. Faking attention does not bring the message home; real attending will.

7. When possible, minimize distractions. For example, if the sound system is not working well, or the room temperature is uncomfortable, let someone know. If the person next to you is chatting, let him know of the distraction. Take a proactive attitude and do something about external noise that is hampering your listening.

8. Accept the challenge of difficult material. Tell yourself, "In the past these formulas have been difficult for me to understand, but tonight I'll do my best to understand and remember them."

9. Be open-minded about emotional words. A speaker might use obscene or emotional language that diverts you from the point being made. Keep focused on the message, remembering that your goal is to capture the main ideas of the speech.

10. Use the time differential between listening and speaking effectively. Productively use that extra time between speed of speech and speed of thought. With this extra time, think of examples and illustrations that tie in with the points being presented.

Summary

Identifying listening roles and being aware of which listening role we are in are essential for effective listening. This chapter focuses on the first of five listening roles—the comprehensive role—which is listening to understand and remember information.

In face-to-face and mediated communication, comprehensive listening focuses on information found in main points, supporting material, and inferences. Vocabulary, concentration, and memory are presented as three variables affecting comprehensive listening, and concentration can be improved by focusing our time and energy on the message and minimizing internal and external distractions. Memory is improved by the use of mnemonic devices and linking, and, when possible, note taking. Questioning and listening to detect are also examined. The chapter concludes with ten guidelines for effective listening.

Notes

1. William A. Welker, Ed.D., "Listening Skills: Learning to Actively Pay Attention," *http://wphs.ohio.k12.wv.us/warwood/skills34.htm,* November 24, 1999.

2. Guy H. Lafrancois, *Psychology for Teaching,* 3rd ed. (Belmont, Calif.: Wadsworth Publishing Company, 1979), pp. 168–170.

3. A. Paivio, *Imagery and Verbal Processes* (New York: Holt, Rinehart and Winston, 1971), p. 332.

4. Kittie W. Watson and Larry R. Smeltzer, "Barriers to Listening: Comparison between Business Students and Business Practitioners." Paper presented at the Fourth Annual International Listening Association Convention, St. Paul, Minnesota, March 4, 1983.

5. Russ Canute, Counselor, Iowa State University, Ames, Iowa, personal interview, October 5, 1983.

6. George F. Tuttle and Johnny I. Murdock, "A Competency-Based Model for Teaching Listening within Organizational Environments." Presentation made at the Sixty-Ninth Annual Speech Communication Association Meeting, Washington, D.C., November 10, 1983.

7. *Harvard Milton College Study Skills Program Level HI* (Reston, Virginia: National Association of Secondary School Principals, 1983).

8. Robert L. Montgomery, "How to Improve Your Memory," *U.S. News and World Report* (August 23, 1979), p. 55.

9. Roy M. Berko, Andrew D. Wolvin, and Darlyn R. Wolvin, *Communication: A Social and Career Focus,* 2nd ed. (Boston: Houghton Mifflin Company, 1981), p. 76.

10. D. E. McHenry, "The Effects of Certain Learner, Task, and Response Variables on Immediate and Delayed Aural Comprehension of Meaningful Verbal Material," Ph.D. dissertation, University of Denver, 1974, cited in Paul G. Friedman, *Listening Processes: Attention, Understanding, Evaluation* (Washington, D.C.: National Education Association, 1983), p. 11.

11. Francis J. DiVesta and G. Susan Gray, "Listening and Notetaking: II. Immediate and Delayed Recall as Functions of Variations on Thematic Continuity, Note Taking, and Length of Listening-Review Intervals," *Journal of Educational* Psychology, vol. 64 (1973), pp. 278–287.

12. A. Conan Doyle, *A Study in Scarlet: The Complete Sherlock Holmes* (London: Magpie Books Ltd, 1993).

13. A. Conan Doyle, "How Watson Learned the Trick." In E.V. Lucas, ed. *The Book of the Queen's Doll's House Library* (London: Methuen, 1924).

14. Nichols, R. G. and L. A. Stevens, *Are You Listening?* (New York: McGraw-Hill, 1957), http://www.listen.org/pages/poor_listening_habits.html

Chapter Nine
Awareness Exercises

Name_____ ID#_____

Before writing your responses, spend some time paying attention to your own comprehensive listening and the comprehensive listening of others. Notice how much time you spend listening comprehensively.
    Listening awareness exercise. Please answer these questions thoughtfully.

1. List and describe two comprehensive listening settings you have been involved with in the last month.

   A.

   B.

2. Describe an inference you made that was incorrect.

3. Describe an inference you made that was correct.

4. Describe a misunderstanding that came about as the result of an incorrect meaning of a word.

5. Describe a comprehensive listening setting where you used your time efficiently.

6. Describe a comprehensive listening setting where your mind wandered.

7. Describe a comprehensive listening setting where your mind did *not* wander.

8. Describe a mnemonic device you have used to help you remember a series of facts.

9. Describe a link, or association, you have used to remember a fact or series of facts.

10. Outline a procedure for preparing for a comprehensive listening role. Use the listening guidelines.

Chapter Nine
Awareness Database

Name_____ ID#_____

1. When I have just met someone, I remember the person's name.

   A.   B.   C.   D.   E.
   often   seldom

2. What percent of my listening time do I spend listening comprehensively?

   A.   B.   C.   D.   E.
   less than 10% 10%–20%   30%–40%   50%–60%   70% or more

3. How do I rate myself as a comprehensive listener?

   A.   B.   C.   D.   E.
   very efficient   poor

4. I prepare myself when I know I am going to listen comprehensively.

   A.   B.   C.   D.   E.
   often   seldom

5. I find myself outlining messages (either mentally or taking notes) when I am listening.

   A.   B.   C.   D.   E.
   often   seldom

6. I can make most comprehensive topics interesting.

   A.   B.   C.   D.   E.
   often   seldom

7. I have trouble keeping calm during an emotionally charged speech.

   A.   B.   C.   D.   E.
   often   seldom

8. If I have trouble hearing a speaker, I correct the problem.

   A.   B.   C.   D.   E.
   often   seldom

9. If I am listening to material that is hard to understand, I put in extra effort to figure it out.

   A.   B.   C.   D.   E.
   often   seldom

10. Speakers with boring voices do not have anything important to say.

    A.   B.   C.   D.   E.
    often   seldom

Chapter Ten

Listening Therapeutically

The therapeutic listening role offers an upset person a trusting, secure environment to talk about problems. Unlike the comprehensive role, where getting information for ourselves is the main goal, the therapeutic role exists for the sender. *In therapeutic listening, our primary concern is with the sender's expression of feelings.* In this chapter we will, (1) discuss the parameters of therapeutic listening, (2) explain listening for feelings, (3) develop a definition of therapeutic listening, and (4) offer some therapeutic listening guidelines. Before beginning the discussion, imagine yourself a listener in the following situations:

A friend you jog with comes into your office and tells you that she will not be able to work out today. You ask her, "What's up? Is there a problem?" She replies,

Well, Hank (her husband) just called and . . . and the X-rays came back from his physical, and . . . well, they're not sure what they've found. The doctor said they want to do a complete scan to verify what they think. Hank's been so careful to take good care of his health, and we've made so many plans. I'm *worried; scared.* We're both going to take the afternoon off and have lunch together and talk. Oh, I'm so *scared.*

A colleague in your department sits down with a cup of coffee, and in the course of a casual conversation says,

That new office procedure for checking out equipment is a real pain. All it's done is add another level of administrative bureaucracy and double the amount of time and paperwork to get a job done. What used to take me ten minutes to get what I need, now takes three or four days. I'm *disgusted* and *frustrated* about being ignored around this place. They give me deadlines and then make it impossible to get anything done on time. I'm really *overwhelmed* with all the nonsense they give me.

You are having lunch with a friend who is separated from his wife and going through a divorce. In the course of the conversation, he says,

I'm really *disappointed* that things didn't work out. After twelve years you'd think there would be something left to build on, but I guess there isn't. I feel *hurt* that I've invested so much time and energy into a relationship only to see it go down the drain. I go home at night and feel so *lonely* and *forsaken.*

You are a supervisor and one of your employees meets with you and shares some of her thoughts:

Well, as you know, I submitted my plan for the new operation, and it was rejected. Maybe I didn't take enough time researching it, I don't know. But I spent almost four months on that project, and I think it was a good one. Anyway, that's all history, and I'm pretty *demoralized* and kind of *insecure* about submitting any other proposals. I feel *inferior* and *inadequate* at this point. Maybe I should just turn my attention to something else.

You and a fellow worker are driving to a meeting. Since the meeting is about an hour's drive away, a number of subjects are discussed. As you get to know each other better, your passenger brings up something that has been on his mind:

Did you see the amount of money they spent on the new City Hall? I really think the mayor went way off the center line on this one. We've got potholes in the streets that will destroy anything but a truck, and he spends seven million on refurbishing six offices. I'm really *annoyed*. No. I'm *enraged* about this misspending of taxpayers' money. I'm also *resentful* that he got the money appropriated without a public hearing. But I guess I'm not the first one to be *mad* about it; there have been three *bitter* editorials in the last three weeks about the situation.

The Therapeutic Listening Role

In each of these situations the words and nonverbal messages indicate that we as listeners should be in the therapeutic listening role, a role *that focuses on the sender* and allows him or her to talk through concerns and problems. The therapeutic listening role encourages the sender to unburden problems and concerns.

Listening for Feelings

The therapeutic listening role is concerned with the sender's *feelings*. For example, in the first conversation, the woman unburdened her feelings of *fear* regarding the uncertainties of her husband's health. In the second, the man disclosed the *stress* he was feeling with the new procedures. In the third scene, the man going through the divorce revealed his feeling of *sadness*. The fourth example, the woman whose plan was rejected expressed feelings of *inadequacy*, and the fifth, in the car, revealed the passenger's strong feelings of *anger* at what he considered inappropriate spending of taxpayer money. In each of these conversations, the feelings in the messages are at least as important as the content of the message.

The measure of success in the therapeutic listening role is more than the retention of information, as it is in the comprehensive listening role. We are successful at therapeutic listening when we create a climate where the sender is able to express feelings about life issues. Success in therapeutic listening hinges on *empathy*—the degree to which the listener becomes a rational and emotional mirror that invites the troubled speaker's discussion of a problem without being judgmental. Carl Rogers, a psychologist, offers a succinct definition of empathy:

> It [empathy] means entering the private perceptual world of the other and becoming thoroughly at home in it. It involves being sensitive, moment by moment, to the changing felt meanings which flow in this other person, to the fear or rage or tenderness or confusion or whatever that he or she is experiencing. It means temporarily living in the other's life, moving about in it delicately without making judgments. . . .[1]

To the extent that the empathic climate encourages a free and open expression of feelings, therapeutic listening is successful.

People involved in all phases of business, professional, and family activities need to recognize the importance of therapeutic listening. Preoccupation with problems by clients, co-workers, supervisors, employees, and family members can lesson their overall functioning effectiveness. Someone who understands the therapeutic listening role can help increase the concerned person's efficacy by allowing him or her to unburden the problem.

Therapeutic listening should stay within the bounds of normal, everyday problems: relationships, anger at a procedure, financial problems, illnesses, and so on. A listener in the therapeutic role should be sensitive to serious problems that might be life-threatening or have other serious implications. *If problems of this magnitude exist, the listener should refer the sender to a professional counselor.*

Therapeutic listening *focuses on the sender's feelings*. To emphasize this idea, listen to this message from a junior in college who started the conversation by talking in general terms about his college experiences. Changes in the content of the message indicate that we are no longer in the comprehensive listening role. As he unburdens his feelings, the message shifts to therapeutic.

I'm in class maybe sixteen hours a week, but I have Tuesday and Thursday afternoons free, so there's plenty of time to study . . . but I just don't have much enthusiasm. My grades are just okay—maybe even a little below par. I know I could do better if I wanted to. I don't know why my disappointment with the school and some of the faculty members can get to me so much. It's not like me. Ever since I can remember—even in primary school, when I didn't have any idea what an engineer was—I've wanted to be an engineer. Theoretically, I should be happy as a lark that I made my third year in engineering, but I'm not.

In this conversation, this student has been exploring his disappointment with himself and with his performance in school. He is concerned with such issues as his dislike for the school and for some of the teachers. Listening empathically, what would we determine are this man's primary feelings? What, if anything, would we say to him? Can we sense how listening to him and letting him unburden his feelings can improve his productivity at school? We need to realize that even though we are probably not trained psychiatrists, psychologists, or counselors, the need for therapeutic listening enters the lives of all of us who interact with people.

Typically, our educational backgrounds are more focused on comprehensive listening for content than on empathic listening for feelings. Consequently, in therapeutic listening, it is important to understand how some content words are in fact expressions of feelings. Some examples of content words and the feelings they reflect are presented in the following list.[2] With this list in mind, we can reread the five conversations at the beginning of this chapter and understand how the sender's words alerted the listener to the fact that s/he was in the therapeutic listening role, and we can also determine how the emphasized words revealed the feelings being expressed. Figure 10.1 presents this in tabular form.

Becoming familiar with the feelings these words express will help alert us to the fact that we are in the therapeutic role and give us insight into the nature of the sender's concern.

Being alert to cues that the therapeutic listening role is needed can help people work through problems and improve their outlook. Not attending to important therapeutic cues could allow problems to grow out of proportion. In this example, a drill instructor regrets ignoring cues for therapeutic listening.[3]

As a Drill Instructor at the Marine Corps Recruit Depot in San Diego, it was my duty to deal on a very personal level with a wide variety of people in some very unusual circumstances. Because of the very nature of Marine Corps boot camp, misunderstanding due to faulty listening and culture shock was more the rule than the exception. What follows is one of the more memorable events of my tour of duty.

My role as a therapeutic listener was extensive. Although it was my duty to administer discipline in an almost inhuman manner, it was just as much my responsibility to listen to their problems and try to find an answer or refer them to someone who could.

••• Figure 10.1

Feelings of Anger

Aggravated	Hostile
Angry	Intolerant
Annoyed	Irritated
Belligerent	Mad
Bitter	Mean
Bugged	Peeved
Cool	Perturbed
Cruel	Resentful
Enraged	Spiteful
Furious	Vengeful
Hateful	Vindictive

Feelings of Sadness

Abandoned	Grief(stricken)
Alienated	Hopeless
Alone	Humiliated
Ashamed	Hurt
Awful	Lonely
Blue	Low
Crushed	Neglected
Defeated	Rejected
Depressed	Sad
Despondent	Small
Disappointed	Sorrow
Down	Unhappy
Forlorn	Unloved(able)
Forsaken	Worthless

Feelings of Fear

Afraid	Intimidated
Alarmed	Overwhelmed
Anxious	Panicky
Apprehensive	Restless
Desperate	Scared
Embarrassed	Shy
Fearful	Tense
Frightened	Terrified
Horrified	Timid
Insecure	Uneasy
Nervous	Worried

Feelings of Inadequacy

Broken	Incompetent
Cowardly	Ineffective
Crippled	Inferior
Deficient	Insecure
Demoralized	Paralyzed
Disabled	Powerless
Feeble	Small
Helpless	Useless
Impotent	Vulnerable
Inadequate	Weak

Feelings of Stress

Ambivalent	Frustrated
Anxious	Futile
Baffled	Helpless
Bewildered	Hopeless
Bothered	Nervous
Caught	Overwhelmed
Confused	Perplexed
Conflicted	Puzzled
Disgusted	Skeptical
Dissatisfied	Trapped
Distressed	Uncomfortable
Disturbed	Unsure
Doubtful	Upset
Exposed	Vulnerable

During my first period of a new platoon, I was faced with one of the usual "whiners." These are Privates who want to go home; boot camp didn't turn out to be what they thought. Our usual answer was, "Too bad, you're here for the duration." It was no different with this one.

I sincerely wish that I had taken the time to listen. It wouldn't have hurt me, and it might have saved this kid's life. The next morning he dove out a third story window to the concrete below.

Of course, listening therapeutically extends into family as well as work-related interactions. For example, listening empathically to children can nurture healthy psychological and emotional development and further their contributions to society. When we think of adults who influenced our lives as we grew up, we can learn about the impact of their therapeutic listening by asking: "Did they listen to us without judging?" "Did they spend time attending to us; allowing us to talk?" *People Reading,* a book about listening, highlights the need to listen to the feelings of children.

Listening to a young person can easily be an act of love. Listening with concern but without judging is an art, and it helps the child explore his motivations, his style, and the accomplishments he has so far achieved. . . . It means giving him a safe place where he can speak at his own speed and explore new options, however unrealistic they may appear to us.[4]

Definition of Therapeutic Listening

Now that we have discussed the basic elements of therapeutic listening, we can bring the ideas together into a working definition:

Therapeutic listening is a holistic, positive, nonjudgmental interpersonal process. The listener attends with empathy to the sender's verbal and nonverbal messages to gain understanding, synthesis of the sender's situation. The therapeutic listening role includes active listening—maintaining comfortable eye contact; an attending posture; staying within conversational distance, while responding with facial expressions, touch, gestures, and encouraging words. The therapeutic listener asks relevant questions, and interprets and summarizes important ideas using the words spoken by the sender.[5]

Therapeutic Listening Guidelines

When we have determined that the listening role is therapeutic, we can practice some behaviors that make this role effective in helping someone.

1. *Allow time to think.* We should reflect on what the person has said and resist the temptation to respond quickly. We should ask ourselves, "What feelings are there?" "What is the basic message?" Taking time to think does not mean that the conversation loses its spontaneity. We should speak any time to help, but we should be sure we have thought before speaking. For example, if we are trying to clarify what the sender has said, rather than saying, "You're telling me that you hate school," we might say thoughtfully, "Let me see if I understand what you're saying."

2. *Short responses are usually best.* We should keep the communication going back and forth, and avoid giving speeches. We should also try to keep the speaker from rambling.

   The therapeutic listener needs to think things through and respond frequently, but the responses should be short and to the point. *Remember, we are helping by listening, so our talking should be kept to a minimum.*

3. *Responses should be adapted to the speaker, by trying to share the emotional tone or climate with the person.* We avoid imitating, but try to recognize and adapt to the mood of the speaker. If someone in the course of a dialogue says, "Yeah, and to top the day off, I got notified that I'm being audited for last year's taxes," we should avoid a response like, "You should use my tax accountant; I never get audited." A response like that might make the speaker feel worse, making him or her feel even less worthwhile. Instead, the listener should make a general summary comment: "It sounds like you're under a lot of pressure."

4. *As therapeutic listeners, we need to decide when it is time to end the interaction.* Someone discussing a difficult problem may become emotionally drained and need a break. At this point, it might be wise to suggest a break; get a cup of coffee; set up a time to visit again.

5. *Be sensitive to shifts in listening roles.* When the content of a message tells us that our role is therapeutic, we form an empathic bond with the sender and act as sounding boards to help the sender unburden problems. We avoid evaluating and offering solutions. Usually few, if any, decisions by the listener are made during a therapeutic interaction. [6]

6. *Avoid the impulse to talk.* With most problems being discussed, we are listening to let the sender express feelings. Except for paraphrasing part of the message for understanding, the listener should remain silent and attentive.[7]

7. *Protect your privacy.* Caring, empathic listeners are in demand, and you can end up giving too much time to others. Prioritize your needs to gauge the amount of your time and energy you can give to someone else's needs.

Shut Up and Listen!

Interactions in our daily lives will frequently put us in the therapeutic listening role. To be effective therapeutic listeners, we build a climate of acceptance and trust, so the sender is comfortable talking about feelings. Once feelings are expressed, the sender can often gain new insights into problems. Jennifer (Kubik) Bergerson, a psychology major, shares her thoughts about therapeutic listening in this essay, "Shut Up and Listen!" The first part lists nine guides for therapeutic listening; then she follows with examples that apply these guides.

In preparing for the essay I have written down times within the past few months where I have been in the therapeutic role, and times which I have sought out a therapeutic ear. After recording these situations I analyzed them, trying to decipher which factors were important in allowing therapeutic listening to take place. I also looked at the factors that led to the situation having a positive or a negative outcome.

I will first discuss the factors I found to be important and influential. I will then give a few examples of good and bad situations that occurred throughout the last couple months involving therapeutic listening. Finally, I will analyze these situations and conclude with what I learned from taking a closer look at therapeutic listening.

There are several factors that play into the role of therapeutic listening. Many of these factors have the common thread of safety. I found that if the sender did not feel safe, he or she simply would not unburden. There are nine other factors that I found to be the most important and influential. Many of these factors are very closely related, work hand in hand with each other, and overlap each other. The nine factors are the following:)

1. Time and Availability

The listener must be in a position where he/she has enough time to sit down and really listen to the sender. I found that usually the sender has a very good sense of how available the listener is. Listening to someone is much more productive if it is not contending with time factors or hurried mannerisms.

An example of the shortened time factor hindering listening happened in the following situation: A friend knocked on my door when I was getting ready to walk out the door. I could tell she looked stressed and wanted to talk. I said, "What's up? I only have a few minutes because I have to leave for class, but let's talk." She responded, "No, Jenn, it's no big deal. I will just talk to you when you get back." I found out later that day that she had gotten a bad grade on a test that she needed to get a good grade on in order to pass the class, and she needed to tell someone. I simply could not be an effective listener because I didn't have much time I could devote to her.

2. Confidential Environment

This is an environment where both the listener and sender feel safe from anyone having the ability to "overhear" or "eavesdrop" on the conversation. This is an environment that is safe from interruptions.

Examples of the lack of confidential environment getting in the way of therapeutic listening are the following situations: My friend Ericka and I are at dinner when she starts to unburden, but sees that there are girls from our floor sitting around us. Ericka says, "Maybe we should talk about this another time." Just because the environment was not "safe" my friend felt like she could not unburden. Another example of an environment that didn't encourage therapeutic listening was the following situation: There always seems to be a lot of people in my room right after dinner. My roommate and I have just learned that this isn't a good time or place to talk because our conversation will always be interrupted.

3. Established Trust

In seeking out a therapeutic listener I found that I always sought out someone that I knew I could trust. If the sender has already had a positive experience with the listener she is seeking, the chances are good that the person will return and feel confident about her decision. This is merely the trust that the person is a wise choice to confide in.

4. Nonjudgmental Listener

This is a listener who is not there to judge the sender or the message. In addition, the listener is not there to solve the problem or offer too much advice. This concept is mentioned in this chapter as being one of the most important factors in being a good empathetic listener; I found the same to be true through my observations. I found out that when I myself got any type of advice or judgment from the listener, it lessened my chance of continuing to disclose, and ever to come back to that person to unburden.

5. Listener Reaction

I found that a listener who is not in a hurry (time/availability), is not too emotionally involved or aroused, avoids judging, and who can easily accept emotions that aren't always rational and well thought out are the most effective therapeutic listeners. I found that when I listened to others, how I reacted to their emotions made a great deal of difference as to how much they would disclose. As much as I thought their emotions in a situation were immature, irrational, or just plain crazy, I tried not to convey that thought in my facial expressions or body language. When I showed it, they were less likely to disclose and sometimes even willing to change what they originally said to make it fit into what they thought I would think was appropriate. On the other hand, when I just stayed calm and showed no judgmental emotion they continued talking and disclosed more. As a result, people disclosed openly to me.

(continued)

6. Confidentiality

This is where the sender is assured that the message will not be spread to anyone else. This is a lot like established trust, but different in that the sender believes that his or her feelings won't get broadcasted. I felt this factor deserved a category of its own because it is more than trusting in the personality of the listener, it is *trusting in the confidentiality of the situation*.

7. Undivided Listener Attention

This is where the listener is not distracted by any noise internally or externally. I found it hard to listen therapeutically when I was preoccupied with my own thoughts. Many times my mood dictated how good I was at giving my attention to the sender. An example of how inattention led to unsuccessful listening is the following: I was getting ready for school when a friend of mine wanted to talk. I welcomed her in, but warned her that I had to finish getting ready while she was talking. She started to tell me about her day, but I could tell it was hard for her to continue because I was not giving her my full attention.

8. Out for the Good of the Sender

This factor also goes along with the nonjudgmental factor. This is when the sender believes that the listener will be on his or her "side." If the listener does make a judgment, it will be in the sender's benefit if any advice is given.

9. Receiver/Sender Commonality

I found that many times when I sought out people with whom I could unburden, I looked for people that may be in my same situation or could easily relate to what I was feeling. An example of this was when I was in a position where I felt overwhelmed by a supervisor's demand to have all the phone calls made by Thursday. I knew that I had three tests that week and that I also had many other commitments. The first person that I sought out was a friend and fellow college student who was also involved in a lot of things. I knew that she would be able to see where I was coming from, because her experiences were similar to mine.

The first part of this essay focused on nine factors that I found to be most important in good therapeutic listening. Next, I will give examples of a positive and negative listening situation. After each situation, I will analyze it and try to explain what factors were present, making it positive or negative.

The setting is about 10 o'clock in the morning. I have already showered, gotten ready for class, eaten breakfast, cleaned my room, and written in my journal. I am now just relaxing until my class at 11. One of my friends who had class early in the morning knocks on my door. I answer it, and she greets me with "Jenn, I am burning inside." I welcome her in, shut the door, turn off my stereo, move the blanket off of the chair, and pull it closer to listen. "I am getting so tired of Beth setting her alarm for 6 o'clock in the morning when she doesn't get up until 8. I am about to say something to her. She is always so inconsiderate." There is a pause.

I respond, "Oh my gosh," "I get so frustrated with mine sometimes, too." This statement gives her freedom to continue to disclose.

"Jenn, she is a nice person and all; we just have nothing in common! I just don't understand her at all. She has an 8:00 class, but doesn't go . . . ever. She'd rather stay in our room and get ready for three hours while I am trying to sleep. I just can't stand her!"

I felt that this situation was very positive in terms of therapeutic listening. When we learned that "All you are for yourself, is only what you can be for others," I am finding to be very true. When my friend came to the door, all my needs were met and I had time to give her. I was able to give her my full attention, because I had no internal or external noise that was overpowering my ability to listen. We already had established trust in each other, along with being in a similar situation (we both lived in the dorms with a roommate). The situation took place in a confidential environment, free from distractions.

The setting is in my room after dinner. My roommate and I are discussing what our next semester class schedule will look like. My roommate, Lisa, states, "I am going to hate my schedule; it is going to be so hard. I am never going to be able to get good grades."

I responded by saying, "Well, then don't take so many hard classes. The ultimate choice is yours." Our conversation was over.

In this situation I spoke before I realized that I was in the therapeutic role. The conversation did not continue because I am sure my roommate felt like I was judging her, and that I wasn't listening, since I was too quick to talk and offer my own advice. My reaction dictated whether she would continue talking or not. She probably felt that I wasn't out for her own good. It would have been a more positive situation if I would have realized I was in this role right away.

As I looked closer at therapeutic listening, I became more aware of the listening roles I was in at different times. I was surprised how many times I just said "Hi" to someone I knew in passing and we'd stop and talk and very quickly one of the two of us was in a therapeutic role. I also became aware of my own level of complaining, so I found myself trying to unburden in a less negative fashion.

In putting this essay together, I learned that being a good therapeutic listener will greatly enhance chances of people coming back to you and liking you. In some situations I consciously tried just to listen and do as little talking as possible. I was surprised that many people didn't even notice that I wasn't talking at all. Hours would pass, and as long as I was listening attentively, the other person was satisfied, even if I wasn't in the therapeutic role any more.

As I looked at some of the factors that I described, I started to think about how intelligently designed a counselor's office is. The environment is comfortable, safe, free from interruptions, and confidential. The other factors come into play when a counselor's personality is introduced as calm and nonjudgmental. Also, in a counseling session the sender has the listener's full attention. As I observe and analyze different situations involving therapeutic listening, I get excited about my future. I know that if I realize when I am in the therapeutic listening role, I can practice these helpful skills every day.

Summary

The therapeutic listening role is listening to help, and it focuses on the sender's need to unburden problems. This role emphasizes empathy and nonjudgmental listening. Empathy is the listener's attempt to experience the same feelings that the sender is expressing, and nonjudgmental listening means suspending evaluation—that is, not judging the goodness/badness or rightness/wrongness of the message. The sender's feelings are an important part of therapeutic listening, and certain words and nonverbal behaviors can alert us that we are in the therapeutic role, and can help us understand these feelings.

On the job, at home, or in other relationships, we often interact with people who can be helped by talking about their problems. Within limits, we can listen therapeutically to help someone unburden and perhaps reach decisions about problems, and as a result increase their productivity. Some guidelines for therapeutic listening include taking time to think, offering short responses, adjusting to the sender, knowing when to end the interaction, avoiding the impulse to talk, and being sensitive to listening role changes. The person who takes the time to listen to help another unburden problems will experience strengthened relationships and improved morale and productivity.

We Listen with Our Hearts

When I listen with the heart
I stop playing the game of non-listening
In other words, I step into the other's skin;
I walk in his shoes;
I attempt to see things from his point-of-view;
I establish eye contact;
I give him conscious attention;
I reflect my understanding of his words;

"We Listen with Our Hearts" by Loretta Girzaitis, 1972. Reprinted with permission.

I question;
I attempt to clarify;
Gently
I draw the other out
as his lips stumble over words,
as his face becomes flushed,
as he turns his face aside.
I make the other feel that
I understand that he is important,
that I am grateful that he trusts me enough
to share deep, personal feelings with me.
I grant him worth.

(Loretta Girzaitis 1972)

Notes

1. Carl R. Rogers, *A Way of Being* (Boston: Houghton Mifflin, 1980), p. 142.

2. *Active Skills for Staff Development: A Cognitive Viewpoint* (St. Paul, Minn.: Department of Education), pp. 8–9.

3. Stephen E. Nicol, "Some Thoughts on Listening," unpublished report, Iowa State University, Ames, Iowa, 1993.

4. Ernest G. Beier and Evans G. Valens, *People Reading* (New York: Stein and Day, 1975), p. 154.

5. http://www.ncbi.nlm.nih.gov/entrez/query.fcgi?cmd=Retrieve&db=PubMed&list_uids= 1494998&dopt=Abstract.

6. Gerard Egan, *The Skilled Helper: A Systematic Approach to Effective Helping*, 3rd ed. (Monterey, Calif.: Brooks/Cole Publishing Company, 1986), pp. 105–106.

7. William McCormack, pediatrician, personal interview, Ames, Iowa, November, 1989.

Chapter Ten

Awareness Exercises

Name_____   ID#_____

Before responding to these questions, spend some time paying attention to your therapeutic listening and the therapeutic listening of others. Notice how much time you spend listening therapeutically. Please answer these questions thoughtfully.

1. Describe a situation in which you were a therapeutic listener.

    A. The setting

    B. The nature of the problem

    C. How you listened

    D. The outcome

2. When you share your problems with someone, describe the characteristics of that person.

    A. Personality

    B. How s/he listens

    C. The outcome

3. Describe a person with whom you would not want to share a problem.

4. Describe a person who listens to your problems.

5. Describe someone you know who is empathic.

Chapter Ten
Awareness Database

Name_____ ID#_____

1. People come to me with their problems.

   A.   B.   C.   D.   E.
   seldom   often

2. I am comfortable talking about my problems.

   A.   B.   C.   D.   E.
   seldom   often

3. I understand someone else's point of view.

   A.   B.   C.   D.   E.
   seldom   often

4. I am comfortable listening to people's problems.

   A.   B.   C.   D.   E.
   seldom   often

5. When I hear something I really disagree with, I keep my opinions to myself.

   A.   B.   C.   D.   E.
   seldom   often

6. I express my feelings.

   A.   B.   C.   D.   E.
   seldom   often

7. People tell me their feelings.

   A.   B.   C.   D.   E.
   seldom   often

8. Listening to problems helps me understand my own problems better.

   A.   B.   C.   D.   E.
   seldom   often

9. Men find it more difficult to express feelings than women.

   A.   B.   C.   D.   E.
   seldom   often

10. Problems can be solved without talking about them.

    A.   B.   C.   D.   E.
    seldom   often

Chapter Eleven

Listening Critically

When we sense that we are being pressured or persuaded, we are in the critical listening role. Unlike the comprehensive and therapeutic listening roles, the critical role requires the listener *to evaluate a message and make a decision*. The decision might be simple and low risk—take a break and get a burger, or go to a movie. It could be significant—buy a car or house, get married, text a short message while driving, have another beer before driving home. The comprehensive and therapeutic roles are invaluable for human growth—they bring us understanding and empathy. The critical role helps us make wise, thoughtful choices, so it is crucial to know when we are in the critical role and what variables come into play in our decision making. When listening critically, we should consider speaker credibility, message logic, fallacies, and data.

The Critical Listening Role

Communication situations might signal a listener to change from one listening role to the critical role. Unless the listener is alert to the critical nature of the message, the listener might make a decision without understanding and evaluating the speaker's intentions and the message. For example, someone calls for an appointment to inform you of a new system of recording and reporting information. You anticipate and prepare for a comprehensive listening situation, and at the appointed time, she arrives and begins her presentation.

As the information is being discussed, you become a bit uncomfortable and eventually realize that this "informative" interaction is a persuasive appeal to buy some software. Once you realize that your listening role is now *critical* rather than *comprehensive*, you activate the critical listening behaviors necessary for a responsible, thoughtful decision.

In another situation, the conversation might move from therapeutic to critical. For example, someone stops by your home to tell you what a difficult meeting he had at work the previous night. His peers and his supervisor rejected an idea he had been working on for the past month. His self-esteem is low, and he needs to talk about the matter. You realize that you are in the therapeutic role and listen empathically. You talk for an hour, and when he is ready to leave, he comments that he feels much better and is going home to do some gardening. On his way out to your yard, he notices a stack of old bricks and asks if he could buy some from you to put a border around his garden. His request makes you uncomfortable, because the listening has just shifted from the *therapeutic* to the *critical* role.

If you had not been aware of this shift from the therapeutic to the critical role, you might have decided to help him by selling or giving him the bricks. However, since you really want to keep the bricks, you reply, "No, I want to keep them for a sidewalk I'm making." This example emphasizes the idea that we must be alert to listening role changes, especially when the change goes to the critical role. If we are not alert to the critical nature of a message, an unsatisfactory decision could be made.

Critical listening can occur in a variety of settings. Some of them are obviously persuasive, and some of them may have little or no apparent persuasive intent. Our lives are filled with persuasive messages from sales people, telephone solicitations, problem solving discussions, friends trying to get us to go somewhere, requests to donate to one group or another, appeals asking us to volunteer for certain activities or clubs, and pressure to buy into new policies or procedures. All of these messages are pushing us to make decisions. The decisions may be short-term and relatively unimportant—"How many boxes of Girl Scout cookies should I buy," or they may be decisions that impact the rest of our lives—"Should we adopt a child?"

When we are in the critical listening role, we are acting as judges hearing arguments. The arguments may not be as formal and dramatic as an actual trial, but the considerations are similar. In making a decision, we ask, "Can I believe this person?" "Do I share the values being expressed?" "Are the conclusions reasonable and logical?" "Does the proposal meet *my* needs?" "Can I afford this?" "What are the long-term implications of this decision?" "Should I be exploring alternatives?" "Who else will be affected by this decision?" "Can I take more time to decide, or is it a `one time only' chance?"

In order to make the best decision, we need to listen holistically. We listen to the believability, or *credibility*, of the sender, the logical structure and arrangement of ideas, the reasoning patterns, and the validity of evidence.

Speaker Credibility

"What you are speaks so loudly, I can't hear what you say," is an idea that demonstrates that frequently we listen to the person more than to the words being spoken. As critical listeners, we pay attention to the credibility of the speaker. A speaker with a positive, long-standing reputation, who is a well-known authority, is more believable than a speaker who is unknown.

In judging whether to believe a speaker, we need to examine five aspects of credibility: competence, character, intention, personality,[1] and dynamism:

1. *Competence.* Competence is the product of the knowledge, background, and achievements of the speaker. A person who has spent years exploring a topic through research and practice would be considered competent. However, competence in one field of experience is usually not transferable to another. For example, a famous pilot endorsing a specific brand of air conditioner may be relying on her expertise as a pilot to transfer to an unrelated subject, air conditioning. Consequently, one might make a poor decision to purchase a certain type of air conditioner based on the testimony of someone who is an expert at flying airplanes, but who actually knows little about cooling equipment.

2. *Character.* Character comes from the speaker's honesty. We ask: "Do I *trust* the speaker?" When critically listening to someone we trust, we will generally accept that the person has *our* best interests in mind. Trust is difficult to measure and understand, but it is central to many of our decisions. Recall decisions you made because of people in your life that you trust—that is, people who follow through on their promises and commitments. Think of how you listen to them. Picture how you listen to those you do not trust, and the influence they have on your decision.

3. *Intentions.* The intentions of the speaker are closely related to character and trust. We ask: "Is the persuader's genuine intent to make my life better, more comfortable, easier?" "Is the coach really concerned about me, as a person?" "Does the

coach want to win at any cost?" "Is the salesperson working for a sale or genuinely interested in my needs?" We listen critically to the intentions of the speaker and make decisions accordingly.

4. *Personality.* Our exploration of personality types in chapter six reminds us that some types might be more persuasive on a given topic than others. Given the topic, we might be persuaded by an outgoing, dynamic personality, or we might go along with a more sedate, low-key, thoughtful personality.

For example, the charm and enthusiasm of a Seven—an Enthusiast—might override the practical aspects of a decision: "Let's go hiking now: we can get our work done later!" A One—Perfectionist—might offer specific details that put the more expensive sound system well ahead of another: "The treble is more natural and authentic and mimics the desired acoustical richness of an actual performance." A Troubleshooter Six might urge you to buy a state-of-the-art Global Positioning System (GPS) for your cross country trip: "Lowering the time and frustration of getting lost, not to mention getting into dense local traffic, easily makes it worth it." An authoritative Eight, a Boss, might simply eliminate other choices by mandate: "You'll need the policy that covers hail damage; it's a must around here." A somewhat seductive Romantic Individualist Four might help you decide to get a painting that ". . . will warm the room and create a calm, mellow feeling." The Two—Helper/Giver—might carefully observe what you're needing and just present it to you: "I noticed you seemed uncomfortable in that office chair; here's a comfy one you might want to try." A Five—Observer—might say little unless asked to give an opinion. Given the Five's sense of thoughtfulness and wisdom, however, the opinion might carry great weight in the decision: "My years of studying the pros and cons of filtration systems have shown me that BioCon delivers what it promises." The Three—Producer—pushes for the product or process that gets the job done as quickly as possible: "This mini-compressor is light and easy to set-up—five minutes, tops; the pressure's up to standards, and it's stowed in the trunk in about thirty seconds. You can't beat it." The Mediator's—Nine's—persuasive approach is laid back and thoughtful—listening to your comments, letting you come to your own choice: "It sounds like you're leaning toward vacationing in Arizona, but I'm not sure you've let go of going to Alaska for sure. Can you tell me what you're thinking?" In any given persuasive situation, a personality might encompass the traits that make someone appealing to us and the topic.

5. *Dynamism.* Dynamism is the energy behind the message. It is not necessarily volume or animation, but it is intensity, sincerity, and genuineness. It is a willingness on the part of the speaker to let the strength of his or her feelings come to the surface. Someone who is shy and totally introverted is viewed as less dynamic and less credible than a sender who has a high level of intensity and energy behind the message.[2]

In making judgments about the credibility of an unknown speaker, we listen for indications of expertise and knowledge. The critical role involves listening for messages that establish the believability of the speaker. We ask, "Can I rely on this speaker for this decision?" "Has the speaker had success with the topic being discussed?" "Did the speaker answer my questions with depth, knowledge, and wisdom?"

In a 2014 Gallup poll respondents were asked to, "Please tell me how you would rate the honesty and ethical standards of people in these different fields—very high, high average low, or very low?" Here is a list of fields that received Very high and High responses:[3]

Nurses	80%
Medical Doctors	65%

Source: "Honesty/Ethics in Professions," *Gallup Poll*, December 8-11, 2014, http://www.gallup.com/poll/1654/honesty-ethics-professionals.aspx

Pharmacists	65%
Police officers	48%
Clergy	46%
Bankers	23%
Lawyers	21%
Business executives	17%
Advertising practitioners	10%
Car sales people	8%
Members of Congress	7%

Of course events change perceptions of credibility. From 1977 to 1985, clergy were ranked highest, but perhaps sex scandals and irresponsible statements by TV evangelists played a part in their credibility drop. In 1999, nurses took the lead from pharmacists—except for 2001, when firefighters came out on top—possibly because of their work after the September 11 attack.

Credibility, then, is a measure of the believability of the sender. The first step in the critical listening role is to determine the level of credibility by examining the sender's competence, character, intentions, personality, and dynamism. Next, we examine the logic being used in the decision-making message.

Logic

As critical listeners we listen to the structure, or logic, of persuasive messages. To help understand logical structure, Stephen Toulmin, a logician, defined six parts of logic that should be critically examined by the listener: data, claim, warrant, backing, rebuttal, and qualifier.[4]

Data

In the structure of a persuasive message, data are facts, opinions, statistics, and testimony which are used as the basis of proof for a claim. Data are tangible, measurable, and can be examined and verified, and the probability of their being connected to other events can be calculated. Here are some examples of data:

Fact: The temperature fell to −30 degrees last night.

Opinion: I think she would be a good addition to our staff.

Statistics: Between 40 and 45 percent of the crops are planted.

Testimony: My twenty-five years in forecasting and studying weather data lead me to believe that we'll probably have a cool, dry summer.

Claims

Claims are what the sender wants us to do. They are the solutions, conclusions, or actions to be considered. A claim is the goal of the persuasive message. Examples of claims are, "Try this plan to solve the problem"; "There can be no other choice"; "Let's have one more for the road"; "I'm pretty sure it's going to rain"; "Buy this car before the new models arrive." Claims are drawn from analogy, sign, cause-effect, induction, or deduction. As critical listeners, we determine the validity of a claim by examining how it was reached by the sender.

Claims from Analogy

An *analogy* infers that if two things are alike in some respects, they could be alike in others. For example, an analogy could be used by an electrician who claims that a house needs new wiring. The electrician uses an analogy comparing electrical systems, which the homeowner knows very little about, with the use of water, which the homeowner *does* understand. In this dialogue in which the electrician compares electricity with the flow of water, the homeowner decides not to replace her wiring because the analogy is not valid where electrical fuse protection is involved. Here is a persuasive dialogue that might take place between the electrician and the homeowner. The electrician is the first to speak:

"Picture a new house with a swimming pool," he says. "Great water demands, right? Now picture the pipes coming into the place; they're small, about this big." He closes his thumb and finger to about a quarter inch. "What's going to happen when the owner tries to fill the pool and the hot tub at the same time?"

"You didn't tell me there was a hot tub," the homeowner mentions.

"Well, there is, anyway. Sorry about that. But what's going to happen?"

"Not enough water can get through the pipes."

"Precisely," says the electrician, nodding and smiling. "So the pool and tub take three weeks to fill. Or . . . "

"Or what?"

"Or the pipes coming into your place break. Pipes can handle only so much water, and wires can handle only so much electrical current."

"And my wires are too small? They need to be replaced with bigger ones?"

"Excellent thinking," again, he smiles. "They could get hot and cause a fire."

"But do pipes have fuses or circuit breakers to protect them?" asks the homeowner.

"No," the electrician answers.

"There's where your analogy between plumbing and electricity fails," the homeowner tells the electrician. "If my wires got overloaded, a fuse will save them from getting too hot and starting a fire, but pipes will just burst."

We must listen carefully to analogies to be sure the comparisons are valid, because the key is to determine if the analogy is similar in all of the aspects involving the decision. The analogy above was only partially valid since some water systems lack protective devices found in electrical systems.

Claims from Signs

Signs suggest facts, conditions, or qualities that are not immediately evident; they are indications of something. An example of a claim from a sign is, "You're carrying an umbrella [sign]; it must be raining [claim]." The critical listener must listen carefully to be sure the signs support the claims being drawn, that other signs point to the same claim, and that contradictory signs are explained.

We frequently look for signs when making claims or conclusions. In this example we have a case of contradictory signs pointing to different claims:

I could tell by his dirty bib overalls and unkempt appearance [signs] that he was out of work [claim]; as he walked toward me [sign], I guessed that he was probably going to ask me for some money [claim]. When I saw him walk over to the limousine as his driver opened the door for him [sign], I realized that perhaps I had drawn the wrong conclusions from his clothing and behavior.

As critical listeners, we must carefully explore the validity of claims drawn from signs. We listen to determine if the signs are really pointing to valid conclusions, or if several claims could be drawn from the same sign.

Claims from Cause-Effect

Claims from *cause-effect* argue that "This, and only this, caused that." For example, "Cigarette smoking causes lung cancer [cause-effect], so stop smoking [claim]." "Getting a university education [cause] assures the graduate a high paying job [effect]. Therefore you should continue your education [claim]." "The price of oil [cause] is slowing the economy [effect]. We must work to lower oil prices [claim]." The critical listener needs to determine if the stated cause is a *real* cause, and if it is the *only* cause. We may reject the idea of working to lower oil prices, because other data indicate many causes of a slow economy.

Claims from Induction

A message that uses specific instances or facts to draw a general conclusion is using *induction*. An example of a claim drawn from inductive reasoning is: "I talked to the girls at my table [specific instance], and everybody's going to Joe's after the game [claim]," or "I contacted three of the guys who took that seminar, and there's nothing worthwhile to be gained from going to it."

In both cases the speaker is making a general claim (". . . everybody's going to Joe's after the game," and ". . . there's nothing worthwhile to be gained from going to it"), derived from specific details: the girls at the table and three who attended a seminar. In cases of induced claims, the critical listener must listen for the number of individual testimonies that led to the claim. Do the instances represent the whole? That is, how many is "everybody"? And are three opinions enough to determine the value of a seminar? Do the people polled represent the entire group?

As active critical listeners, we need to question the speaker to determine the kind of sample used. Also, we need to determine if significant exceptions are being explained. Maybe some of the girls not going to Joe's have gone before and found it a real waste of time and money. Maybe those who *are* going to Joe's have never gone before and do not know what to expect.

The generalized claim about the seminar that has "nothing worthwhile" needs the same scrutiny. What are the standards for "worthwhileness"? The number of jokes the seminar leader tells? The number of friends in the seminar? The fact that someone received a bad experience in another seminar could even prompt that generalization.

Claims from Deduction

Deduction structures a message from general information to specific conclusions. For example, "Our basketball games are always exciting, so I'm sure tonight's basketball game is going to be exciting!" is a specific claim about tonight's game based on the speaker's general knowledge that the team plays exciting, fast-paced basketball. However, as critical listeners, we need to be aware that in spite of the generally exciting character of the games, this one could lack excitement. Even great teams have occasional letdowns.

We are basing a decision on deduction if we stop for a cup of coffee ". . . because," says our traveling companion, "all of the service areas have good coffee." Probably, she has not tried all of the service stops, but has apparently sampled some of them and found they served good coffee. From these favorable experiences she has formed the general idea that all the service areas have good coffee, and she infers by deduction that this specific stop also serves good coffee.

In this inspection of critical listening, we have looked at data—the facts and proof being used—and we have examined claims and conclusions, and how we arrive at them. Now we will explore *warrants*, which are the link between the data and the claim.

Warrants

Warrants are statements that are generally believed by the listeners. They connect the data and the claim. Often warrants are not stated by the sender, so as critical listeners, we need to study the structure of the arguments to determine the warrants being used by the sender. Once we understand warrants, we have made substantial growth in analyzing the decisions we make when listening critically.

Claim and Warrants from Analogies

The *warrant* is the link between the data and the claim, and it is a general statement. In the earlier analogy about water and electricity, the electrician is persuading a homeowner to rewire the house; the electrician uses an analogy, saying that substantial use of water requires larger pipes.

The argument goes like this: You are using substantial amounts of electricity [data]; therefore your house needs to be rewired with bigger wire and more circuits [claim].

The unstated warrant in this argument is, "The physical activities of water are the same as the physical activities of electricity." This warrant links the data to the claim with a general statement that encompasses both the data (which involve water) and the claim (which involves electricity). In addition to claims and warrants from analogies, we will examine four more claims and warrants that are found in persuasive messages. These are claims from: (1) signs, (2) cause-effect, (3) induction, and (4) deduction.

Signs suggest facts, conditions, or qualities that are not immediately evident; they are *indications* of something else. Under the discussion "Claims from Signs," we used this paragraph to illustrate that signs can lead to faulty claims.

> I could tell by his dirty bib overalls and unkempt appearance [signs] that he was out of work [claim]; as he walked toward me [sign]. I guessed that he was probably going to ask me for some money [claim]. When I saw him walk over to the limousine as his driver opened the door for him [sign], I realized that perhaps I had drawn the wrong conclusions from his clothing and behavior.

The logic in this paragraph looks like this:

Data [sign]:   dirty overalls, unkempt appearance.

Warrant, unstated: personal appearance is related to employment.

Claim: He is out of work.

Data [sign]:   walking to limousine; driver opening door.

Warrant, unstated: expensive possessions and employed attendants indicate success.

Claim: He is a successful, well-rewarded person; the first conclusion was not correct.

Claims and Warrants from Induction

Inductive logic builds from specific instances to a general claim. The claim discussed earlier, "Everybody's going to Joe's after the game," has the warrant:

Warrant: More than 85 percent of a sample means "everybody."

Data: Eighty-six percent of those I talked to are going to Joe's after the game.

As critical listeners, we can examine this warrant by questioning the sampling techniques: Why is 85 percent representative of the whole population? How many people were sampled? Was it a random sample? Why aren't the other 15 percent going?

Claims and Warrants from Deduction

Claims that go from the general to the specific are arrived at through deduction. Our enthusiastic speaker in this category claimed:

Claim: Tonight's home basketball game is going to be exciting!

Warrant: All home games are exciting.

Data: We are playing a home basketball game tonight.

Listening critically, you find that you are uncomfortable with the claim, so you question the validity of the warrant. You might not accept the warrant that all home games are exciting. So you reject the warrant as stated and recast it:

Warrant: "*Some* of our *conference* home games are exciting."

You reject the speaker's claim and change it to:

Claim: "Tonight's game *might* be exciting."

And based on the changed claim, you decide not to go to the game tonight.

Data, claims, and warrants are the backbone of critically listening to logic. Toulmin adds three more parts for logical analysis: backing, rebuttal, and qualifier.

Backing

Backing is data that prove the warrant, because sometimes, as critical listeners we might reject a warrant at face value. The electrician in the earlier example needed to offer more backing for his warrant: "The physical activity of water parallels the physical activity of electricity." To increase the believability of the warrant, backing can be added, which might include some testimonials from qualified experts. The electrician could have provided backing in the form of a picture showing similarities between electricity and water. If possible, he could have given examples that show that some water systems have safety plugs that release when the pressure becomes too much for the system. This would certainly have helped in his persuasive efforts when the homeowner mentioned the fuse/circuit breaker information.

Notice how understanding warrants—a job that takes a good deal of thought and energy on the part of the critical listener—can help us get to the core of a persuasive message.

Now we move to the appeal to go to Joe's house after the game. The answers to the questions we posed as critical listeners can provide the foundation for the backing. The warrant, which was unstated by the sender, was "More than 85 percent of a sample means 'everyone.' " What kind of backing would we listen for to accept this warrant?

Here is some backing that we might find acceptable:

Backing: According to a widely used book on survey statistics: "when a sample exceeds 85 percent, the survey is said to include virtually the entire population."

This backing might help us accept the warrant, and the data might be sufficient to persuade us that "Everybody's going to Joe's house after the game," and, of course, we should go, too.

Next, we move to the basketball game. We critically listened to the enthusiastic sender and generated this warrant: "All State home games are exciting." We heard the data: "State is playing at home tonight," and then the claim: "Tonight's game is going to be exciting."

We have disagreed with the validity of the warrant, saying, "Some of State's home conference games are exciting." If we were to mention that only *some* of the games are exciting, the speaker could respond by providing backing for the warrant:

Backing: A poll in the state's major newspaper showed that 90 percent of the state's population thought that their team played hotly contested, competitive home conference games, which were exciting.

Backing: John Filborne, the president of the student body, believes all of our home games are exciting.

Given this backing for the warrant, we as critical listeners might accept the claim that tonight's game is going to be exciting.

Backing is a special form of data that support the warrant, and a warrant is a generalized claim, often unstated but central to the effectiveness of critical listening.

The last two parts of Toulmin's model are rebuttal and qualifier; they are fairly simple and apply to the claim.

Rebuttal

A *rebuttal* restricts the argument to certain conditions which could affect the claim, and the rebuttal is usually recognizable by the word *unless*. It softens the argument by acknowledging that the outcome is not a sure thing. "My claim is valid *unless* one of these issues arises." So now we hear a claim with rebuttal:

Claim with Rebuttal. Tonight's basketball game is going to be exciting [claim], *unless a key player is sick or misses the game for some reason* [rebuttal].

Claim with Rebuttal. Everybody's going to Joe's house after the game [claim], *unless it goes into overtime and gets too late* [rebuttal].

Qualifier

A *qualifier* gives the listener the degree of probability, either in actual percentages or with words like, "possibly," "more than likely," "probably," "almost certainly," "there is a good chance," and so on. The qualifier does just what it means—it qualifies the claim.

Claim with Qualifier. Eighty-five percent [qualifier] of the group is going to Joe's after the game.

Claim with Qualifier. There is a good possibility [qualifier] that tonight's game will be exciting.

Claim with Qualifier and Rebuttal

Of course, claims can have both a qualifier and the rebuttal.

I think there's a good chance [qualifier] that tonight's game is going to be exciting [claim], unless Johnson's elbow isn't healed [rebuttal].

Figures 11.1 and 11.2 show a summary of Toulmin's system of logic as adapted to critical listening.

(D) Data: What we have to connect us with reality: facts, opinions, comparisons, statistics, testimonies, examples, illustrations, analogies, narratives, observations, any forms of proof.

(C) Claim: The solution or conclusion drawn from the data. To a lesser or greater degree the claim is potentially controversial.

(W) Warrant: The bridge or "mental jump" from the data to the claim. How we get to a conclusion. Often not stated by the sender.

(B) Backing: Data that strengthen the acceptability of the warrant. Sometimes listeners will not accept a warrant at its face value, so backing could be used as proof of the warrant.

(R) Rebuttal: An escape hatch that modifies the claim. The claim may not be true under all circumstances, so the rebuttal acknowledges those circumstances. (For example, "Unless the game goes into overtime.")

(Q) Qualifier: Gives the degree of probability to the claim. "Possibly . . . Probably . . . sixty-five times out of one hundred . . . 70 percent chance."

Now that we have explored critically listening to logic, which is the *structure* of persuasive message, we turn our attention to ten fallacies of reasoning that can occur within the structure.

••• Figure 11.1

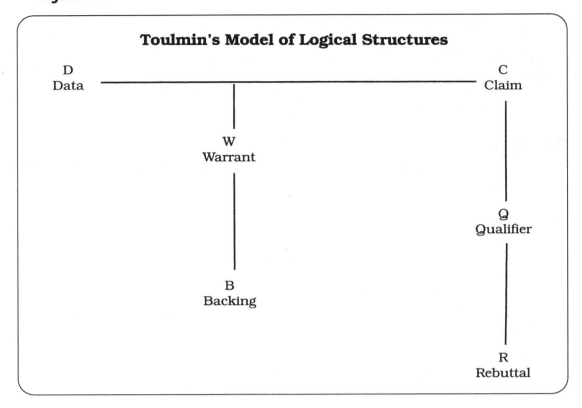

••• Figure 11.2

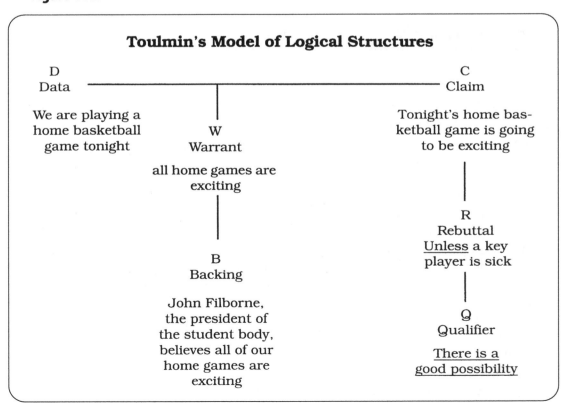

The fallacies to be discussed are: (1) Ignoring or shifting the burden of proof, (2) Begging the question, or assuming, (3) *Argumentum ad hominem*, or attacking the person, (4) Straw man or red herring, (5) Unjustifiable emotional appeal, or pulling on the heartstrings, (6) Hasty generalization, or faulty induction, (7) Stereotyping, or they are all the same, (8) Disjunctive reasoning, or either/or, (9) Oversimplified cause, or it is obvious, and (10) Unexamined analogies or, are these really the same?[5]

Fallacies of Reasoning

Fallacy #1: Ignoring or Shifting the Burden of Proof

The critical listener needs to be sensitive to the sender's responsibility to prove assertions that s/he makes. The assertion might be noncontroversial: "I think it's going to rain," or highly controversial: "The depletion of ozone will destroy life as we know it in ten years." In every case, the responsibility to prove an assertion lies with the sender.

Listen to these arguments to understand how the burden of proof has been ignored by the sender and shifted on to the listener. In each case where the proof is ignored or shifted, the active listener needs to shift the burden back to the sender with feedback and questions:

Daughter: "Dad, just give me one good reason why I can't have the car tonight."

Dad: "No, Honey, you need to show me why you should be able to have the car."

Friend: "I'll never be able to quit smoking. How can I?"

Friend: "I don't know, how can you?"

Fallacy #2: Begging the Question, or Assuming

A question or issue has been "begged" when *a portion of the assertion being given is assumed, without proof, to be true.* Here are some examples of question begging:

Professor: Students accused of cheating on exams should be thrown out of school, no "ifs," "ands," or "buts." They shouldn't get any of this appeal to the next level stuff, because when they cheated, they gave up their rights as responsible students on this campus, PERIOD.

Student: But it's *assumed* I've been cheating; I was just looking out the window.

Listening critically, we notice that the sender equates being *accused* of cheating with actually cheating. Begging the question or assuming implies that accusation and guilt are one and the same. Listen to this person trying to persuade us to give him a ride to work. He begs the question by equating the sign—cloud build-up—with actual rain.

Man! Look at those clouds building up in the west. I think you'd better take me to work; if I don't get a ride, by the time I get there I'll be soaked.

Circular argument is a special way of begging the question by wrapping one unproved assertion around another and coming right back to the first one:

We need to control weapons with stiff laws. I've heard the argument against gun control for years. The groups that are against gun control say that controls will penalize and restrict the sportsmen who would comply with the control laws, leaving the criminals to wander around freely with guns. This is shabby reasoning. If we had gun control laws, the criminals *couldn't* be running all over with guns, because the weapons would be regulated by law.

Fallacy #3: Argumentum ad Hominem, or Attacking the Person

This Latin legal term means "argument against the man." We have all heard politicians attack their opponents rather than the issues at stake. (Such an attack might be legitimate if the opponent offers only unsupported personal opinions as proof.)

The critical listener should notice how frequently this device is used in the legal setting also. Attorneys will attempt to discredit a witness by pointing out undesirable character traits, a lack of trustworthiness, or a past criminal record. We need to listen to whether the argument rests on solid evidence and reasoning and accept it or reject it on those terms and not on unrelated past activities. These two examples show how *argumentum ad hominem*, attacking the person, can draw the listener to faulty conclusions.

> You know, a leopard can't change his spots. We've dealt with Chester Grenspat for years and we know he can't be trusted as far as you can throw him. So, no matter what he proposes regarding this matter, vote against it; it will not be in our best interests.

> The search of my home was illegal, and the drugs and drug money that police found in my home should not be counted as evidence against me. After all, the person who informed on me has a criminal record.

Notice that in both cases, the sender is asking the listener to make a decision based on someone's past record, rather than on the facts and structure of the argument.

Fallacy #4: Straw Man or Red Herring

The straw man and red herring fallacies are closely related. They both are structured to redirect the focus of the issues being argued. They differ only in the degree of change they have on a topic. Straw man takes the listener into a *related* but distorted or exaggerated topic. The sender builds a scarecrow—a straw man—which becomes an altered target for discussion, and the topic in its original form might be ignored. Red herring goes beyond distortion of the original and *replaces* it with a new topic.

As listeners we need to be alert to these fallacies, because if these topics, which have been changed by either straw man or red herring tactics, are discussed and decisions are made based on them, *the actual issues have not been addressed.*

First, let's take a closer look at straw man manipulating. In this example, three people are discussing the reliability of cars:

> Marge, an auto mechanic claims, "In general, the Japanese cars are more reliable than most American brand cars."

> Howard, a local labor union steward nods affirmation. He agrees with that statement: "Yes, they do seem more dependable."

> However, Jeremy, an accountant, who is having his car fixed by the mechanic, disagrees with this viewpoint, and says, "You're just questioning the reliability of the automotive labor and workmanship in our United States."

If Marge, the mechanic, and Howard do not listen critically, they will spend their time and energy trying to show that labor in the United States is not up to others' standards. They will be fighting a straw man—the unreasonable extension of the original assertion that had to do with automobile reliability—and will now be discussing a much different but somewhat related argument about U.S. labor, workmanship, and reliability.

Red herring takes the manipulation further by introducing a new topic into the discussion. Anyone who has hunted with a dog knows that competing scents can confuse the animal and send her on the wrong trail. This form of distraction is sometimes called *red herring* because, like a dog going after the wrong scent, it can take the critical listener completely away from the main issue.

Listen for the fallacy in this argument: In a discussion about the value of transcendental meditation (TM), one person says that she did not find TM very beneficial. The other person, who finds TM a valuable part of her life, continues the discussion but throws out a red herring by moving into quite different topics that were not included in the original discussion.

All right, as long as you're discrediting transcendental meditation as a form of relaxing and getting in touch with yourself, we might as well do away with the benefits of other systems of relaxing and getting to know ourselves. Napping, listening to music in a quiet setting, even the peace of going to church might as well be brought into the discussion because they all have some of the same effects.

In this scene, the first speaker states a simple personal claim: "I don't find TM very helpful."

The listener takes the simple statement to a new level by packing it with issues of napping, music, and church attendance. Certainly, if the first speaker begins to defend these new topics, a good deal of time and energy could be wasted, and any conclusions would be meaningless, since the original issue (TM) has been lost.

As critical listeners, we should attend to the main issues and not get side-tracked. The best defense for the straw man or red herring fallacy is to listen carefully to be certain that the original issue stays in focus. Point out to the sender that the discussion is wandering off the original course.

Fallacy #5: Unjustifiable Emotional Appeal, or Pulling on the Heartstrings

Emotions are a natural and valuable part of human nature, and there is certainly nothing wrong with reacting to emotional messages. Emotion can be very persuasive; its use is legitimate. Emotional appeal when used to encourage someone to buckle up before driving or to get them to give up smoking is certainly noble.

However, pulling on the heartstrings has led to poor decision making. Many tragedies are the result of emotional appeals where cautious, critical listening was abandoned to emotional manipulations. What happened to critical listening in this situation?

In late 1978 the world was shocked by a horror that as a fictional plot would have been rejected by the most charitable editor of fantasy fiction as too preposterous to be considered. Who would believe that nearly a thousand adult human beings would stand by while others murdered their children and close friends and then would voluntarily drink grape-flavored Kool-Aid that they knew had been mixed with cyanide? Yet on the instructions of an egomaniac [Jim Jones] who called himself both a minister and a god—and was believed—the inhabitants of a failed utopia called Jonestown in Guyana, South America, did just that. . . .

. . . the main reason people follow a Jones is that they *abandon critical judgment* [emphasis mine] on the assumption that their leader is infallible. Consider the Unification Church of the "Reverend" Sun Myung Moon. He tells his fanatical followers that a "New Messiah" is coming and that he will be a Korean male born this century. He says that this "Third Adam" will become the father of a "Perfect Family" that will redeem mankind. Moon, who has had several marriages, is certainly a father—seven times over. When asked uncomfortable questions, Moon replies to his disciples—"I am your brain." Obviously, the busloads of young people who are daily carted off to posts throughout Manhattan (from the church's headquarters at the former Hotel New Yorker) to solicit funds for the millennium believe this statement and are happy with it. *Would they, too, drink cyanide if Moon commanded them to?*[6]

Emotional appeal when not listened to critically, can, in extreme cases, cost lives; moreover, emotional messages can also be the source of poor decisions on a less dramatic scale:

Bill looked at his car, which was totally destroyed by his best friend, Jason, who had been drinking. The car had been rolled twice and landed upright in a field. Fortunately no one was hurt.

Bill recalled the emotional appeals that led to the decision he had made to lend the car to Jason. He knew Jason had been drinking, but Jason assured Bill that he was all right. Bill lent him the car after an emotional scene:

Tears had welled up in Jason's eyes as he told Bill that he had to see his aunt (who had raised him since he was six) one more time in the hospital. "She's dying, Bill, I just want to say 'Good-bye.' "

Bill abandoned his best judgment, gave in to the emotional appeal, and decided to loan Jason his car.

Fallacy #6: Hasty Generalization, or Faulty Induction

Inductive reasoning examines individual cases and uses them to make a generalized claim. When the sender makes a generalized claim from *too few specific cases* or cases that are not appropriate, the fallacy of hasty generalization exists. Here are three examples of hasty generalizations:

Men are lousy cooks [claim]. Yesterday, I asked my brother to fix some soup and grilled cheese sandwiches for the kids. Well, he and one of his buddies attempted the job, and they boiled the soup all over the stove and burned the sandwiches [generalization from only two cases].

Those people from the east end of town are pleasant and helpful [claim]. Just the other day, I had a flat tire over there and a man gave me a ride to a service station right away. And about two months ago, my wife had to return something she had bought in a store there, and they were just as nice as they could be [generalization from only two cases].

Miller has won the vote in Story County [generalization from only one case]. Let's hear it for our next governor! [claim]

Fallacy #7: Stereotyping, or They Are All the Same

Stereotyping is a way of thinking that focuses on *similarities* rather than *differences*. It categorizes people or things without considering individual differences. For example, some stereotyping was used in explaining the straw man fallacy, when the auto mechanic, union steward, and accountant were discussing the reliability of American and Japanese cars. In this example, the union steward and the accountant did not behave as we might expect. The union steward, who stereotypically would be a strong defender of American products, agreed that the Japanese cars were more dependable. Moreover, the accountant, who stereotypically would not have a strong viewpoint about auto reliability or labor, expressed a supportive view for American labor. These views might not fit the stereotypical picture of a union representative and an accountant.

Critical listeners need to be alert to stereotyping: all union representatives are alike; all accountants are alike. In the example of the cooking class related to hasty generalization, one might be more willing to accept the hastily generalized claim that men are lousy cooks, because this claim fits an already existing stereotype: "Men are no good in the kitchen."

The realization that no two things or people are alike will help us avoid decisions based on stereotyping. Realizing this, when we listen to these comments: "He's a Harvard man," "She's a liberated woman," "He's a hairstylist," "She's a sorority woman," "He's an alcoholic," "He's a high school dropout," or "She's in her third marriage," we can realize that individuals within these groups are distinctly different and should not be considered the same. To make decisions based on reality rather than stereotyping, we listen, and focus on *differences*, not similarities, *within* groups.

Fallacy #8: Disjunctive Reasoning, or Either/Or

Disjunctive messages place something or someone in "either one camp or another." For example, "Jake is not doing well in his new assignment in purchasing. He's *either* stupid *or* lazy." In reality, Jake might not fit into either category. When we listen to this disjunctive comment, we need mentally to add more "*ors.*" For example, ". . . or, Jake has not had sufficient training," ". . . or, Jake has been sick," ". . . or, Jake is having personal problems."

Few claims are either one or the other; there is usually some middle ground, some room in between the extremes. Even when we flip a coin, a small possibility exists that the coin will not land heads or tails, but on its edge. Following are some examples of disjunctive statements that ignore the middle ground and put people in one camp or another:

"She's either a dedicated professional or a housewife."

"If the job can't be done the way I want it, then don't do it at all."

"Look at the muscles on him; he must take steroids or work out eight hours a day."

"Look at the diamond on her. She either is rich or she deals in drugs."

Fallacy #9: Oversimplified Cause, or It Is Obvious

As critical listeners, we need to listen for the two most frequent oversimplifications of the cause-claim relationship: (1) mistaking a minor or contributing cause as the main cause of a problem, and (2) attaching a problem to one cause when there are *several* significant causes involved.

When solving a problem, we must be as certain as possible that we are directing our energies at the actual cause of the problem. For example, in diagnosing an illness, the physician thoughtfully listens to the patient describe the symptoms. She listens with her stethoscope and with her hands, all in an attempt to make a decision to treat the actual cause of the problem, and not a minor cause. As critical listeners, we must put the same care and attention into our listening to find the actual causes of problems we are solving. These examples show that *apparent* causes of problems may not be the *actual* causes:

"If you loan me $100, I could get myself out of this fix I'm in." (Is lack of money the cause of the problem?)

"A new computer will really streamline your purchasing process." (Is slow computer capability the problem?)

"You got that cold from going out without your hat." (Did the hatless head cause the cold?)

We want to listen critically to isolate all of the major contributing causes of a problem. The following examples each address a contributing cause, but ignore other causes:

"This country would be out of debt if we could just lower oil prices." (There are other causes of debt.)

"Just take one of these pills a day, and you'll lose ten pounds in a month." (Weight is the product of a number of causes.)

"This new computerized thermostat will bring those heat bills right down to minimum." (Weather extremes and insulation are two other causes of high heat costs.)

Fallacy #10: Unexamined Analogies, or Are These Really the Same?

We have discussed analogies earlier, but let us review for a moment. An analogy takes parallel ideas or situations and says this one is like that one in many respects. Earlier, we used the analogy of water and electricity, and we found that they were alike in some ways, but not in all ways. Consequently, in that situation, the analogy failed to persuade. We critically listen to determine if there is *one important difference in the analogical comparison*. If there is, the analogy fails, and the listener should reject the claim. For example, the following analogy makes the claim that some intelligent being smarter than the people and objects of the universe made the universe and everything in it:

If you were walking on a deserted jungle path and found a mat woven out of plant stalks, one over the other, to make a rectangle two feet by three feet, you would assume that some intelligent being smarter than the plant stalks had worked with the stalks and formed them into the mat, wouldn't you? Well, look at the intricate design of the universe. Isn't it reasonable that some intelligent being smarter than the people and the objects of the universe fashioned all of that?

This analogy suggests that the pattern and structure of a woven mat parallels the pattern and structure of the universe. Of course, no one knows that. We can recognize a mat immediately, but the limits and structure of the universe are largely unknown. Consequently, at this point, the analogy cannot be accepted as valid.

Examining Data

As critical listeners, we must constantly be attentive to the logical structure and reasoning of persuasive messages. Now we examine listening to the data within the structure of the message. We will discuss data in the forms of (1) examples and illustrations, (2) testimony, (3) definition, (4) statistics, and (5) visual aids.

Examples and Illustrations

Examples and illustrations are specific instances that explain or clarify part of a message. An example is a short explanation; an illustration is longer and more detailed. Senders use them to make abstract ideas clearer.

As a critical listener, ask yourself—Does the example or illustration represent the whole? Is it typical? Or is it an extreme example?

Is the example relevant? It might be typical and representative, but how does it prove the assertion being made? Sometimes a speaker may tell an interesting story or joke, but as critical listeners we need to ask how it relates to the topic being discussed.

Jessica Tuchman Mathews, an environmental scientist, discusses the greenhouse effect and makes the claim that rising temperatures on the earth could greatly affect plants and animals. Notice that her examples are representative and are not extreme. She says that plants and animals will be affected by rising temperatures:

> [N]othing that we know about evolution suggests that plants and animals can adapt to such rapid change. There have been big temperature swings before over geological time, but there you're talking millions of years. Now we're talking decades. For example, we know something about how fast trees can move to adjust to different climates, how far the wind blows the seeds in a year, and how far they can progress. It's a tiny fraction of how far they would have to move in order to keep up with their changing habitat. So you would expect massive extinctions.[7]

This illustration is relevant and is adapted to the whole concept of greenhouse effect. As critical listeners, we would probably accept the claim that the greenhouse effect would be substantial.

Testimony

There are two types of testimony that we use to make decisions. First is *expert* testimony; second is *witness* testimony. Expert testimony reports factual findings *and recommends future plans, policies, or procedures*. Witness testimony provides factual information *without recommending future plans, policies, or procedures*.

Expert testimony might range from the physician who tells us that we should be exercising more often, to the grocer who tells us that the Colorado peaches that just arrived are especially good and we should buy them while they are fresh, to the mechanic who recommends an engine overhaul for our car. From these expert testimonies, we form our plans: Do we jog more? Buy the peaches? Get the engine overhauled? Our decision is based, in part, on the credibility of those giving testimony.

We also rely on witness testimony to determine factual information. Witness testimony helps us determine whether something did or did not occur: "I saw Mr. Jacobson's car turn directly in front of Mrs. Thurman's car, causing an unavoidable situation." "The last time I ate there, I found a bug in my salad." "I saw him pouring the cheap wine into the fancy French wine bottle." Or, "Mom, I saw Suzy kick Hal on the playground." Based on our perceived accuracy of the witness testimony, we decide if we should eat there, buy wine there, or punish Suzy.

When listening to testimony, ask yourself, Is it complete and objective? Are there partially quoted portions that change the overall intended meaning? If the authority being quoted or paraphrased were sitting next to you, would s/he be comfortable with the words being attributed to him or her?

Does the testimony come from an authority *in the field* being discussed? Just because an engineer is testifying does not mean the person is an expert in this particular area of engineering. Does the testimony come from a neutral, unbiased source? Or does the source have *stock in the company*—that is, something personal to gain from the testimony?

Definition

We need to listen closely to definitions because they can prompt decisions. In this text, *listening* is defined as *using both hemispheres of the brain to assign meaning to all sense input.* By accepting this definition, we have accepted the ideas that we listen with both sides of our brains, with our eyes, our noses, our skin, our tongues, as well as with our ears. Ultimately, accepting this operational definition is a decision to change one's outlook of listening and to expand listening behavior to include both sides of the brain and all five senses. The definition does, in fact, carry a persuasive message.

When critically listening to a definition, ask yourself: Does the definition add to my understanding of the concept? Does it clarify and delineate the idea? Are there any aspects of the definition that I cannot accept?

Statistics

Basically, statistics are numbers that summarize findings or data into four categories:

Central Tendency.   This shows the pattern of the gathered data with the mean or median. The mean is called the average; it adds the score and divides by the number of entries. The median is the middle score. That is, half the scores are above the median and half are below.

Correlation.   Correlation shows the strength of a relationship between two variables. For example, a high correlation might exist between cholesterol and heart disease. One caution when listening to correlation statistics is not to confuse the correlation with causation; other factors could be involved.

Differences.   The range, which is merely subtracting the lowest from the highest score, can help us by showing differences. When the range is high, there is greater diversity; when the range is low, there is more similarity.

Percentiles.   Percentiles help us picture the percentage of scores that are below a particular score. For example, a tire manufacturer might tell us that on a durability scale its tires scored 480 points, a score that puts its tires in the ninety-seventh percentile. This means that 97 percent of the competition's tires were below this manufacturer's tires in durability.

Some of the reasoning and logical cautions discussed earlier regarding data apply here. Ask yourself as you critically listen: Were the statistics taken from a large enough sample? Does the sample represent the total population? Are the statistics current? Currency is especially important in areas of quickly changing technology. Who collected the statistics? Was the collector unbiased?

Visual Aids

We listen to visuals with our eyes. A visual might be attractive, but is it relevant? Does it support an idea or a claim? Is the visual an important part of the message? It might be interesting, but how does it apply here? Is the visual clear? Can it be easily understood? The way a graph is set up can minimize or maximize compared data. Watch to determine that the scales on a graph are equal both vertically and horizontally.

Listening Critically to Campaign Speeches

Our lives are full of situations where listening is a part of decision making. The decisions we make range from when and where to go shopping to which people will lead our country. In a country that has so much freedom of choice, we must be especially aware of applying our critical listening skills to government leadership. The following speech given by an expert in political analysis, Dr. Ray Dearin, highlights the importance of listening critically before voting, and it offers some suggestions to sharpen our critical listening skills before voting:

> *Ray D. Dearin is a Professor Emeritus of Speech Communication at Iowa State University, where he teaches courses in Rhetorical Criticism and Political Campaign Communication. The following essay is based upon a lecture he gave to an undergraduate class in Listening on September 28, 1988.*

Let me begin by thanking Dr. Paul Kaufmann for inviting me to speak to you this morning on a subject I have been paying a lot of attention to lately. Since I am teaching courses in rhetorical criticism and campaign rhetoric, and since a presidential campaign is now going on, I thought it might be appropriate to share with you some ideas about critical listening as it applies to the kind of political rhetoric we hear every four years at this time.

I suppose I should first tell you how I have come to know all that I intend to tell you. Whenever a person discovers an idea for the first time, that is called *originality*. When a second person comes along and uses the idea, it's called *plagiarism*. When a third person uses it, it is called *lack of originality*. With a fourth person, it is known as *drawing from a common stock*. And when you get to the fifth person who uses it, then it is called *research*. I want you to know that what I tell you this morning is based on a lot of "research" on my part. My approach will be to look at some of the basic principles upon which most campaign speeches are built and then apply some critical listening standards to these speeches.

Three Key Features of Campaign Speeches

Of all the many principles and devices that typify modern political speaking, three features are so pronounced and pervasive that they stand out sharply. These key elements are the use of *contrast, repetition,* and what I call the *mood of indignation*. Let's look more closely at these persuasive stratagems.

Contrast

The primary principle of political speaking is *contrast*. You might expect this, since every election contest has candidates who try to paint the bleakest, darkest picture of gloom that will surely occur if their opponents are elected, while the brightest, most prosperous times you can imagine will be likely to follow if they are elected. Although the contrast seems to be about policies or issues, when you examine the arguments closely you will inevitably find that the contrast is achieved syntactically; that is, certain words or expressions are being played off against one another in ways that emphasize conflicting ideas. Frequently this effect is achieved through the use of balanced sentence constructions, antitheses, and phrases turned around or inverted. I'll give you some examples of these devices in action.

Although most of you were probably not yet born when President John F. Kennedy delivered his inaugural address in January 1961, you can doubtless recite one of the memorable lines from that speech: "Ask not what your country can do for you; ask what you can do for your country." When you examine this idea, you will see that its meaning is conveyed by a rather simple rhetorical device: the use of an antithetical sentence construction. "Ask *not*," Kennedy beseeched his listeners, "what your *country* (**A**) can do for *you* (**B**) ask what *you* (**B**) can do for your *country* (**A**)." **AB** forms a balanced contrast with **BA**. Exactly the same rhetorical form was used elsewhere in Kennedy's speech when he said: "Let us never negotiate (**A**) out of fear (**B**), but let us never fear (**B**) to negotiate (**A**)." Professor Kaufmann and I are old enough to remember

---

"Listening Critically to Campaign Speeches" by Dr. Ray D. Dearin, reprinted with permission.

that this same scheme was used in the Salem cigarette commercials on television in the 1960s. Accompanied by a little jingle, the ad proclaimed: "You can take Salem out of the country, but you can't take the country out of Salem." After hearing this ditty a few times, you found yourself walking around whistling the tune.

The **AB:CD** form of antithesis is probably even more common in public speeches in general, and in political discourse in particular. It involves a direct contrast between two concepts, not just an inversion of these ideas. On January 17, 1980, the Reverend Jesse Jackson came to Iowa State University to give a speech. To this day I can still remember something he said in his talk. "We need will power **(A)** to cop in **(B)**," said Jackson, "not pill power **(C)** to cop out **(D)**." This same formal principle of sentence arrangement was employed by Winston Churchill, who ranks alone as the consummate English orator of the twentieth century. For example, in a speech in 1925 Churchill sought to contrast socialism and communism. He said: "If I were asked the difference between socialism and communism, I could only reply that the socialist tried to lead us to disaster by foolish words, and the communist wished to drive us there by violent deeds." See if you can identify the **AB:CD** pattern in this sentence.

In practically every political speech the principle of contrast appears as the driving force. If you listen carefully, you can often detect it throughout the entire speech, or at the level of individual paragraphs and sentences, and often in the specific contrasts that are developed between words and concepts. It is also the basis for a lot of humor. Former President Ronald Reagan used it when he said: "Politics is not a bad profession. If you succeed, there are many rewards. If you disgrace yourself, you can always write a book."

Repetition

The second principle of campaign speaking I would like to call your attention to is *repetition*. The recurring use of particular sounds, words, phrases, or even a whole sentence has become a staple of political rhetoric. The repetition of specific sounds, or *alliteration*, is widely used by public speakers who want to hold the attention of their listeners and create a vivid, memorable effect. No contemporary political communicator has carried the device of alliteration farther than Jesse Jackson. Notice how Jackson combines the principle of contrast with the repetition of the "s" sound in this passage:

> "Both tears and sweat are wet and salty, but they render a different result. Tears will get you sympathy, but sweat will get you change."

And think of how the repeated "p" sound must have sounded to Jackson's listeners at the end of the following idea in one of his speeches:

> "We need a value system that will allow us to fulfill our essential human and humane tasks. To be producers, to be providers, to be protectors."

Sometimes Reverend Jackson gets a little carried away with his alliteration, as in this passage:

> "We must contrast the politics of the five B's—blacks, browns, budgets, busing, and balance—with the five A's—attention, attendance, atmosphere, attitude, and achievement."

But when his repetitions work, they lend a striking quality to his speechmaking. In a distinctive way of expressing the importance of personal motivation in the lives of young people, Jackson combined the repetition of the initial consonant sound as well as the last syllable of a word to produce this gem: "Children must know that it is not their aptitude but their attitude that will determine their altitude."

Repetition in political rhetoric can be used to create effects similar to those in nursery school rhymes. Thus, Senator Edward Kennedy said of the Republicans: "They lavish tax breaks on the greedy and deny bread to the needy." And President Richard Nixon once proclaimed, "The wealthiest nation in the world should be the healthiest nation in the world." These devices, while catchy, do not approach in grandeur the style and sentiment expressed in Dr. Martin Luther King, Jr.'s speech to the crowd in front of the Lincoln Memorial in Washington, D.C. in 1963. In his address King used the recurring sentence, "I have a dream," to stir the imagination of both the assembled crowd and the millions who would hear or read this speech. King's dream of racial equality was expressed in one of the most common of rhetorical forms, but the tone established in his address has given this thought a revered place in the annals of American oratory.

As long as we are talking about repetition, I guess I should point out one feature of humor—political and otherwise—that you've probably already noticed: most jokes have three lines, with the third one being the punch line. This fact is sometimes called the *rule of three*. It can be traced back at least to Julius Caesar, who is supposed to have said: "I came. I saw. I conquered." As a vehicle of humor, the rule of three appeared in the joke that was popular a few years ago that went like this: "Do you know the three most frequently told lies? They are: 'The check is in the mail.' 'Sure, I'll still respect you in the morning.' And 'I'm from the federal government, and I'm here to help you.' " This reminds me of the wit of Senator Robert Dole, who once came into a room where three former presidents were standing together. The presidents were Gerald Ford, Jimmy Carter, and Richard Nixon. Dole took one look and said, "Hear no evil, speak no evil, and *evil*." Senator Dole's sharp tongue contrasts with the gentle humor of Ronald Reagan, who went around the country giving speeches during the Carter administration. Once Reagan said, "Well, Jimmy's in the White House, Amy's in the tree house, and Billy's in the dog house." Whether the device of repetition involves the recurring use of a sound, word, phrase, or sentence, or whether it simply establishes an expectancy in the audience that a third idea will be used to bring closure to the thought sequence, the result of its use is the enhancement of an idea. You will find that repetition is one of the most common techniques used by political campaigners to drive their points home.

Mood of Indignation

The third feature of political rhetoric I will discuss does not come from a manipulation of language but from a manipulation of our emotions. Have you ever noticed how political speakers try to get us really worked up? They seek to arouse our emotions and get us to bypass our rational thought processes. Cicero recognized the importance of the passions two thousand years ago when he wrote: "For men decide far more problems by hate, or love, or lust, or illusion, or some other emotion, than by reality, or authority, or any legal standard, or judicial precedent, or statute." This seems to be the guiding assumption behind much political discourse today.

In his keynote speech to the Republican National Convention in 1988 New Jersey Governor Thomas Kean sought to arouse indignation towards the Democratic presidential nominee, Michael Dukakis, and his advisers. Kean related the following account:

> "Last week, in a rare moment of candor, a prominent Dukakis Democrat explained their strategy to a reporter from *Congressional Quarterly Magazine*. What he said shocked me, and I have to share it with you. He said Democrats' advice to special interests was, and I quote, . . . 'Just Shut Up. Gays. Women. Environmentalists. Just shut up, and you will get everything you want after the election. In the meantime, just shut up so we can win.' Now I ask you, should this country tolerate such cynicism?"

Governor Kean is trying, of course, to arouse righteous indignation not only among Republican delegates at the convention, but also on the part of the millions of viewers at home. He is indulging in a familiar practice that is used by politicians in both of the major parties. He is arousing anger and resentment against the ideas and actions of the opposing candidate.

All three of these techniques have one thing in common. They attempt to get us to go along with our speaker's thinking without analyzing very carefully what is being said. Contrast causes us to polarize our thinking. We are led to see an issue as having only two sides, only one of which is the right one. Repetition causes us to accept an idea because it is drilled into our heads. And the mood of indignation leads us to react in a knee-jerk fashion that substitutes emotion for sound analysis and reasoning as we consider an idea. With a clear understanding of these rhetorical devices, we are now in a position to consider ways to improve our ability to listen critically to the political messages that bombard us during a campaign.

Two Principles of Critical Listening

Of all the principles of critical listening that could be mentioned, two stand out as crucial in the evaluation of political speeches. These principles relate to the prudent use of the excess attention we have as we listen to a speech, and to the emotional state in which we attend to a speaker's ideas.

Using Excess Attention Wisely

This first principle is sometimes known as "capitalizing on the thought-speech differential." It derives from the fact that we can all think much faster than any speaker can talk, and that we need to put this extra thinking capacity to work. Instead of using it to let our minds wander over peripheral or unrelated matters, we can use this mental energy to examine the premises and conclusions of the speaker's arguments. Suppose we encounter instances of reasoning such as these:

All Democrats raise taxes.

Al Gore is a Democrat.

Therefore, Al Gore will raise taxes.

Republicans favor tax breaks for the rich.

George W. Bush is a Republican.

Therefore, he will give tax breaks to the rich.

In these cases your excess attention can be put to good use. You can evaluate the major premises and ask, "Do all Democrats raise taxes?" and "Do all Republicans favor tax breaks for the rich?" You might remember, for example, that John F. Kennedy, a Democrat, lowered taxes, a fact that Republicans often point to in order to show that the economy got a boost when this was done. And your critical evaluation of the second argument might cause you to try to think of proposals George Bush might have made to "give tax breaks to the rich." Is he actually on record as favoring such a policy?

When a speaker uses inductive reasoning, ask yourself whether the examples cited are sufficient to lead to the conclusion that is advanced. Here is a fairly typical specimen of the kind of inductive logic found in political speeches. This passage is from a speech Alexander Haig, a former U.S. Secretary of State, gave at the 1988 Republican National Convention in New Orleans. Haig contrasts the dismal state of foreign affairs under the Democratic administration of eight years earlier with the more hopeful situation of 1988:

"When I last spoke to a Republican convention in 1980, we saw a nation thrown off balance by blunder and gloom. The Soviets were on the march everywhere. Afghanistan had been sieged. Soviet surrogates were triumphant in Campachia, Southern Africa, and Central America. A cruel war raged in the Persian Gulf. Our allies were disheartened and freedom was in retreat. And all the Democrats could offer was indecision and malaise. Today, eight years later, the policy of peace through strength has begun to pay off. The Russians are leaving Afghanistan. Their surrogates in Africa and Asia are in trouble. The Soviets are negotiating our arms control agenda of reduction and cuts, not their agenda designed to increase Soviet superiority. Democracy, not Communism, is on the march. George Bush helped to make this happen, and he is, indeed, the safe candidate for America."

Capitalizing on the thought-speech differential, you could examine the examples set forth by Haig, asking whether the instances are sufficiently numerous, representative, and accurate to lead to the conclusion he wants us to reach.

Evaluating analogies uses our critical thinking capacity in other ways. For example, George Bush likened the American economy of 1980 to a "sick patient" in his acceptance speech in 1988. He said:

"My friends, eight years ago this economy was flat on its back in intensive care. We came in and gave it emergency treatment. Got the temperature down by lowering regulation. Got the blood pressure down when we lowered taxes. Pretty soon the patient was up back on his feet, stronger than ever. And now who do we hear knocking on the door, but the doctors who made him sick. And they're telling us to put them in charge of the case again. My friends, they're lucky we don't hit them with a malpractice suit."

Is this a good analogy? Are there similarities between a sick patient and an economy? Certainly there are more differences than similarities. As critical listeners, we can understand the point Bush is trying to make and even be amused by it while still recognizing that this "argument" offers little substantive evidence but plays upon a few superficial resemblances between two very different conditions of life.

Switching Off Emotional Attitudes

Another thing I suggest that you learn to do while you are listening to political rhetoric is to switch off your emotional attitudes that get in the way of clear, analytical thought. This habit, of course, is especially needed when the speaker is indulging in the mood of indignation discussed earlier. But each of the principles of rhetoric we examined has as its purpose the creation of an emotional link between the audience and the speaker's thesis. Especially when you are very partisan and are inclined to favor the speaker, it is all the more imperative that you retain a critical detachment. You need to resist the tendency to suspend your judgment and get swept along with the emotional currents that are being generated by the speaker.

One of the primary means political speakers use to generate an emotional response is to use a *slogan*. A slogan is always used to take the place of rational thought. Many kinds of slogans have been used in American elections. Some were promissory; they held out a promise of the good things that would follow the election of a certain candidate: "Forty Acres and a Mule," "The Full Dinner Pail," Huey Long's battle cry, "Every Man a King," and Dwight Eisenhower's promise in 1952, "I Shall Go to Korea." Sometimes slogans have used the device of alliteration, which we identified earlier: "Peace and Prosperity," "Ban the Bomb," "Beat the Bosses," "Love That Lyndon," "Tippecanoe and Tyler Too," and "Win with Willkie." Other slogans have issued warnings to the American voters: "Don't Let Them Take It Away," "Coolidge or Chaos," "Save the American Way of Life," and "No Third Term." Sometimes slogans even pretend to be rational, appealing to your reason: "Let's Look at the Record," "Let's Talk Sense to the American People," and "Experience Counts." But all of these slogans attempt, in one sense or another, to elicit a visceral, nonrational reaction from the audience. Occasionally, the response is contrary to the desired result. Thus, when a billboard appeared in Champaign, Illinois, favoring Barry Goldwater for President in 1964 with the slogan, "In Your Heart You Know He's Right," some wag added below, "But In Your Guts, You Know He's Nuts!" Although the response was not the one desired, it was just as emotional as the one sought by the creator of the Goldwater campaign slogan. A knee-jerk response to a slogan, whether negative or positive, is difficult to avoid in the heat of a fiery political battle, but if we are to be intelligent respondents to such speeches and advertisements, we must maintain a critical detachment that will allow us to evaluate them without the distortion that comes from the intervention of strong personal motives and feelings. In order to preserve this detachment, we must switch off our emotional attitudes toward the speaker and his or her party and the message.

Conclusion

In closing, I would say that the difference in sense and nonsense is probably not any greater in political rhetoric than in other kinds of persuasion. The same kinds of communication techniques—contrast, repetition, and the use of the mood of indignation or another strong emotion—all show up in sales presentations, advertising campaigns, sermons, pep talks to athletic teams, and so forth. But the consequences may be greater—the stakes higher—in political campaign communications than in these other contexts where we are asked to form views or make decisions. If we get a lemon for a new car or a faulty freezer or television set, the results are annoying, but if we are persuaded to elect a governor, a senator, or a president, the consequences are enormously more consequential—and more difficult to remedy. As Will Rogers used to say, "When Congress makes a joke, it becomes a law." So we need to pay close and critical attention to the speeches we hear from those to whom we are asked to entrust our public offices.

I have suggested that we use our excess attention wisely to evaluate the appeals we hear from politicians, and that we need to suspend our strong emotional feelings in order to preserve a detached and critical frame of mind. From such a perspective, we will be in a better position to scrutinize both the political messages we hear and the rhetorical means used to convey them. Of course, you should apply these same principles of critical listening to what I have said in this talk. I hope you will not be like the Siamese twin I heard about who was a poor listener—everything he heard went in one ear and out his brother's. I hope that's not true this day, but that you will be able to apply some of these principles as you try to become a more analytical and critical listener.

Summary

Many of life's decisions are made on the basis of the ability to listen critically. As effective listeners, we must be alert to the critical listening role and apply the appropriate decision-making skills. The quality of our decisions, and our lives, depends on the ability to listen critically.

Listening critically requires that we make decisions based on speaker credibility, logical structure, reasoning, and valid data. Speaker credibility consists of competence, character, intentions, personality, and dynamism. Logical structure includes examination of data, warrant, claim, backing, qualifier, and rebuttal. Fallacies of reasoning are ignoring the burden of proof, *argumentum ad hominem*, straw man, red herring, emotional appeal, hasty generalization, stereotyping, disjunctive reasoning, oversimplified cause, and unexamined analogy. Finally, listening to data in the form of examples and illustrations, testimony, definition, statistics, and visual aids is discussed as an important aspect of critical listening.

Effective critical listening can improve quality in our daily living by promoting responsible decisions regarding relationships, productivity, purchases, and use of time. Chapter 12 discusses critical listening as it applies to spending money.

Notes

1. James C. McCroskey, "Scales for the Measurement of Ethos," *Communication Monographs*, Vol. 33 (1966), pp. 65–73.

2. *Ibid.*

3. http://www.gallup.com/poll/1654/honesty-ethics-professions.aspx

4. Stephen Toulmin, Richard Rieke, and Allan Janik, *An Introduction to Reasoning* (New York: Macmillan, 1979).

5. James M. McCrimmon, *Writing with a Purpose* (Boston: Houghton Mifflin Company, 1980), pp. 236–242.

6. James Randi, *Flim-Flam! Psychics, ESP, Unicorns, and Other Delusions* (Buffalo, N.Y.: Prometheus Books, 1982), pp. 94–97.

7. Bill Moyers, *A World of Ideas: Conversations with Thoughtful Men and Women about American Life Today and the Ideas Shaping Our Future*, Betty Sue Flowers, ed. (New York: Doubleday, 1989), p. 292.

Chapter Eleven
Awareness Exercises

Name_____ ID#_____

1. Describe a recent situation when you made a decision after listening to someone.

    A. The setting

    B. The decision you made

2. Describe a person whom you trust to help you make decisions. What characteristics does this person have?

3. Build an argument using data, warrant, and claim.

    A. Data

    B. Warrant

    C. Claim

4. Write an example that shows the shifting of the burden of proof.

5. Write an example that shows the straw man fallacy.

6.   Write an example that shows the red herring fallacy.

7.   Write an example that shows stereotyping.

8.   Write an example that shows *argumentum ad hominem.*

9.   Write an example that shows hasty generalization.

10.   Write an example that shows begging the question.

11.   Write an example that shows oversimplified cause.

12.   Write an example that shows disjunctive reasoning.

13.   Describe a single interaction when your listening role changed from comprehensive, or therapeutic, to critical.

14.   Describe a time when you listened and made a poor decision.

15.   Describe a persuasive presentation where data were used effectively.

16.   Describe a time when you listened and made a good decision.

17. Build an argument using data, warrant, claim, backing, qualifier, rebuttal.

A. Data

B. Warrant

C. Claim

D. Backing

E. Qualifier

F. Rebuttal

Chapter Eleven
Awareness Database

Name_____ ID#_____

1. I am aware when I am in the critical listening role.

   A.   B.   C.   D.   E.
   seldom   often

2. I have made decisions without being aware that I was making decisions.

   A.   B.   C.   D.   E.
   seldom   often

3. How many decisions in a day—from radio, TV, friends, salespeople, relatives, girlfriends, boyfriends—do you make as a result of listening?

   A.   B.   C.   D.   E.
   0–2   3–5   6–10   11–14   15 or more

4. I am an effective critical listener.

   A.   B.   C.   D.   E.
   seldom   often

5. When in a persuasive setting, I pay attention to the credibility of the sender.

   A.   B.   C.   D.   E.
   seldom   often

6. I make compulsive decisions (that is, decisions with little thought).

   A.   B.   C.   D.   E.
   seldom   often

7. I find it easy to "go along with the crowd."

   A.   B.   C.   D.   E.
   seldom   often

8. I wait a day or more before making an important decision.

   A.   B.   C.   D.   E.
   seldom   often

9. I am impressed by visual aids.

   A.   B.   C.   D.   E.
   seldom   often

10. I make wise purchases.

   A.   B.   C.   D.   E.
   seldom   often

Chapter Twelve

Listening as a Consumer

This book is about the principles and practices of face-to-face listening, and except for cell phone use, the discussion hasn't wandered into the digital world of websites, email, twitter, and other mediated tools. However, with so much electronic marketing available, we can easily apply the consumer listening ideas there, as well.

What's happening is this: creative electronic approaches to marketing are taking on the flavor of responsive face-to-face communication. These programs mimic warm-blooded human interactions so well that the listening principles that work in face-to-face settings apply equally in these virtual settings. So, we'll discuss consumer listening as though it's all face-to-face, and make reasonable adaptations to cyber world marketing as well.

Applying critical listening skills to purchasing has never been more important because the twenty-first century is experiencing an explosion in advertising and marketing strategies. In this Information Age, consumers are finding themselves drowning not only in the number of products on the market, but also in the expanded opportunities to buy products, with eBay and Amazon just two of thousands of Internet possibilities. Using new technology, companies and organizations have expanded capabilities and are working on innovative approaches for getting their products and services to buyers. One business expert in a speech titled "How to Become an Effective Listener" remarked:

> Living in the "Information Age," we are bombarded with a blizzard of data bits every day. Because we feel overwhelmed, we start to block out whatever we believe is less than immediately useful. But you will never be able to sift the wheat from the chaff unless you truly listen to what is being said."[1]

This chapter looks at critical decisions when spending money on products or services. To raise awareness of the key elements in making responsible purchases, we will discuss the consumer listening role, listening to our motivations to purchase, listening to selling techniques, and using consumer research to gain information to sharpen our consumer listening.

The Consumer Listening Role

We are in the consumer listening role when we are deciding *if, when, how,* and *where* we are going to purchase a product or service.[2] Television, radio, telephone, newspapers, Internet search engines, mobile devices, and salespeople, are all positioned to persuade us to make a decision to buy. The pressure is on, and we must listen carefully to ourselves and others to make sensible decisions on how and where to spend our money.

Advertisers and market researchers want to know what buyers value, desire, and need. In addition, businesses want to know how much consumers will spend to fulfill these desires and needs, as well as what type of advertising promotes their products. With sophisticated data gathering, consumer and marketing research is becoming finely targeted and detailed.

Messages to purchase come from a variety of different sources. In the last decade there was a shift from TV advertising to direct appeals in the marketplace. This eliminated the usual travel time used to reflect about making a purchase. In addition to friendly folks offering samples of various foods at Sam's Club and other outlets, there are

> . . . product pitches on your shopping cart, electronic ads above the aisles, and coupon dispensers attached to the shelves. In-store radio and television deliver hit songs and news along with cues to pick up Pampers or Pepto-Bismol in aisle two. The leading hawker of the hype, Act Media, sells ad space in 26,000 stores to such companies as Kellogg and P&G much as TV networks sell commercial time. Says Chief Executive Wayne LoCurto: "Does it make any sense to spend millions of dollars talking to people in their living rooms and cars and then let them wander around a supermarket with 30,000 product choices without something to remind them to buy your product?"
>
> Campbell Soup, which has used all of Act Media's programs, report sales increases of 7% to 10% from various in-store promotions. Says Herb Baum: "We believe there's no better time to reach consumers than when they're in the store with a fistful of dollars."[3]

The use of the Internet as a marketplace also eliminates time for consideration before purchasing an item or service. Through e-commerce, consumers merely "click" a button to order. According to the *U.S. Census Bureau News,* retail e-commerce sales for the third quarter of 2014 totaled $71.9 billion—we're doing a lot of electronic button clicking buying.[4] In addition to e-commerce growth, consumers in the twenty-first century are also seeing a growth in Internet marketing as an innovative approach to influence buyers' decisions. One may wonder, "How can words and images on a screen influence purchasing habits?" The answer upon which many businesses are basing their strategies is to continue to give the customer electronically personalized attention.

> The Internet is a virtual nirvana for one-to-one marketing and is becoming a key component to many organizations' communications strategy. Technology is enabling marketers to deliver specific information, products and services based on a single individual's needs. This is often accomplished by learning more about a site visitor as they travel through a site and then using a dynamic page environment to customize a home page, or show different banner ads, for example. Possibly the most intriguing opportunity in this environment is to track and archive information and tie it to a name and e-mail address.[5]

Wal-Mart, Amazon, eBay, and thousands more have added one-to-one Internet marketing to increase their sales. These websites create a feeling of personal interaction online. They remember past visitors and "greet you at the door" by name and customize to your personal needs.[6] In addition, auction sites create an interactively exciting and potentially addictive competitive atmosphere where the bidder can *win* a prized item. Let the bidding begin!

The continuous expansion of marketing techniques and purchasing locations means the consumer-listener must be focused and prepared before making a purchase. This preparation should include listening to our motivations for shopping and researching the products or services to be purchased.

Listening to Our Motivations to Shop

As we discussed in Chapters 6, 7, and 8, how we communicate intrapersonally impacts the effectiveness of all other communication. It follows, then, that consumer decisions to spend money rely on internal motivations. These internal messages must be carefully monitored before a purchase is made to determine our reasons for shopping, which range from necessity, to enjoyment, to addictive-like compulsion.

About 24 million Americans are classified as "hard-core shoppers."[7] These *shopaholics* shop for shopping's sake rather than to fill real needs. Browsing the aisles somehow makes them feel good. Bumper stickers proclaim: "When the going gets tough, the tough go shopping."[8]

For some, the motivation to shop is biochemical—purchasing actually gives the shopper a chemical high:

> . . . shopping can be traced to the brain chemical dopamine. Dopamine plays a crucial role in our mental and physical health. The brains of people with Parkinson's disease, for instance, contain almost no dopamine. Dopamine also plays a role in drug use and other addictive behaviors. Dopamine is associated with feelings of pleasure and satisfaction, and it's released when we experience something new, exciting or challenging. And for many people, shopping is all those things.
>
> Knowing that shopping triggers real changes in our brain can help you make better shopping decisions and not overspend while in a dopamine-induced high. For instance, walking away from a purchase you want and returning the next day will eliminate the novelty of the situation and help you make a more clear-headed decision.[9]

Another reason for the increase in unwise spending is convenience. A little over a generation ago, Christmas shopping was hard work. Shoppers had to bundle up, hassle with ice and snow, and trudge from store to store, perhaps in different parts of town. Today, bright, warm, well-lighted malls entice the shopper into rows of stores easily accessed with only one park of the car. The shopper can spend an entire day under the roof of one mall and not visit all of the stores. The Internet has also brought an additional ease to shopping. One doesn't even have to leave home to buy clothes, stereo equipment, cars, and other favorite items. With this technology, shoppers merely have to point and click. Add to this ease of access the option of high ceiling credit cards, and all the ingredients for unwise, addictive spending come together.

As technology continues to fine-tune consumer adaptation and intensifies marketing pressure, the need to listen to our motivations before we shop becomes more and more crucial. For example, we need to ask ourselves: Why are we shopping? What personal needs are being met? Is my shopping compulsive? Do I shop to escape boredom? Is this trip to the mall or the Internet really necessary? Is the act of spending exciting? Answers to these questions will offer insights into our reasons for shopping, which might range from a real need to an addictive satisfaction.

> The word "addiction" is not used lightly here. There are even support groups, such as Shoppers Stoppers, in Dayton, Ohio, that help people who are trying to stop their compulsion to spend beyond their means for things they don't need. "Shopping is an addiction comparable to drug abuse," says a consulting therapist at Miami Valley Hospital. "It is done without regard to the consequences."[10]

To spend responsibly, we first need to listen to our motivations. We listen to ourselves to find out if our spending is thoughtful or compulsive. Are we spending responsibly or for other reasons: feelings of powerlessness, worthlessness, boredom, loneliness, or a need for attention. The following two examples show how a man made foolish purchases because of boredom and how a woman spent irresponsibly because of resentment.

The man:

> I was alone and bored last Saturday. My girlfriend was out of town at a wedding, and my best friend was on a fishing trip. I was tired of reading, there was no new email, and the TV had nothing to offer. I didn't feel like doing anything at home, so I hopped in the car and wandered to the mall. I hit Best Buy and ended up getting a real "deal" on a 65-inch Smart TV which I didn't need (I already have a good TV and DVD player) and couldn't afford (I put the $2800 purchase on my already stressed credit card). On top of that, I ended up in the sports store and bought a pair of air basketball shoes for $290, which I didn't need!

The woman:

> I was furious with him for leaving me for two days to go fishing. He can afford to do that, but he's so stingy when I want to go shopping. So I went shopping in a major way and bought all those goodies that I never buy myself—and I put them all on *his* credit cards. Shoes, dresses, slacks, make-up, and purse. Even a nice camera to capture those precious moments! I buy him things with my money, so I decided it's all right for me to help myself to his money. The whole shopping spree made me feel a lot better.

Consumers need to face their motivations to determine their reasons for spending. Frequently, obsessive shoppers are venting their discomfort or anger at a friend or spouse. "They tear into the racks instead of their family." Noel, a thirty-three-year-old housewife in the process of a divorce, tells her story about shopping as an escape from her relational problems: "As my frustration increased with my marriage, so did my spending," which added up to $50,000. Shopping sprees can be used to cope with anger, loneliness, boredom, or depression.[11]

After listening to themselves, some shoppers might discover that they crave attention—even a salesperson will do. Listening to the friendly and helpful words of a caring salesperson can be attractive and fill the need to be listened to by someone who is interested. The salespeople say, "May I help you?" They "ooh" and "ah" and fuss. You become the star in your own production.

In addition to craving attention, motivation to shop can come from low self-esteem. According to psychiatrist Carole Lieberman, "People shop to make up for what they don't have on the inside. They're trying to fill up because they feel empty."

Personal motivations for shopping vary from individual to individual; however, additional personal insight can be gained by understanding that women and men are different in their approaches to shopping. Research suggests that compulsive shopping is more common among women than men. Women spend on clothing and accessories to enhance appearance. Men spend on electronics, tools, and mechanical devices, and they also earn a sense of power by picking up the tab for the meal. "They try to boost their self-esteem by buying an image of power."[12]

Listening to ourselves can give us crucial insight into why and how we spend money. The urge to buy can come like hunger and demand satisfaction. "Once I can see it in my mind, it won't go away until I buy it," reported a woman who had seen some jewelry in a store. Some people listen to themselves and realize that shopping is "exciting," "thrilling," and "wild." One person said it was like "falling in love with a product."[13]

Most shoppers probably do not fall in love with products, but if we listen carefully to ourselves, we may find some purchasing is illogical and compulsive. Figure 12.1 offers ten questions as a guide to help structure intrapersonal consumer listening.

Once we have listened intrapersonally and analyzed our motives for shopping, we can turn our attention to the messages that are designed to persuade us to purchase products or services. As already mentioned, detailed, painstaking market research equips sellers to plan and carefully adapt these persuasive messages specifically to our age, income, education, profession, interests, past purchases, income, marital status, sex, hobbies, location, and more, so we must listen with sharp, critical intensity to assure that we are making our purchases responsibly.

Listening to Selling Techniques

To be responsible consumer listeners, we should be aware of nine techniques that are often used to persuade us to spend our money. Remarkably, most advertising fits into one or more of these categories. (The discussion of the Fallacies of Reasoning and Criteria for Examining Data found in Chapter 11 ties in closely with these techniques.)

Here are the nine selling techniques: (1) promoting a sense of belonging as described in the *band wagon* technique, (2) keeping it simple and straightforward as life was in *the good ole days,*

••• Figure 12.1 Consumer Listening Questionnaire

Directions: Circle the appropriate number after each question, and add up your score at the end. Do you:

		Never	*Sometimes*	*Always*
1.	Shop to excess?	0	1	2
2.	Shop when you don't need to?	0	1	2
3.	Buy items you don't need or won't use?	0	1	2
4.	Feel guilty about your shopping?	0	1	2
5.	Shop when you're angry, depressed, or lonely?	0	1	2
6.	Get limited or no pleasure from shopping?	0	1	2
7.	Have debts that make home life unhappy?	0	1	2
8.	Hide your shopping from friends or family?	0	1	2
9.	Go to work late or leave work early to shop?	0	1	2
10.	Have a problem with alcohol or drugs when you can't shop?	0	1	2

If you scored between 0 and 4 points, you probably have your shopping under control, although you may be trying to reach for a fast remedy sometimes.

If you scored between 5 and 10 points, you should take a close look at your shopping habits. You are probably headed for two kinds of trouble. First, you are probably not taking the time you need to take care of the underlying problem behind your shopping. Second, you are creating a new problem by compulsively shopping.

If you scored over 10 points, you do have a serious shopping disorder that will not get better on its own. It is time to take care of yourself as you would your best friend, your sister, or your daughter.[14]

(3) appealing to the hard-working middle class who are just *plain folks*, (4) referring to the recommendations of so-called experts—*testimonials*, (5) *emotional appeal*, (6) expecting the credibility of one symbol, product, service, or person to *transfer* to another, (7) making the product or service even better—*new and improved*, (8) selecting only information that shows the positive side—*card stacking*, and (9) showing that the product or service is unbelievable—*that's incredible.*[15] These techniques are attractive reasons for spending our money, and if we can see the message for what it is—a manipulation—we can make a decision based on our real need for the product or service.

Band Wagon

This selling technique encourages someone to buy a product, service, or idea because everyone else is buying it—hop on the wagon and come with us. It plays on the idea that we all want to "fit in" with the group. For example, recently, this author found himself in Chicago's O'Hare airport with a two-hour layover. The unstructured time offered a chance to observe people finding their way to various destinations. Remarkably, many of these business travelers were dressed in similar attire—men in tan slacks with blue blazers; women in blue suits with white blouses. Haircuts and hair styles were also similar for men and women. These similar appearances were the result of subtle pressure to fit in with everyone else in the "traveling businessperson" category.

Younger people are particularly vulnerable to these pressures. Children want the current videogame or jeans like their friends have. College students have a particular style of backpack, sunglasses, or hat that fit the college scene.

Adapting to a particular culture can be wise as long as we are aware of what we are doing. As listening consumers, we need to question our motives for buying a product or idea. We ask ourselves, "Is this clothing or behavior necessary for me to fit into the setting I have agreed to be in?" "Am I comfortable with the expectations of the group I am identifying with?" The intent of these questions is: "How many of my personal values am I willing to give up to fit in with this group's expectations?" If buying into the clothing, hairstyle, tattoos, and behaviors of a group allows one to keep a clear sense of who s/he is, then being persuaded to conform could be a sensible choice.

Good Ole Days

This selling strategy promotes a product or service that claims to bring the consumer back to the simpler times of the past—those good old days that we remember with fondness. The messages tell us if we buy the product, we will be getting back to the basics—those good old days when grandma baked at home. There are many examples of this selling technique, even on the plastic wrapping of *Farmhouse 12* grain bread, which reads, "The master bakers at Pepperidge Farm have been making delicious breads for over 60 years . . . breads baked the old fashioned way bursting with flavorful ingredients . . . are the embodiment of this tradition."

Certainly, technology has brought advancements and comforts that were unheard of just a few years ago. Nevertheless, an attraction for a basic, simpler, nontechnical lifestyle is built into a number of consumer messages. The strong interest in antiques—be it furniture, cars, airplanes, boats, machines, or vintage clothing—provides a viable consumer market, and what these advertisements are saying is, "Not even technology can make this better." In some cases, this is a valid point. For example, the trend away from man-made fabrics back to cotton and other natural fabrics verifies that some time-proven products are superior. Finding a carpenter who is a craftsman in the "old style" is viewed as worth more, because the final product is beautiful, solid, and functional. However, not all products and services from the past are superior, and the consumer should weigh a decision to buy after comparing the past with state-of-art qualities.

Plain Folks

This selling technique appeals to the hard-working, grass roots, no-nonsense person. For example, plain folks promotions that tell us that their product has "No fads or fancy stuff," or "This meets your needs head-on," or "The truck is built tough for the hard-working man," are identifying with the common person. The North American culture values practical, functional, and basic goods and services. We see these values in Western movies and the image of the cowboy on his horse framed by a mountain scene. We see the typical mother with three kids climbing into a van with functional options that assure the safety of her family along with having enough room for groceries and the family dog.

Plain folks messages often compare simple, down-to-earth behavior with frivolous, elitist behavior: the everyday Jane *versus* snobby Susan. For example, these ads might say: "Who needs to go first class? I can get there in business class just as well." Through these messages, the listening consumer could be convinced that s/he is making a purchasing decision based on culturally approved, practical needs.

The other side of the plain folks message appeals to the fun and nonpractical. These messages say the consumer is not plain or ordinary. For example, advertisements tempt the listener to "spoil herself." They say to the executive, "You deserve the best at the end of a trying day." "First class travel belongs to first class people." In essence, the messages are saying, "You are not a plain person; you are special. Reward yourself." A purchase based on this message would be motivated by the belief that, in this instance, I am special; I am going to dispense with practicality and spend the money just for fun.

Testimonials

This persuasive technique relies on a credible source to endorse a product or service. The testimonial, usually in the form of "I choose this service over all others, because . . . ," may come from a well-known celebrity, a professional, an athlete, an expert, or a salesperson. When listening to a testimonial, the buyer should ask: "Is the testimonial complete and fair? Is it from someone with first-hand knowledge of the product? What does the source of the testimony have to gain from the product endorsement?"

Emotions

Emotions appeal to our feelings—love, hate, power, freedom, fun, and like all appeals, they can be worthwhile. Certainly, the feelings of love and caring used in promoting the use of seat belts or abstaining from drinking alcohol and driving are noble. However, we need to be aware of the nature of the appeal: it is, after all, an attempt to bypass logic and tap into our feelings. Services that are sold emotionally might be insurance—"The greater the love for your family, the more life insurance you will buy." Examples of products sold emotionally are greeting cards: "For those who care enough to send the very best," and caskets: "The casket you buy is a measure of your caring and love"or the vehicle you purchase might be a Jeep where "There will be a seat left open, a light left on, a favorite dinner waiting, a warm bed made . . . because in your home, in our hearts, you've been missed. You've been needed, you've been cried for, prayed for. You are the reason we push on."[16] In each case, we must determine if the emotions are, in reality, a valid reason to buy the product or service.

Transfer

This selling technique attempts to increase the desirability of a product or service by associating it with a well-known and well-accepted symbol or phrase. The seller's hope is that the listener will transfer the high regard for the symbol to the product being sold.

Many logos for products and retail outlets are positive symbols that are intended to transfer a sense of sophistication, integrity, quality, or economy to the consumer. For example, the Target logo of three red and white concentric circles carries the association, "Right on target" with purchases here. The phrase, "Proudly made in the USA" implies quality and a sense of pride in the product.

During election years, consumer listening is directed toward "buying into" one political candidate or another, and one of the most impressive uses of transfer occurred in a political campaign of the 1950s. During this campaign, Senator Richard Nixon appeared on television to defend his use of campaign contributions that were put into a questionable fund. Mr. Nixon, who was being considered for a vice-presidential candidacy, defended these contributions and convinced the American public that he should be the vice president.

Unquestionably, his success in selling the television viewers was greatly helped by the use of symbols. He sat at a massive wooden desk, symbol of solidarity and high position; his wife, Pat, was at his left, and periodically, the camera would pan over to her—Mr. Nixon's symbol of faithfulness, loyalty, and family. The most impressive symbol in this television speech was a cocker spaniel puppy named Checkers. In this speech—which has since been titled the "Checkers Speech"—Nixon acknowledges that his family did indeed receive the puppy as a political gift, but, even if it destroyed his political future, he was not going to return it. Checkers became Nixon's strongest symbol: a symbol that transferred to him as being kind, caring, loyal, respectful of life and nature, highly principled, and willing to sacrifice his career for something, a cute puppy, that he and his family loved.

The television viewers listened and bought the message that Nixon was acting honestly and in the best interests of the country. He went on to become vice president, even though his political career didn't reflect the virtue of honesty which checkers symbolized.

New and Improved
....

This technique tells the potential buyer that the product or service being sold is state of the art. It is the outgrowth of the latest technology. Again, the listening consumer should be alert to this technique and ask: "Should I wait until the new models come out or risk purchasing an obsolete model?"

The discussion about the good ole days emphasized the idea that the newest is not always the best. We now need to determine if the *change* in a product or service is, in fact, an *improvement*. Is it a change for the better?

Some of the fastest-changing products that claim new and improved are computers, TVs, and cell phones. It seems that every month new and significant changes are brought to the public's awareness. When considering the purchase of one of these new and improved devices, the critical listener needs to weigh the value of the faster speeds, increased memory, and added features. Do you *need* these innovations, or will the current set-up serve your purposes just as well?

Card Stacking
....

This technique misleads the listener. It presents half-truths or does not provide pertinent information. The term *card stacking* means putting the playing cards in winning order for the dealer. Card stacking might use expert testimony, but only that part of the testimony that is favorable toward the item being sold. For example, a dentist is quoted as saying, ". . . the majority of dentists surveyed preferred brand Y toothpaste. . . ." From this expert testimony, the listener believes brand Y is the best; however, the testimony *not* quoted in the advertisement goes on to say, ". . . in terms of price and accessibility." "But," the dentist continues, "if decay prevention and tooth appearance are the concern—which I believe they should be—then brand X is highest on my recommended list." The advertisers have stacked the cards in their favor by omitting the last portion of the dentist's message, which substantially changes the intended meaning. This technique is frequently used in ads for movies and concert programs.

That's Incredible
....

This technique focuses on the language of selling. Catchy phrases and powerful adjectives and modifiers infer that the products or services are something more than they actually are. For example, the automobile that has "the awesome power of the turbo V-6" offers a message of strength, but the specific details of the power and performance are missing, left to be inferred by the listener. Listener inference is part of the incredible message: "The store designed for those who strive to be on the cutting edge." Here, the listener might infer that an incredible experience awaits the customer at this store.

Another example of *that's incredible* involves pain capsules. If all nonprescription pain capsules take about the same amount of time to give relief, one manufacturer may claim "that no pain capsule gives relief faster than brand X." The actual meaning of the claim is true, but the wording of the claim makes it possible for the consumer to infer that brand X works faster than the other brands.[17] This selling technique uses language that puts the product or service far beyond the ordinary and gives the impression of implied superiority. Here are some other examples of that's incredible:

Outdoor parka: "Nothing can compete with our Pac-Lite."

"Finally, a weight loss enhancer that really works!"

"Looks just like a genuine Yellow Diamond featuring 31 brilliant cubic zirconia stones; this sophisticated ring looks like it cost a small fortune."

"One little capsule a day can ease dozens of your worst health worries:
High Cholesterol/Constant Fatigue/Heart Trouble/Colds and Flu/Memory Loss
Poor Circulation/Aging Skin/High Blood Pressure."

These incredible messages may seem innocent enough, but without some alert consumer listening, the buyer may infer beyond the content of the message and make an unwise purchase.[18]

Effective consumer listening is the result of three stages of preparation. We have explored two of these: first, listening intrapersonally for reasons for buying, and second, understanding the techniques used to market products and services. The third step involves researching the product.

Consumer Research

We turn to professional experts for information and advice, because they are knowledgeable in a particular field. The physician listens for information about symptoms and makes an educated decision to treat the problem; the attorney listens to a description of a situation and decides on a legal approach to the problem; the auto mechanic listens to the details and proceeds with diagnostic efforts. In each case, *before* a sensible decision can be made, these people use listening skills to find specific information about the topic.

As listening consumers, we might not become experts (such as physicians, attorneys, or mechanics) on the products or services we buy, but gaining knowledge about a potential purchase will help significantly in the final decision. With the knowledge gained from research, the consumer can listen critically to facts and ignore the irrelevant information. Depending on the complexity and cost of the purchase, this research can be finished quickly by surveying several models of a product, or it can be a fairly detailed and lengthy effort that might require outside professional consultation.

There are a number of readily available sources for acquiring consumer information: hard copy and online journals such as *Consumers' Research* and *Consumers' Digest*, Internet reviews of products and services, as well as personal reviews, blogs, and discussions. These sources explore the pros and cons of almost every product and service. Importantly, they also show the consumer an organized approach for researching a potential purchase. This organized approach involves carefully examining the range of variables that could encourage or discourage the purchase.

Under the heading *products*, we will research a relatively low-cost item—mouthwash (just as an example that anything can be researched); then, one of the highest-cost items—a car. Under *service*, we will research auto body repair.

Mouthwash.[19]   Annual sales of mouthwashes are about $629 million, and one alone grossed $321 million.[20] The two top selling mouthwashes are Warner-Lambert's "Listerine" and Procter & Gamble's "Scope." Basically, these products are diluted water-alcohol solutions of chemicals, and on the store shelves are a number of less expensive—half the price—mouthwash products whose compositions duplicate those of the leading brands.

The question is, "Which one should I purchase?"

Several studies have determined that the private-label mouthwashes are as effective as their brand-name competitors. The most effective brand in plaque-reduction is Listerine, which reduced plaque an average of 25 percent and gingivitis 29 percent. Scope and Cepacol showed a 14 percent reduction in plaque and a 24 percent reduction of gingivitis. Based on these studies, the private-label imitations of Listerine, Scope, and Cepacol should be equally effective in reducing plaque and gingivitis in each of their respective categories.

With this information, the consumer is prepared to listen critically to sale messages about mouthwashes, having researched the product in credible sources. As with any purchase, the final choice will be the result of the consumer's internal motivation, the sales techniques targeting the product, and the researched information. Next, we consider a research model for a large purchase—an automobile.

An Automobile.[21]   This research assumes that you as the buyer know in general what you want and are now in the process of getting information on the more subtle details that influence the buying decision.

First, you as a consumer should read car enthusiast and road test reports to decide on the general model type, equipment, fuel efficiency, and price range you want. Next, start visiting dealers for test drives; perhaps rent a car you are considering. Once you start looking at specific cars, you begin a practical evaluation.

Start your evaluation when the car is parked and locked. Does it have keyless entry? If keyed entry, does it take one key for the door and one for the ignition? Are the door, trunk, and hatch smooth to open, or are they heavy and awkward? Do they close quietly and tightly?

Once inside, are you really comfortable? Does the seat adjust well? Is the steering wheel lined up with your position in the seat? Does the seat adjust comfortably? Will you be comfortable for a long drive? Is the rear seat accessible in a two-door model? Try placing packages or a child's seat in the back seat of a two-door model. In a sleek hatch-back model, is the hatch heavy and awkward? Is it large enough to handle packages and luggage that would fit in a trunk?

In the driver's position, are the mirrors functional? Are the sideview mirrors easily adjusted? Do they give a full and complete picture?

Next check the safety equipment. Adjust the seat and put the belt system in place over your body. Adjust the belt and take up slack. Notice if the belts "load" properly; the shoulder belt should rest halfway between the shoulder-arm joint, not too close to your neck. Determine if the belts are easy to unlatch and stow each time you remove them. Check the belt system in the rear seats. Are they easily used? Is there provision for securing a child seat? Retracted seat belt systems are often an obstacle, and sometimes the use of the rear seat area is too difficult for elderly passengers. The number of passengers that a vehicle can carry is found by the designated seating position (DSP) represented by each set of seat belts. If buying a van or recreational vehicle, notice if the number of DSPs is sufficient for your use. Are theft and security systems operating? The safety system is like insurance. Be sure you have the best possible.

Now you can begin the road test. Be aware of the ease of latching the belt system, starting the engine, moving away from a stop, and maneuvering out of a parking space. Does the transmission move smoothly into drive? Is the clutch smooth in engaging first gear? How do the brakes feel? Do they have a solid and secure feeling? Are there any unusual noises or surges from the engine? Is the car quiet and tight? In traffic, is there adequate visibility of the front, back, and sides? Are there no obstructions that add guesswork to parking? Can you park it easily? On the road, is the ride comfortable, not too mushy or stiff? At night, is the instrument illumination adequate? Can you read the instruments and control markings?

Finally, research for possible hidden costs. Research insurance prices for the make and model you are considering. (Added safety and security features will lower the insurance cost.) Full coverage on a full set of aluminum wheels might amaze you. In addition, ease of repair, frequency of theft, performance, and luxury can all add substantially to insurance costs.

The consumer who has carefully researched is now ready to listen critically to the details presented by a salesperson and to substantially increase the probability of making a sensible purchase.

Having explored some of the research possibilities of two products—mouthwash and automobiles, we turn to a service—auto body repair. As with products, the purpose here is to have a way to approach your research for the best service decision.

Auto Body Repair.[22]   Automobile body repair is a service that is used by every adult at one time. The chances of getting into an accident are one in four, and even without an accident, sooner or later the car may need cosmetic work to eliminate rust and normal wear and aging.

In researching where to go for body work, here are some steps that will help guide the listening consumer toward a comfortable decision.

1. Get recommendations first. Frequently, the most reliable advertising is through people we know. A visit with friends and relatives will often lead to a reliable body shop. Referrals from a mechanic, insurance agent, or car dealer can also be helpful.

2. Watch the shop in action. Visit the shop and observe these six areas:

    a. Is the lot fenced in, or is it open? A shop that is concerned with security is likely to be just as careful in doing quality work.

    b. Do signs indicate membership in reputable associations? Memberships of organizations like the Automotive Service Association (ASA) are expected to comply to a code of ethics and responsible automotive consumer service practices.

c. Are there indications that the shop employees are certified mechanics? The National Institute for Automotive Service Excellence (NIASE) offers a certification program for mechanics, including auto body repair personnel and painters.

d. Are cars waiting for repair damaged from a variety of sources? Cars with rust, fender benders, and major collisions will give you an idea of what the shop is capable of handling.

e. Is the shop relatively clean and organized? Are precautions taken such as having the painting booth well removed from the sanding area to avoid contamination?

f. What equipment is used? The best shops have state-of-the-art equipment. Down-draft spray booths and laser alignment equipment, as well as sophisticated welding and paint mixing systems are indicators of a well-equipped shop.

After observing in these six areas, listen carefully while you visit with the manager and repair technicians about these topics:

- *Dent repair.* A good shop will not usually fill major dents with body putty, but will either pound out the dent or replace the part.
- *Body fillers.* For little dings, hammer and dolly marks and minor damage, body fillers should not exceed more than one-half inch.
- *Sand blasting.* To clean rust thoroughly, the shop should use sand blasting *and* some sanding.
- *Metal protection.* Metal conditioners and primers should be applied to bare metal to prevent rust.
- *Preparation.* Areas to be painted should be sanded first and primed, so that the paint will adhere well.

Next, get a detailed estimate. Ask that all parts and labor be clearly itemized and be sure the shop will notify you if the costs might exceed the estimate. Today, some shops offer written warranties, and a ninety-day or longer written warranty on paint is a reasonable request.

Clarify parts warranties. Get manufacturer's warranties, and be sure the highest-quality replacement parts are used.

As this model shows, researching a service is more complex because, now, in addition to a product, you must evaluate the experience and skill of the technicians doing the work, which can have substantial effect on the final performance and look of the car. With the information gained from this research, the listening consumer will be in a solid position to make the best decision on where to have the car fixed—or any service, for that matter.

Summary

This chapter applies critical listening to the process of making a purchase. The consumer listening role involves making decisions on when, how, and where to spend money.

Before reasonable buying decisions can be made, the consumer should listen in three stages. (1) Listening intrapersonally for motivations for shopping may range from need to compulsion. (2) Persuasive messages which encourage the purchase of a product or service. These persuasive techniques include *band wagon, good ole days, plain folks, testimonials, emotional appeals, transfer, new and improved, card stacking,* and *that's incredible.* (3) Consumer research which provides information about the product or service. The listener who uses this three-step process will increase the likelihood of spending money more wisely, whether in a face-to-face or internet setting.

Notes

1. Robert E. Guzik, "Are You Listening?" *http:www/svobodamag.com/features/0720are.html.*

2. Marion Plunkett, "Learning through Listening," *Marketing* (Maclean Hunter, October 19, 1998), vol. 103, no. 39, p. 29.

3. http://www.footedge.com/footedgestage/newsamerica/index.html

4. http://www.census.gov/retail/mrts/www/data/pdf/ec_current.pdf

5. Interviews with Rob McClelland (Technology) and Marianne Kocal (VP), Meyocks & Priebe Advertising, Des Moines, Iowa, November 11 and December 18, 1999.

6. Don Peppers, "Wal-Mart Clicks on Main Street," http://www.1to1media.com/view.aspx?DOCID=12174

7. http://www.motherjones.com/news/feature/2000/05/shopaholic.html

8. Jeffrey A. Trachtenberg, "Shop Until You Drop?," *Forbes,* vol. 141 (January 11, 1988), p. 40.

9. Tara Parker-Pope, *Wall Street Journal* (Dec. 6, 2005), http://www.azcentral.com/health/wellness/articles/1206wsj-shopping06-ON.html

10. Trachtenberg, p. 40.

11. Anastasia Toufexis, "365 Days Till Christmas," *Time,* vol. 132, no. 82 (December 26, 1988), p. 82.

12. *Ibid.*

13. Anne H. Rosenfeld, "Mind Openers: An All-Consuming Passion," *Psychology Today,* vol. 22, no. 12 (May 1988), p. 12.

14. Georgia Witkin, Ph.D., "The Shopping Fix," *Health,* vol. 20 (May 1988), p. 74.

15. John L. Price and George Mann, "Thinking Skills and Propaganda Detection," presented at the Annual Conference of the Mid-South Educational Research Association, Little Rock, Arkansas, November 8–10, 1989, pp. 5–6.

16. http://www.digitalsparkmarketing.com/creative-marketing/advertising/emotional-appeal/

17. Robert G. Wyckham, "Implied Superiority Claims," *Journal of Advertising Research* (February/March, 1987), p. 54.

18. *Ibid.*

19. Dr. Irving Allan Kaye, "Fresh Breath for Less," *Consumers' Research,* vol. 74, no. 2 (February 1991), pp. 29–30.

20. http://www.happi.com/current/feb022.htm

21. Richard Williford, "Do You Really Want *That* Car?," *Consumers' Research,* vol. 74, no. 8 (August 1991), pp. 20–22.

22. Walter W. Watt, "Finding an Auto Body Repair Shop," *Consumers' Research,* vol. 73, no. 2 (February 1990), pp. 30–33.

Chapter Twelve
Awareness Exercises

Name_____   ID#_____

Review Chapter 12 and how you spend your money, and respond to the following:

1. Describe an in-store promotion you have observed. (Example—pizza slices at the grocery store)

2. Describe a situation where you or someone you know made an unnecessary purchase.
    A. Why was the purchase unnecessary?

    B. What were the *real* reasons for the purchase?

3. Describe an example of fitting in band wagon advertising:

4. Describe an example of good ole days advertising.

5.   Describe two example of plain folks advertising.

6. Describe an example of testimonial advertising.

7. Describe an example of emotional appeal advertising.

8. Describe an example of transfer advertising.

9. Discuss an example of new and improved advertising.

10. Discuss an example of card stacking advertising.

11. Discuss an example of that's incredible advertising.

12. Describe a product or service you plan to purchase in the future. Outline, in detail, the steps you will follow to research this purchase.

Chapter Twelve
Awareness Database

Name_____ ID#_____

Gender Identification

_____ male   _____ female   _____ other

1. I tend to buy products that are demonstrated in the store.

    A.   B.   C.   D.   E.
    often   seldom

2. I find shopping fun and recreational.

    A.   B.   C.   D.   E.
    often   seldom

3. Spending money relieves tension.

    A.   B.   C.   D.   E.
    often   seldom

4. I think carefully about purchases that add up to more than $25.00.

    A.   B.   C.   D.   E.
    usually   seldom

5. I am aware of advertising techniques.

    A.   B.   C.   D.   E.
    often   seldom

6. I research most products prior to purchase.

    A.   B.   C.   D.   E.
    often   seldom

7. I believe television media and radio advertising.

    A.   B.   C.   D.   E.
    often   seldom

8. I research major purchases ($1,000 or more).

    A.   B.   C.   D.   E.
    often   seldom

9. I buy on impulse.

    A.   B.   C.   D.   E.
    often   seldom

10. I read consumer educational publications.

    A.   B.   C.   D.   E.
    often   seldom

11. I think about my motives for shopping.

    A.   B.   C.   D.   E.
    usually   seldom

12. If I don't have cash or money in my checking account, I'll put purchases on a credit card.

    A.   B.   C.   D.   E.
    usually   seldom

13. I pay my credit card off every month.

    A.   B.   C.   D.   E.
    usually   seldom

14. I keep my shopping within a planned budget.

    A.   B.   C.   D.   E.
    usually   seldom

15. I save money for special purchases.

    A.   B.   C.   D.   E.
    usually   seldom

16. Shopping is work.

    A.   B.   C.   D.   E.
    usually   seldom

17. My credit cards are close to maximum.

    A.   B.   C.   D.   E.
    usually   seldom

18. I make shopping lists before going shopping.

    A.   B.   C.   D.   E.
    usually   seldom

19. I am satisfied with my purchases.

    A.   B.   C.   D.   E.
    usually   seldom

20. Friends influence me on purchases.

    A.   B.   C.   D.   E.
    often   seldom

21. I purchase online. (Amazon, etc.)

    A.   B.   C.   D.   E.
    often   seldom

22. I bid on eBay.

    A.   B.   C.   D.   E.
    often   seldom

Chapter Thirteen

Listening Appreciatively

Listening appreciatively is listening to enjoy. Each day, we have the chance to take little vacations that may not involve travel but give us time to leave our daily responsibilities and give us a different perspective. We close the office door, turn on some music, look at a favorite picture on the wall. We jog and enjoy the sounds of spring, or are entertained with an iPod; we relax and visit with a friend; we share jokes and stories. Perhaps we go to the theater, a concert, a movie, a production featuring an entertainer or a comedian, or an exhibit that centers on a favorite hobby. We might watch TV or listen to the radio or rent a movie. To add further understanding to appreciative listening, this chapter discusses: (1) the appreciative listening role, (2) the steps of appreciation, (3) the individual nature of appreciation, (4) knowledge and appreciation, (5) the link between appreciation, learning, and fun, and (6) humor and appreciation.

The Appreciative Listening Role

Appreciative listening is listening for enjoyment and pleasure. This role differs somewhat from the comprehensive, therapeutic, critical, and consumer listening roles, because the appreciative listening role is *initially* based on a nonrational and intuitive *attraction*. The attraction, at first, can happen by chance, but as our interest grows, the steps that lead to the appreciative listening role can lead to choices that substantially affect our enjoyment in life.

The Steps of Appreciation

Interviews with a variety of people show that appreciative listening develops in three steps that progress from casual interest to a deep-felt appreciation.[1] Awareness of these steps can help us understand how we come to appreciate and how we can prepare for the appreciative listening role.

Step one is *attraction*. This step draws our attention to something or someone, and is primarily a function of the right brain: it is nonevaluative and nonlogical. It is an emotional reaction that pulls us. As a result of this attraction, we *might* have a desire to gain knowledge about the subject and move to the next level.

The second step of appreciation is *contact*, which is a combination of right and left brain functioning. Because of the emotional right-brain attraction, we become interested in this subject and begin to learn about it through continued listening, observing, involvement, or participation. In this step, we are learning about what attracts us, and we are using the right and left brain to add to our understanding about this attractive person or topic.

The third step is *critical evaluation.* Here, the left brain hemisphere dominates. As we learn more about the subject, we begin to judge it; we rely on intrapersonal messages and we prioritize our own internal values—"Is this good or bad for me?" "Is this a wise way to spend my time?" "Is this exciting to me?" Next, we might survey the accepted social norms—"Is it an acceptable or unacceptable interest?" This step in appreciative listening takes continual information from step two—contact—to provide a basis for comparison and evaluation, and it takes sustained energy from step one—attraction—to supply the motivation to pursue the interest.

Now, we can take a look at how these steps might take place in an actual situation:

Step 1. Attraction   The simple act of seeing a glider flying overhead is preparation for the attraction step. If you choose to ignore the glider, you have not reached this first step. However, something stimulated you to take interest in the glider, prompting you to be attracted. The stimulus could be anything and could have been there for you hundreds of times, but for any number of reasons, this time you were attracted to it. It may have been a type of glider you had never seen before, or you could have simply been noticing it against a sky that you thought was especially beautiful.

Step 2. Contact   At this step you watch the glider and learn about it. This initial knowledge can be as simple as just seeing that it flies and can actually gain altitude. Even without riding in a glider, you decide it would be fun, so you attend an air show, take a class to learn more about flying, or go to the glider field to watch the operation and visit with some of the pilots.

Step 3. Critical Evaluation   You think soaring is fascinating, but do you want to continue perusing this? Now you have reached the critical evaluation step. With each sighting of a glider you compare it to your past experiences and become a critical judge, weighing the pros and cons of what you are observing. Perhaps at this point in the process, you notice a coupon in the newspaper advertising glider rides for $50. You clip it out, deciding later if this is how you want to spend your money, basing your decision on what you enjoy, what you think is difficult, and what you think is exciting. You can use the coupon or exit the cycle, moving on to different interests.

Another example of a situation leading to appreciative listening could have happened to you as a third grade student attending your older sister's band concert. At the concert, you become *attracted* to the drums. At the *contact* step, you watch drummers at concerts and on TV and notice how they contribute to the music. In middle school, you are asked if you want to play in the band, and you make a *critical decision* that you want to play the drums. As you go through your school year playing in the band, you are just an average drummer, but later as an adult you still can appreciate the drummer's contribution to music.

This example shows how you may be "forced" into a listening environment, since, as a child you probably had little choice in deciding whether to attend the concert or not attend. When you saw the drummer, you reached the attraction step. Your listening to the drummer that night was contact, and even though it may not have been extensive contact, you learned more about playing the drums. Next, you moved to the critical evaluative step, which led you to conclude the drums were fun and interesting. At this point in the process, you made a temporary exit, or pause, until you were asked to play in the middle school band.

Importantly, these steps of appreciation apply to our relationships as well. We can choose to appreciate and to stop appreciating people in our lives. If we find someone attractive, we will follow the three steps—attraction, contact, critical evaluation—repeatedly, until we approach a level of desired appreciation. Again, we can stay with the relationship or exit. If the attraction remains, we keep connecting and decide to continue growing in the relationship. However, if our attraction decreases, we can exit the relationship at any step, deciding that we have taken it far enough.

Figure 13.1 shows what the appreciative listening process looks like.

••• **Figure 13.1**

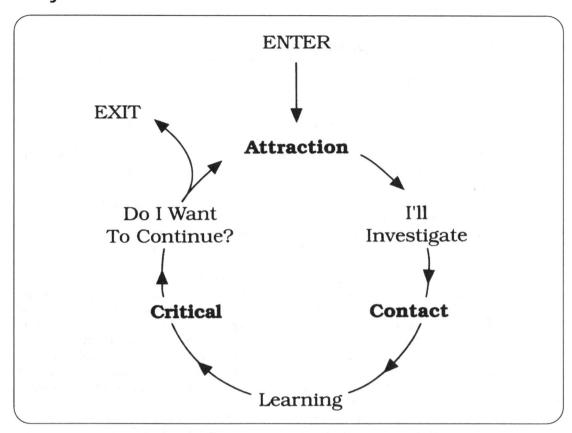

The Individual Nature of Appreciation

Appreciative listening is highly individualized. In a *comprehensive* listening setting, two efficient listeners would be able to compare notes after a lecture and find that they understand and recall the same central ideas. However, two listeners discussing something they appreciate, say, a play or concert, can have differing impressions of the event. Music, for example, will impress personality types in different ways: some may find it stimulating and exciting; others might find it loud and meaningless; still, others might not react to it at all.

Appreciation is individualized and is noticed early in life. The baby in her crib listens to her music box and is quieted and soothed. She listens and assigns some meaning to the music box tune. Another child might listen to the same music box and not be soothed at all. Rather, it might stimulate the child to want to touch and play with it. Appreciation varies from person to person. Some are more prone to appreciate color and design, while others appreciate the workings of machines. We come into the world with certain predispositions regarding what we appreciate, and our environment can encourage or discourage them.

Diverse appreciation is part of life. Newspapers and websites promote a variety of different events that involve appreciative listening—concerts (ranging from rap to symphonic); intimate dinner theater or grand productions from early Greek and Shakespeare to modern comedies and musicals; and movies ranging from animated musicals to horror.

Some appreciative tendencies are inborn, but we also *learn* to appreciate. In the process of growing up, we tend to value what our family valued. The interests enjoyed by our parents often are enjoyed by us. As we grow through life, we form our own set of criteria for appreciation. Our friends and school courses introduce us to new entertainments, different art forms, and hobbies. Perhaps we take a course in music appreciation, art appreciation, geology, drama, or oral interpretation. Inherited differences combine with learning to help us listen and appreciate a variety of offerings.

Knowledge and Appreciation

Appreciative listening is linked closely with knowledge—we need some knowledge to appreciate. In general, we want to know more about what attracts us. We may listen to a musician because she is unique, and has a style we have not heard before. She possesses a stylistic knowledge that we appreciate, just as a classical artist can be appreciated for her knowledge of an art form. The idea that knowledge is needed for appreciation is true with any topic of appreciation. For example, both the mechanic who appreciates a smoothly running engine or a cook who appreciates the power and utility of a food processor understand the engineering and care that went into their development and manufacture.

Appreciation also comes from comparative knowledge. For example, we see a sunset, we compare it with other sunsets, and we evaluate it as one of the most beautiful. We see a play performed, and we compare it with other performances and make a judgment. To appreciate someone or something, we compare them with our past knowledge, and we evaluate based on this comparison.

The amount and type of knowledge can also affect appreciation. A person may have knowledge that leads him to judge something as unattractive. For example, someone who has the idea that opera consists of loud singing in a foreign language will probably never go to an opera and have the chance to appreciate it. A friend invites him to go to a performance, but he refuses to go. He says he has heard bits and pieces of that opera, and it is "not for him." His friend knows he dislikes opera and is aware that he knows very little about it, so the friend explains the plot and some aspects to listen for: humorous scenes, interesting music, and intricate costumes. With this knowledge, he might be attracted enough to attend an opera and *begin* to appreciate some of its qualities.

In this example, we see that some knowledge about opera can increase attraction. However, if we know more about opera, will we enjoy it more? There is no clear-cut answer to this question, and the question leads to other questions. If listeners are knowledgeable about opera, is the probability greater that they will activate the left brain and be in the critical listening role? With this added knowledge, will they make decisions on how it *should* be played, and consequently, not appreciate it? Or does appreciation increase with knowledge?

A dilemma exists in the relationship between appreciative listening and knowledge. As one poet wrote, "We murder to dissect," that is, once we have studied a topic thoroughly (dissected it), we cannot listen and appreciate it any more (we have murdered our ability to appreciate; we are too critical). With knowledge comes the possibility that appreciative listening will become more critical.

However, knowledge does not always lead to critical assessment. Someone with considerable knowledge can understand the difficulties in staging the performance. Even though the performance might be less than perfect, this mature critic can appreciate the efforts and difficulties involved in the production. Knowledge and appreciation can also work together. Some knowledge is needed to sustain attraction, and as the knowledge increases beyond the initial attraction, the listener tends to judge the details of the appreciated subject. In time, knowledge becomes a source of mature appreciation.[2]

Appreciative Listening: Learning and Fun

Appreciative listening comes initially from attraction to something that is fun—listening to music, or going to a play, a concert, or a movie. In the process of having fun, we learn about people, life's peculiarities, a favorite hobby, and any of the thousands of attractions that are available.

Richard Bach, in his book, *Illusions: The Adventures of a Reluctant Messiah*, expands the idea that appreciative listening is fun and learning. In this excerpt, one of the main characters, Don Shimoda, and his new friend, Richard, have decided to relax for an evening by going to the movie, *Butch Cassidy and the Sundance Kid*. The author uses this scene to illustrate that appreciative listening is fun and learning. At an exciting part in the movie, Don touches Richard on the shoulder and asks him:

"Why are you here?"

"It's a good movie, Don. *Sh.*" Butch and Sundance, blood all over them, are talking about why they ought to go to Australia.

"Why is it good?" he said.

"It's fun. *Sh.* I'll tell you later."

"Snap out of it. Wake up. It's all illusions."

I was irked. "Donald, there's just a few minutes more and then we can talk all you want. But let me watch the movie, OK?"

He whispered intensely, dramatically. "Richard, *why are you here?*"

After the movie, Donald and Richard discuss the reasons for appreciative listening: fun, learning, or both.

"The other people, any people anywhere who go to any movie show, why are they there, when it is only illusions?"

"Well, it's entertainment," I said.

"Fun. That's right. One."

"Could be educational."

"Good. It is always that. Learning. Two."

"Fantasy, escape."

That's fun, too. One.

"Technical reasons. To see how a film is made."

"Learning. Two."

"Escape from boredom . . ."

"Escape. You said that."

"Social. To be with friends," I said.

"Reasons for going, but not to see the film. That's fun, anyway. One."

Whatever I came up with fit his two fingers; people see films for fun or for learning or for both together . . .[3]

Once we have decided that a diversion from our daily demands and responsibilities is in order, we need to survey the arena of possible appreciative experiences available to us. We might appreciate the vivid message of a polished speaker; a casual talk about a hobby; the humor of a comedian; a story dramatically told. We might be listening to life's joys and problems when the lights go down in the theater as the play begins. We might appreciate the vigor and energy of a rock concert; the soothing mix of tones at a symphony. The choices available for appreciative listening are as varied as people's interests; one need only to explore them. Figure 13.2 shows some appreciative listening choices gathered from people of all ages.[4]

Humor and Appreciation

What we appreciate is usually learning or fun. Humor—those scenes that we find amusing and make us laugh—is a rich source of fun and learning, and being attracted to humor is the start of an appreciative interest that is healthy and can keep life's worries in perspective. Appreciating the humor in life can help us stop worrying.[5]

As we learned from Chapter 8, stress can contribute to respiratory problems, high blood pressure, rheumatism, stomach ulcers, the common cold, thyroid complications, and many other physical ailments.[6] One authority on arthritis listed five of the most common conditions that contribute to arthritic problems and they all tie in with stress: marital failure, financial disaster, grief, loneliness, and long-held resentments.[7] Moreover, it is suggested that half of all hospital beds is taken for patients with nervous and mental troubles.[8] The negative effects of stress are clear, and one way to minimize its effects is through appreciative listening to humor.[9]

••• Figure 13.2   Appreciative Listening Choices

visiting museums	going to the restroom after being in the car three hours
soap smell after a shower	nice wet juicy kiss
silence of snow and it hitting you in the face	sound of chopping wood
the feeling of clean sheets in a freshly made bed	hitting a bull's-eye
eating gummy bears	coming to a swishing stop while snow skiing
bees	rippling water under a dock at night
sound of working with wood	creaminess of French silk pie
computer printer	smell of cologne
crowd and band at a basketball game	champagne and roses
baked bread and cookies	well-tuned sport bike
poplar trees blowing in the wind	fresh-cut grass
sound of water	sound of cooking steaks
impressionists' paintings	apple trees in bloom
smell after a rainstorm	thunderstorms
heat of the sun	smell of pine
sleet hitting a window	sunsets
feel of soft fur	smell of wife/husband
changing of seasons, budding trees	taste of pure, clean water
walk in a snowy woods	chocolate
taste of fresh bread with butter melting on it	proportion of Victorian houses
taste and sight of fresh vegetables and fruit	feeling her cat
the chatter of a happy child	sound of loons
feel of squeezing a hand	feel of velvet
fresh ground coffee	petting her black Labrador
smoking a pipe after a meal	hearing what the customers want
feel of a soft woman	hard bike tires
new car smell	crackling fire
feel of his muscles flexing	good golf shot
voices of grandchildren	feel of soft leather

Humor improves health, increases learning, and helps solve conflict. Health research has found that laughing reduces blood pressure, oxygenates the blood, massages vital organs, facilitates digestion, and causes release of endorphins in the brain. (Endorphins produce feelings of well-being.) Moreover, humor is suggested as a possible help in prevention and recovery from illnesses.[10] Not only does humor reduce the effects of worry, it also helps us learn. Laughing and learning seem to work together, helping the listener pay attention and remember the message.[11]

One final aspect of humor is that it can enhance professional effectiveness. For example, teachers and managers who use humor are judged to be more effective by their students[12] and their employees.[13]

Listening appreciatively to humor has the benefits of minimizing stress and worry, increasing learning, and contributing to professional effectiveness. To increase listening appreciatively to humor and realize these benefits, we should look for humor in everyday happenings and even see ourselves as sources of humor.[14] Moreover, we can increase our sense of appreciation for humor by adapting an attitude of playfulness and by listening for the humorous incongruities in situations involving ourselves and others.[15]

Listening Experience

The following essay, "Listening Experience," was first constructed as a lecture about appreciative listening. Notice how the author emphasizes the idea that listening to a performance is a group listening experience, with each listener coming for different reasons and with a variety of backgrounds and experiences.

The late David P. Hirvela was Associate Professor and Director of Theatre at Iowa State University. He taught acting, directing, and arts management. He directed and acted professionally with regional theatres. He authored *The Performing Arts: An Audience's Perspective*.

As defined earlier, listening in the performing arts includes receiving both aural and visual stimuli. Listening, a complex behavior, involves all our senses. It encompasses more than what passes through our ears. Although we listen each day of our lives, listening as a part of an audience presents different demands than our usual daily experiences. What are the components of the performing arts listening experience?

Performing arts listening is a group experience. *Most often a person responds to the performing arts as a member of a group. And, the nature of how we respond will be influenced by the group's behavior. Unfortunately, most of our group listening is associated with sitting in classrooms for twelve to sixteen years.*

The positive and negative behaviors we have learned from classroom listening may initially transfer to the audience experience. Classroom listening has taught us how to remain attentive over relatively long periods of time; how to engage ourselves with the instructor and with our fellow classmates; how to concentrate. However, we have also learned how to look *attentive, but* think *about other things; how to escape boring instructors or lessons through daydreaming; how to focus on the most insignificant distractions.*

Each audience member has different purposes for attending a theatrical event. *The assumption that an audience has a single unified purpose for attending—to respond to the performance—ignores the reasons people attend any performance. Our purposes for being in the audience impact our listening. They affect our attention to the performance and our interest in listening. If you listen with less attention and interest, you reduce the chances that the performance will make its desired aesthetic impression.*

Performing arts listening occurs in a restrictive communication environment. *Sitting in a theater with other people restricts the freedom of your response to what you see and hear. The group discourages verbal response among audience members or with performers. Other audience members may quiet anyone who disturbs the performance by talking. Therefore, you have little opportunity to respond verbally, an uncomfortable condition for some people. Consequently, the audience's situation offers even more restrictions than the classroom listening.*

Performing arts listening emphasizes physical passivity. *Audience members of theatre, dance, and music performances (excluding most popular music events) have little opportunity to move. The formal theatre environment and group expectations encourage listening while sitting. Only extraordinary emergencies permit leaving the theater during a performance.*

This physical passivity contrasts with the freedom of movement allowed with the more informal performing arts. At a rock concert you feel free to stand and shout, dance in the aisles, or even stand on the seats. The rock performance stimulates this activity, and the whole audience participates actively. As you watch a film in a theater, you can get up and leave for more popcorn at any time. This action is accepted by other audience members and is encouraged by the theater management, who show commercials promoting, "Have a snack" and inform audiences that the snack bar has various candy and soda products.

Even greater informality exists with television and radio listening; viewers move whenever and wherever they please during these performance events. Since most of your performance models for listening

From *The Performing Arts: An Audience's Perspective*, by Dr. David P. Hirvela, reprinted with permission.

behavior are typically informal, you may feel uncomfortable and limited in an audience of the formal performing arts. This physical passivity affects your listening.

The listeners to the performing arts have a shortened attention span. *Most audience members have an attention span for sitting and listening to the performing arts that is significantly shorter than our ancestors'. Audiences even as recently as the 1950s attended Broadway plays lasting at least two and one-half hours, attended double bills at the movies, or listened to the radio for three to four hours in the evening. In the early 1900s audiences felt cheated if their theater evening was not a four- to five-hour experience, which might include an orchestral overture and between-act music, a full play, variety acts, and a short play as an afterpiece. Why has our attention span for the performing arts shortened?*

Our individual tempo-rhythms, that is, our internal responses to time, reflect the pace of our technological society. Information speeds around the world in seconds; at work, computers process information in milliseconds. We even expect restaurants to serve our food fast *and on demand. We have less patience with performing arts that do not engage us immediately.*

With entertainment we have developed concentrated attention spans of eight to twelve minutes based on watching television since childhood. The average American spends more than five and one-half hours each day watching television. This television experience teaches us to concentrate on the performance only eight to twelve minutes. Longer concentration is impossible, because commercials interrupt the performance. Television does not permit focusing on the performance for longer time periods. Therefore, we develop a shortened attention span for the performing arts from the very influential early years of childhood. Because of the short attention span, theater performances of two hours, broken only with one intermission, may seem unbearably long. They strain an audience member's concentration. This shortened attention affects how you listen and, therefore, how you receive the performance.

The performing arts experience places new demands on your listening skills. Your listening techniques must adjust to performance situations. New approaches to listening must develop. These adjustments and changes will enhance your reception of the performing arts, and ultimately increase your enjoyment and appreciation.

An Individual's Experience with the Performing Arts

Every time you attend a performance, you bring along your accumulated experiences with that performing art. As each person in an audience is unique, likewise each person's experiences with performing arts vary. Some audience members will have attended many performances; some will be attending for the first time. How does this variation in experience affect audience responses?

The greater your experience, the greater the likelihood that you will involve yourself in the aesthetic elements of performance. Aesthetic involvement increases the range and intensity of your reactions. These reactions feed back directly to the performers and your fellow audience members. If your experience is limited, the range and intensity of your aesthetic involvement with the performance will decrease, which affects feedback.

If intense aesthetic appreciation requires knowledge and experience, how can the exuberant reactions of first-time viewers of any performance be explained? If you remain open to receiving any new experience, you have the potential of being caught up in its energy, excitement, and aesthetic. "Remaining open" in the performing arts usually means allowing your right brain to receive the experience and avoiding left-brain impulses to evaluate. Even a first-time viewer of ballet will be captured by the movement, the spectacle, the beauty of the performers, and the music, without understanding the intricacies of ballet choreography.

As we experience more performances of any art, our aesthetic appreciation grows. We walk into performances more knowledgeable, ready to respond emotionally and thoughtfully. Accumulating performance experiences may reduce our right-brain responses to the immediacy of the performance. We could become left-brain cognitive evaluators of the arts. Be wary. Remember: Our first pleasures in the arts were right brain—intuitive, spontaneous, simultaneous, nonverbal. No matter how many experiences we may have, we must never lose the sense of awe in appreciating a performance.

Summary

This chapter defines the appreciative listening role as listening to enjoy and to learn. The process of appreciation occurs in three steps: attraction, contact, and critical evaluation. We can exit this three-step process at any time, but exiting is usually at the attraction or critical evaluation step. Appreciative listening is unique to each individual's experiences and personality, and it encompasses a wide range of activities. Knowledge of a subject plays an important role in appreciation, and this knowledge might encourage or discourage appreciative listening. To increase sources of appreciation, the listener should actively explore a variety of experiences. Appreciating humor is discussed as a means of reducing stress, improving health, and increasing professional effectiveness.

Notes

1. Steven C. Larson, "Steps Leading to Appreciative Listening," unpublished report, Iowa State University, Ames, Iowa, 1992.

2. James J. Kaufmann, professional musician, personal interview, Ames, Iowa, September 5th, 1992.

3. Richard Bach, *Illusions: The Adventures of a Reluctant Messiah* (New York: Dell Publishing Co., Inc., 1981), pp. 102–111.

4. David Meadows, "Individualized Listening to Enjoy," unpublished report, Iowa State University, Ames, Iowa, 1992.

5. Dale Carnegie, *How to Stop Worrying and Start Living* (New York: Simon and Schuster, 1985), p. 86.

6. John Morreall, *Taking Life Seriously* (Albany, New York: State University of New York Press, 1983).

7. Roger Cecil, *A Textbook of Medicine* (Philadelphia: Saunders Publisher, 1955).

8. Carnegie, p. 89.

9. Larry Peter and B. Dana, *The Laughter Prescription* (New York: Ballantine Books, 1982).

10. James Goodman, "Humor: When Health is a Laughing Matter," *Executive Fitness*, vol. 13, no. 15, pp. 10–11.

11. Anne Ziv, *Personality and a Sense of Humor* (New York: Springer Publishing Co., 1984).

12. James Check, "Positive Traits of the Effective Teacher, Negative Traits of the Ineffective One," *Education*, vol. 106, no. 3, pp. 326–334.

13. Jeremy Abrams, "The Best Lessons I've Learned as a Superintendent," *The Executive Educator*, vol. 9, no. 3, pp. 20–21.

14. Goodman, p. 11.

15. Peter and Dana.

Chapter Thirteen
Awareness Exercises

Name _____   ID# _____

Take some time to recall people, settings, entertainments, or hobbies you appreciate. Recall some reasons you appreciate them.

1. List three events where you were an appreciative listener.

   A.

   B.

   C.

2. Discuss a situation where you went expecting to relax and appreciate, but it turned into a critical listening event.

3. Discuss a situation where the expectation was critical listening, and it became appreciative.

4. List two forms of entertainment that you do not appreciate.

   A.

   B.

5. List two forms of entertainment that you do appreciate.

   A.

   B.

6. What is the best movie you have seen in the last month? Why did you appreciate it?

7. What is your favorite TV program? Why do you appreciate it?

8. Name your favorite hobbies.

9. Why do you appreciate them?

10. Which radio station(s) do you listen to most often? Why do you listen to them?

11. Which TV station(s) do you watch most often? Why do you watch them?

12. What time of the day do you usually do your appreciative listening? Why?

13. What is your favorite music group?

14. Who is your favorite vocalist or soloist?

15. What is your favorite song?

16. Who is your favorite actor?

17. Recall someone you appreciate. Briefly describe what led to the appreciation using these three steps:

A. Attraction

B. Contact

C. Evaluation

18. Recall something you appreciate. Briefly describe what led to the appreciation using these three steps:

A. Attraction

B. Contact

C. Evaluation

19. Describe a time when humor helped reduce stress.

20. Who is your favorite comedian?

21. Who is your favorite author?

22. Who is your favorite painter?

23.   Who is your favorite poet?

24.   Who is your favorite playwright?

25.   What is your favorite short story?

Chapter Thirteen
Awareness Database

Name_____   ID#_____

1. I explore new and different forms of entertainment.

   A.   B.   C.   D.   E.
   seldom   sometimes   whenever
                                                                   possible

2. TV is my main source of entertainment.

   A.   B.   C.   D.   E.
   seldom   usually   always

3. Videos/DVDs are my main source of entertainment.

   A.   B.   C.   D.   E.
   seldom   usually   always

4. I go to plays whenever possible.

   A.   B.   C.   D.   E.
   seldom   usually   always

5. I go to theater movies whenever possible.

   A.   B.   C.   D.   E.
   seldom   usually   always

6. I attend live entertainment whenever possible.

   A.   B.   C.   D.   E.
   seldom   usually   always

7. I go to listen to a speaker whenever possible.

   A.   B.   C.   D.   E.
   seldom   usually   always

8. I go to rock concerts whenever possible.

   A.   B.   C.   D.   E.
   seldom   usually   always

9. I attend symphonies whenever possible.

   A.   B.   C.   D.   E.
   seldom   usually   always

10. I listen to radio whenever possible.

    A.   B.   C.   D.   E.
    seldom   usually   always

11. I enjoy being outdoors.

A.   B.   C.   D.   E.
seldom   usually   always

12. I enjoy reading novels.

A.   B.   C.   D.   E.
seldom   usually   always

13. I enjoy jokes.

A.   B.   C.   D.   E.
seldom   usually   always

14. I enjoy social gatherings.

A.   B.   C.   D.   E.
seldom   usually   always

15. I find architecture interesting.

A.   B.   C.   D.   E.
seldom   usually   always

16. I listen to CDs, MP3, or iPod while driving.

A.   B.   C.   D.   E.
seldom   usually   always

Chapter Fourteen

Listening in a Partnership

In the previous chapters of *Sensible Listening*, we have discussed a background for effective listening and emphasized the ideas that we listen intrapersonally, interpersonally, and holistically to comprehend, to help, to decide, to purchase, and to appreciate. As we become competent in these roles, we increase the probability of making responsive connections with others, and some of our most meaningful connections are partnerships. In this chapter, the importance of listening in the development and maintenance of partnerships is considered by first discussing partnering in our lives, second, by defining partnering, and third, by clarifying the link between listening and partnering.

Partnering in Our Lives

We go through life in a series of partnerships. Some may last thirty minutes or less; some thirty years or more. Short-term partnerships might be between people on the phone discussing a meeting or problem; a neighbor visiting about a community issue; someone asking for directions. In these cases, the partnership may not continue after the goals are reached—the meeting is set; the issue is resolved; the directions are given.

Longer partnerships exist between couples, family members, professional colleagues, owners and contractors, contractors and subcontractors, or any people who share common interests and goals. Of course some of these partnerships are legal commitments: marriages, formal business partnerships, management buyouts, or people buying a business, but whatever the type or duration, a partnership is formed whenever shared goals, values, and cooperation are needed for productivity and satisfaction. A partnership, to be effective, develops a culture of cooperation.

Partnering Defined

A partnership is an agreed-upon process to listen actively and work together to reach common goals. Even though this discussion of partnering focuses on the workplace, the strategies apply comfortably to other committed relationships—couples, spouses, and families, as well. Since most of the research has focused on business partnerships, the vocabulary is business appropriate. The principles, however, certainly apply to family partnering issues as well, and later in the chapter partnering principles are applied in non-business situations. In the workplace, partnerships are frequently formed around projects for development, design, management, or construction. In fact, this kind of project partnering is the most frequent type of partnering in United States' organizations today, because it has significantly helped reach goals efficiently while reducing confrontation.

In business and in other relationships, partnering begins with a commitment from the leadership. It is an assurance by the owner and management of the project to treat the contractor as a trusted team member; moreover, partnering is a commitment by the contractors to a relationship of fairness and openness with the owners and managers. By definition, partnering is not a legal agreement with joint liabilities, but rather an informal relationship—with listening at the core—that leads to mutual acceptance without exploiting either party. A partnership is not necessarily a friendship (although partnerships do occur between family and friends), but it is a commitment-process to treat those involved with dignity and respect.

Following is the definition of partnering developed by The Partnering Task Force of the Construction Industry. Notice that the definition stresses a process with commitment, equality, trust, and respect for each partner's dignity.

> Partnering is a long-term commitment between two or more organizations for the purpose of achieving specific business objectives by maximizing the effectiveness of each participant's resources. This requires changing traditional relationships to a shared culture without regard to organizational boundaries. The relationship is based upon trust, dedication to common goals, and an understanding of each other's individual expectations and values.[1]

Business Partnering

The development of Chrysler's subcompact car, the Neon, provides a vivid and thoroughly detailed narrative of the partnering process. In the development of the Neon, management first listens and commits to the project, and the project leaders nurture a partnership based on commitments, teamwork, trust, and fair play.

The beginning of the Neon partnership began in a test track garage where Robert Marcell, the head of Chrysler's small car team, met with Lee Iacocca, then chairman of the board at Chrysler. Iacocca listened as Marcell built his case to gain Iacocca's commitment to the Neon project.

> He began showing slides of his home town, Iron River, a decaying mining community in Michigan's Upper Peninsula. Up flashed the now-shuttered Homer-Wauseca mine, where Marcell had worked summers during college. Then the abandoned yard, where 1,000 railcars a day were once loaded with ore. And the hospital where, because of the flight of the young from Iron River, five people die for every one that is born. "The town is crumbling," he said, his voice shaking, "because we couldn't compete."
>
> Detroit, Marcell argued, was slowly heading toward the same fate, and abandoning small cars would speed its demise. But if Chrysler could become the first U.S. company in decades to make a profitable subcompact, it could help reverse the trend. It could prove that American carmakers, in toe-to-toe combat, can outmuscle the Japanese. Marcell uttered what became his team's rallying cry: "If we dare to be different, we could be the reason the U.S. auto industry survives. We could be the reason our kids and grandkids don't end up in fast food service." As he ended his pitch, he thought he saw a tear in Iacocca's eye.[2]

As a result of this speech, Marcell gained Iacocca's commitment to the Neon project, and one of the most remarkable partnership efforts in auto manufacturing history began. It was a partnership made up of over 1,000 people—150 managers, 600 engineers, 289 suppliers, and a number of blue-collar workers who contributed to the effort.

Once the first partnership step—commitment to the Neon project—was completed, Marcell proceeded to the next step—building a team. He and twelve engineers first assigned to the project began a process called *concurrent engineering*. This meant building a listening team of engineers, marketers, purchasers and financial experts to work together from the beginning to avoid later delays from disagreements or misunderstandings.

Marcell knew that team building was crucial inside the Chrysler organization and with *outside* vendors and suppliers who would supply nearly 70 percent of the value of the finished car. Consequently, in October 1990, the Chrysler team invited twenty-five suppliers of crucial components such as seats, tires, and suspensions to send engineers to Chrysler's proving grounds in Chelsea, Michigan. These meetings helped those outside Chrysler understand the project needs, and they also helped secure the *trust* needed to build a working team.

> At first, the suppliers were skeptical of the partnership Marcell envisioned, which called for sharing sensitive financial data and ideas in a mutual effort to slice costs. They had all been burned before by customers professing brotherly love. But Marcell's earnestness won them over.[3]

With *commitment, team development,* and *earned trust,* the partnership was well under way to meeting its goals of developing a marketable subcompact automobile in a timely manner.

Central to this partnering process was listening: Iacocca listened to Marcell, engineers and suppliers listened to each other, and of course, Chrysler listened to their most important partners, the potential buyers of the Neon.

> One thing Marcell did know was that the Neon wouldn't sell if it scrimped on features or performance. So the team focused on cutting costs where customers wouldn't notice, or wouldn't care. For instance, small-car owners told researchers power windows weren't important, so the team chose the crank variety. Market research also showed that buyers saw nothing special in the four speed automatic transmission most competitors offer. So engineers adapted an existing Chrysler three speed, saving more than $300 million. The team also decided to sell identical cars at Chrysler and Dodge dealerships instead of offering two slightly different versions, as Ford did with its Escort and Tracer. That saved about $10 million in engineering and tooling. Stylists did away with all but one exterior molding; chopping parts costs $50 per car.[4]

In addition to listening to potential customers, early in the partnering process Marcell also listened to the workers who would be building the Neon, and he included the United Auto Workers as team members.

> As early as November, 1990, he had asked union members there to help engineers make the car easy to build and to streamline production methods. The result, in theory, will be fewer defects. "Engineers are great, but they've never built a car," says Bob Dunlavy, a United Auto Workers quality coordinator.
>
> In January and February, 1992, Marcell enlisted the UAW full-time. Chrysler bused about 90 Belvidere workers to suburban Detroit to help assemble the first production prototypes and suggest how to do the job better.[5]

The trust and teamwork, which was developed throughout the partnering process, created an atmosphere where partners would listen openly to criticism and evaluation. Ideas for improvement were considered, and if a team believed goals could be better reached, the ideas were incorporated into the process.

> Among the many ideas they came up with: a height-adjustable assembly line, so assemblers can fasten on components without fatiguing body contortions that lead to mistakes. Two workers, Ron Swain and Cary Smoot, suggested changes to Neon's door installation equipment so window glass would fit perfectly. That's crucial, since there's no upper door frame to guide the glass, and the slightest gap can cause wind or water leaks. So far, workers have proposed more than 4,000 changes in the car and production process, and many have been implemented.[6]

A review of the Neon project shows that the key steps to effective partnering were considered: commitment to the project and the process of listening in the partnership, as well as the development of trust and respect for the partners. Perhaps the most meaningful comment about this partnering process comes from United Auto Worker Bob Dunlavy:

> "We're proud of what's going on."[7]

The Neon went out of production in 2005, but it remains a role-model of large scale effective partnering.

In order for partnering to work, it needs to become an integral part of the culture which is valued and totally supported by the key players in the organization, whether they are the CEOs and owners of multimillion dollar enterprises, family members at home, or friends who enjoy a hobby together. In all cases, effective partnering uses the full range of listening theory: an understanding of the communication process, intrapersonal, interpersonal, movement, holistic, personality, stress management, and the five listening roles: comprehensive, therapeutic, critical, consumer, and appreciative. Partners listen comprehensively to the details of the partnership; they listen therapeutically to the feelings and concerns of the partners; they listen critically to test the credibility and logic of the partnership and to decide how resources might be used; and they listen appreciatively to enjoy the many aspects of the partnering experience.

Effective listening, then, is an integral part of partnering, and it plays a substantial role in developing the six criteria of partnerships: (1) commitment, (2) communication, (3) conflict resolution, (4) trust, (5) teamwork, and (6) evaluation.

Listening and Partnering

Commitment

Achieving goals begins with participant commitment of two parallel goals—these goals are equally important to working out a partnership. The first of these goals calls for complete commitment to the project. Second, and equally important, is commitment to the process of partnering to reach the project goals.

As discussed in Chapter 6, "Listening to Ourselves," all communication begins within ourselves. In order to become committed to a project, we first listen to determine how this project can meet our needs and goals. For example, we might ask, Will the project fulfill our need for survival by assuring a paycheck? Conserving resources? Saving time and money? Will it fulfill our need to belong? Will it bring us together with people who respect us? Will it fulfill our need for power? Will we be empowered to make important decisions? Will this project fulfill our need for freedom? Will we be allowed to create solutions to problems? Will we be free to be ourselves? Will it fulfill our need for fun? Will we be able to appreciate our achievements? Will we be able to pursue aspects of the project that we enjoy?

Commitment says that we accept the project goals, and we share these goals with our partners. Consequently, we will listen as partners to reach the goals. The goals can cover the range of human endeavors: building a bridge, painting a house, rebuilding a plane, being married, planning a vacation, raising children, making money, keeping warm, making a dress, keeping healthy, losing weight, and so on.

Once we have made our commitment to project goals and to partnering as a means of achieving these goals, we are ready to develop a productive relationship with our partners through effective communication.

Communication

One of the first steps in establishing effective communication is to promote interaction in the partnering culture. Regular meetings, discussions, even newsletters and posted material encourage communication. Just keeping office doors open encourages two-way interaction. Moreover, communication is supported when the culture supports equality. Equality means listening openly, without judgment, and empathically to feelings, listening with interest to comprehend facts and information, and listening to appreciate the insights, interests, and humor of partners.

A partnership, by definition, is based on communication—the act of sending messages and listening to each other. This substantial part of partnering says, "I will exert the energy to connect with my partners. I will take the time to listen to them and listen to my own feelings, so that I can share with them."

Conflict Resolution

Partnering programs use the term conflict resolution, so we'll stay with it; however, the word *conflict* in some situations is probably too strong—it has overtones of the last step before a fistfight. Substitute *difference* or *disagreement resolution*. The definition for *conflict* is "the interaction of interdependent people who perceive incompatible goals and interference from each other in achieving those goals."[8] Basically, this says that conflicts are disagreements that come from having different goals or different approaches to reach goals. Conflict resolution is a structure to solve these disagreements.

Differences occur on a daily basis between family members, friends, and colleagues, Often, they aren't earth-shattering, but they need to be resolved in order to move toward a goal. For example, two people might agree on a goal to go to Chicago to see a play. Within this overall goal are subgoals that might cause disagreements and require a plan for conflict resolution. Which play should they attend? The matinee or the evening production? Should they drive, take a plane, a bus, Amtrak? Where should they stay? What time should they leave? Without some established method of conflict resolution, this partnership could become bogged down in disagreements that waste time and energy.

Any effective partnering process needs an agreed-upon, readily available procedure to resolve conflicts quickly and satisfactorily. *Without a system of conflict resolution, many of these conflicts could become adversarial and drawn-out arguments or dragged out in expensive and time-consuming proceedings.* In interpersonal relationships as well as business dealings, un-partnered conflicts often find their solutions in legal battles that cost substantial amounts of time and money.

The importance of an understood and agreed-upon method of resolving conflicts is basic to effective partnering. When issues go unresolved, they fester and increase in magnitude. If unchecked, they could end up in court. In order to resolve problems quickly and satisfactorily, a responsive problem resolution plan is necessary at the level closest to the problem. The resolution plan will also help keep unproductive, adversarial roles from developing in the first place. Here again, alert listening to conflicting facts and feelings can ward off potentially disruptive conflicts.

In the case of the two playgoers, conflicts are simply resolved by an agreement to meet over lunch to discuss any differences: which play to attend, the mode of transportation, and lodging. In more complex relationships, such as marriages and other couple commitments, conflict resolution is necessary to meet the goals of the relationship. Over time, many couples work out ways to resolve differences. Certainly, not all conflict resolution plans are that simple, and couples might spend a good deal more time and effort building ways to solve problems, but even a plan this simple could work.

Many couples consult therapists to explore and build conflict resolution programs for their relationships. Therapists help the couple listen to themselves and to each other, and ultimately to develop a plan to solve relational problems. Here is an example of a couple who worked out a conflict resolution plan that helped their marriage partnership reach some of its goals. The plan they developed was specific and tailored to their partnering needs. Here is their story.

Susan and Ted are psychology teachers who fell in love. They started living together and after eight months started having serious relational problems. Ted, who had been abused as a child, was full of anger and had an explosive temper. Once he punched a hole in the wall, breaking his hand. He never hit Susan but did push her and, needless to say, often frightened her. Their relationship was punctuated with fights, and the week after their engagement, Susan threw the ring at him.

The therapist they consulted helped them work on two conflict resolution plans, one that helped Ted resolve his temper flare-ups and another that helped them fight symbolically. The conflict resolution program that they developed for Ted's temper was simple and creative. It forced Ted to listen to his anger and share his problem with some of his less intimate partners.

In the last session, Belson [the therapist] addressed Ted's violence. He had Ted bring three male friends to therapy and explain the problem to them. He told Ted to buy a red phone, to serve as his violence hot line—if things got out of control, he was supposed to call his friends. The hot line worked as a deterrent. "I had always kept my temper a secret," says Ted. "This exposed it, made it more real. And if I gave in to it, I would lose face with my friends."

Belson also suggested that the couple find a safe way to fight. They bought a squirt gun; they haven't used it much.[9]

When partnerships involve more people, the conflict resolution becomes proportionally more complex, but the *keys to resolving conflict remain the same: listen and agree on the goals and the methods of reaching them.*

To function effectively, a partnering organization needs a conflict-resolving system that fits the culture of the organization. For example, a commonly used method of resolving conflict in decision-making discussions and debates is a system called *Robert's Rules of Order*, which are carefully structured procedures designed to solve differences. When a group agrees to abide by these rules from the beginning, the members understand that Robert's rules will be the basis for conflict resolution in this group: Ideas will be moved and seconded, and discussion will be limited to a specific time and topic.

All successful groups have established ways to solve conflicts. For instance, in basketball, when conflict arises regarding the possession of the ball, the method of resolving the conflict is to alternate team possession. In conflict cases, the referees resolving the conflict must first listen carefully to the facts, frequently by viewing a replay video of the contested call and then applying the resolution fairly.

Established, fair rules for resolving conflicts help keep partners from becoming adversaries, and these rules naturally make the work environment more productive. One beverage company provides a valuable model for conflict resolution that has built trust and minimized lawsuits for the past forty years. An article in *Personnel Journal* first provides some background and then the specifics of the brewery's' conflict resolution program.[10]

> In 1975, the brewing company created the Peer Review System, a process that guarantees employees fair treatment by allowing them to bring their grievances in front of a group that includes their coworkers. It was an innovative move back then, and it has proved successful.

This conflict resolution system has effectively brought management and workers together in a reasonably equal relationship, and has diminished major conflicts and litigation. The conflict resolution system is based on active comprehensive, therapeutic, and critical listening. The program is clear and definitive, and its application is understood and equally applied in all conflict circumstances. It has nine steps:

1. An employee who is dissatisfied with a company policy decision—not the policy itself—may file an appeal with his or her employee-relations representative within seven working days after the incident.

2. The employee-relations representative then sets up an appeal board by randomly selecting two members of management and three employees from the same job category as the appellant.

3. A hearing is scheduled by the employee-relations representative.

4. At the hearing the supervisor describes the circumstances surrounding the discipline.

5. The employee explains why the supervisor's action was unfair.

6. Board members listen and ask questions of both parties, and may listen to other witnesses if requested.

7. When the board members have listened to all the information they need, they privately discuss the case.

8. They vote on one of three outcomes:

    a. To uphold the action.

    b. To reduce the severity.

    c. To overturn the action completely.

9. The decision of the board is final, and a signed, written summary is given to the supervisor and the employee.[11]

As the examples of the playgoers, the fighting couple, and the brewery point out, a partnership needs listening, commitment, communication, and *a clearly understood system to resolve conflicts.* The fourth requirement for a successful, working partnership is trust.

Trust

In simplest terms, *trust* is following through on commitments: doing what you say you are going to do. It correlates closely with the variables of speaker credibility as discussed in Chapter 11, "Listening Critically." Basically, trust in a partnership is a blend of (1) competence—which comes from knowledge, background, and achievements, (2) character—honesty, (3) intentions—concern for others, (4) personality—positiveness and optimism, and (5) dynamism—intensity, sincerity, and energy. Additionally, the way partners listen seems to affect trust. A poll asking "What builds trust with your partners?" produced these response categories:[12]

Listening objectively to the facts involved

Listening openly, without judgment to a partner

Listening that gives the speaker dignity and respect

Making decisions after listening to all of the information, including the *feelings* involved

Appreciating and enjoying the partner for who s/he is

Trust develops when the partners know they can depend on each other. It grows with the knowledge that a partner will follow through on commitments and will act reliably and helpfully; that your partner will listen openly and objectively to understand, and when decisions and judgments are made, the trusted partner will consider all input and weigh the alternatives fairly and equally before coming to conclusions.

The fact that fair and equal treatment builds trust is emphasized in the closing discussion about the brewery's conflict resolution system. In this discussion, an employee-relations manager emphasizes the idea that partners will use a resolution plan only after experience has shown them that the people responsible for operating the plan are trustworthy.

> Despite the fact that the majority of decisions favor the supervisors, employees trust the system. It took a while, however. "At first, employees' use of the system was low," says an employee-relations area manager. "The first few years that the system was in existence, less than eight appeals per year were held. But then, as the employees gained trust in the process, the numbers steadily grew. For the last several years, we have been averaging approximately sixty appeals per year."[13]

After relationships evolve through commitment, communication, conflict resolution, and trust, interdependent teamwork begins in the partnership. This teamwork creates the activity that leads directly to measurable productivity.

Teamwork

Our discussion so far has provided the basis for a practical definition of *teamwork.* In fact, the terms *partnering* and *teamwork* are nearly synonymous. Partners are committed to a project and to each other. Moreover, they have developed processes to communicate and resolve conflict. However, the idea of teamwork takes partnering one step further by adding a sense of dynamic activity. People can be partners even when they are doing nothing together—not interacting at all. For example, two partners could be alone in the library researching ideas for a common project. At this point, they are partners working independently to find some ways to reach their goal. Moreover, it is possible to have a "silent partner"—someone who is committed to a program but is not active with other partners in the process of reaching program goals. Even though these people are partners, their lack of interaction keeps them from being team members. It is not possible to have a silent or noninteractive team member because, by definition, a team member is *interdependent* while working toward the partnership goals. Consequently, when partners discuss and merge their efforts to reach a goal, they are acting as team.

Teamwork, then, is a partnership interacting together as a unit. When the team is functioning well, all of the partners are utilizing the diverse skills and talents of each partner to the fullest. We have all observed teams when they are functioning at their optimal level: a basketball team that is quickly and carefully listening to nuances of voice, movement, and eye contact, moving down the floor like a flawless machine: a partnership of managers, supervisors, production workers, and vendors combining their thoughts to find a solution to a product design problem, a couple discussing how they are going to take care of the kids during a business convention. In each case, teamwork is partnering in action. It is listening and interacting, and arriving at solutions that probably could not have been found independently.

These synergistic solutions that build interdependently are based on the understanding that each partner has valuable and diverse contributions to make, and if they are actively listened to as team members, the best solution will be generated. Like holistic listening where all the senses combine like a team to give a fuller picture than any of the senses operating alone, synergistic solutions incorporate a range of diverse ideas that is greater than the sum of all the individuals involved in the process. Teamwork, then, evokes a stimulation that energizes each partner to contribute and create beyond what could be done independently.

With the components in place—listening, commitment, communication, conflict resolution, trust, and teamwork—the partnering process now needs monitoring and evaluation. Partnerships grow and mature, and to assure optimal growth, systematic evaluation is necessary to monitor the process and the progress.

Evaluation

Partnering is a process of commitment, communication, conflict resolution, trust, and teamwork. The process of partnering—like any process—needs to be examined and evaluated regularly. *Evaluation is defined as a process of gaining information and using that information to make goal-oriented adjustments.* Many partnering projects perform a final evaluation when the project is finished, and this evaluation is extremely valuable in comparing partnered projects with unpartnered projects. However, evaluation is also necessary *during* the project.

Ongoing partnering evaluation should consist of regular time-outs to listen to the progress of the project. These time-outs might be established at four levels. Level one focuses on *comprehensive listening* to the status of deadlines, costs, and procedures. Level two, *therapeutic listening,* gauges the current feelings in the partnership. This level is concerned with feelings of trust, comfort, satisfaction with relationships, communication, and conflict resolution. Feelings of mistrust, discomfort, dissatisfaction, frustration with the communication, the relationships, or conflict resolution might be expressed at level two, as well. Level three uses *critical listening* to evaluate decisions. The thoroughness and clarity of decision-making is considered here. Questions related to decision input and the quality of decisions in saving time, money, and other resources are considered. Level four incorporates *appreciative listening.* At this level, the reward system and feelings of satisfaction, dignity, and respect are discussed and evaluated. The four evaluation levels can be summarized as the four Cs:

1. Comprehend   Comprehensive listening
2. Care   Therapeutic listening
3. Critique   Critical listening
4. Commend   Appreciative listening

These evaluation time-outs can be formal or informal discussion or written surveys and questionnaires. The evaluation uses a system of gaining feedback—information and feelings—about goal achievement and the partnering process. This feedback is for making adjustments in the partnering process. The evaluation process is needed for keeping a project on course. Regular time-outs allow for comprehensive listening to adjust the group's directions; appreciative listening to visit with partners and share some enjoyable moments; and some therapeutic listening to find out how they're feeling about the project. The point of the evaluation is to "Take time out to see how we're doing in reaching our goals."

As mentioned earlier, partnering affects all relationships, and of course the six listening levels apply to personal partnerships. Here's a look at partnership development in dating and more permanent personal unions.

Personal and Family Partnership

1. Commitment: In the early stages of a relationship, commitment isn't an issue; at this point, the cycle of appreciative listening is just starting, and the couple is exploring what they find interesting and attractive with each other. The relationship might evolve to more intensity or it may fade. If the attraction becomes more serious, commitment is usually not formalized with any kind of ceremony, but it might grow to a mutual agreement to date each other exclusively. As the relationship develops further, the commitment bond is strengthened when the couple becomes engaged, and marriage might take it to the next step by publicly and legally formalizing the commitment.

2. Communication: As in all successful partnerships, couples should plan structured time free from distractions that interfere with communication. This arrangement might simply mean going to a neutral place that's set aside for visiting. The communication plan should be easy and doable: going for a walk, for coffee, or for lunch. When jobs become intense or when children come along, communication times might evolve to include "dates" or mini-vacations away from the job and the kids.

3. Conflict resolution: Every couple will have some conflict, and it's important to have a workable plan for resolution. For example, a plan might stipulate no arguments when one of the two of you first get home from work, and not to have a serious discussion when either or both partners are extremely upset, hurt, or angry.

    The examples earlier in this chapter discussed couples' resolving conflict by not going to bed angry or using a squirt gun to resolve differences. Also, some couples use letters to communicate their feelings and differences. Whatever the plan, both parties should have clear understanding of the plan and be willing to carry it out. If couples can't work out differences, they can seek counseling with a family therapist who will help develop a resolution plan with them.

4. Trust: Trust is developed when partners do what they say they're going to do; it erodes when they don't. In a personal relationship, these trust commitments might be broadly stated. For example the general mandate "to love, honor and obey" carries a long list of implied behaviors for the partners. And since the behaviors are implied, they are subject to individual interpretations by the partners, and these interpretations should be discussed and agreed upon.

    Specific commitments that can be "trust-makers" or "trust-breakers" are easier to evaluate. "I'll pick you up at eight," or "I'll have the kids ready to go when you get here," either happen or they don't, and unless there's a valid reason for a partner not following through, trust is increased or decreased

5. Evaluation: Every couple needs to evaluate their relationship from time to time, and these sessions can be spontaneous—"Hey, we need to visit about some stuff that's been taking more of our time than it should"—or planned for specific times—anniversaries, birthdays, and New Years. Additionally, various venues for couple reflection/evaluation are available—weekend retreats, marriage encounters, or self-planned escapes where movies or literature are discussed in a relaxing setting. Sessions can also be scheduled with a marriage and family therapist who can provide a productive structure for evaluation.

6. Teamwork: Teamwork is just that, working together to reach a goal. The goals can be simple, "Let's get the dinner going so we can enjoy our time with our guests," "How about we go to the conference together and plan to make a little vacation out of it?" Complex teamwork would involve planning and building a house together, or sharing the logistics of planning a family vacation with all the kids, their spouses, and grandkids.

Summary

Partnerships are agreed-upon, carefully structured arrangements to listen actively and work together to reach common goals. At the center are active listening, shared goals, and respect for the dignity of each partner. By definition, partnerships are nonlegal and nonadversarial agreements that focus on reaching goals through cooperation and compromise. Partnerships can be short-lived and exist between any number of people who are willing to listen actively and: (1) commit to goals and the partnering process, (2) work on effective communication, (3) develop a plan for conflict resolution, (4) build trust, (5) work as a team, and (6) establish systematic evaluation of the process.

Notes

1. http://www.spi-co.com/partneringculture.html.

2. "Chrysler's Neon: Is This the Small Car Detroit Couldn't Build?," *Business Week* (May 3, 1993), p. 116.

3. *Ibid.* pp. 118–119.

4. *Ibid.* p. 122.

5. *Ibid.*

6. *Ibid.*

7. *Ibid.*

8. J. L. Hocker and W. W. Wilmont, *Interpersonal Conflict* (Dubuque, Iowa: Wm. C. Brown, 1985), cited in Joseph P. Folger, Marshall Scott Poole, and Randall K. Stutman, *Working Through Conflict* (New York: HarperCollins College Publishers, 1993), p. 4.

9. Phoebe Hoban, "He Said, She Said: Couples' Therapy Is the Flavor of the Month," *New York Magazine* (June 15, 1992), p. 34.

10. Dawn Anfuso, "Peer Review Wards Off Unions and Lawsuits," *Personnel Journal* (January 1994), p. 64.

11. *Ibid.*

12. Paul Kaufmann, "Partnership Trust," unpublished survey, Iowa State University, Ames, Iowa, January, 1994.

13. Anfuso, p. 64.

Chapter Fourteen
Awareness Exercises

Name_____ ID#_____

1. Describe a partnership that affects your life.

    A. Age of partnership—how long have you been in it?

    B. Number of partners

    C. Levels (example: owner, board of directors, general manager, production manager, line supervisor; or parents, children, roommate, and so on)

2. What are the goals of that partnership?

3. What form of commitment has been made in that partnership?

    A. To goals

    B. To the partnering process

4. What system of communication is used in that partnership (face-to-face discussions, memos, video conferences, group meetings, and so on)?

5. How do the partners resolve conflicts?

6. How would you judge the level of trust in that partnership?

7. What signs of teamwork do you observe in the partnership?

8. What steps are taken to evaluate the partnering process?

9. Evaluate the partnership in these areas.
   A. Listening

   B. Commitment

   C. Communication

   D. Conflict resolution

   E. Trust

   F. Teamwork

   G. Evaluation

10. List a large organization (of ten or more people) that you believe function as partnerships (possibly regional or national).

11. List a small organization (fewer than ten people) that you believe function as partnerships (possibly local).

12. List three two-person partnerships.

 A.

 B.

 C.

Chapter Fourteen
Awareness Database

Name_____   ID#_____

Examine your experiences with partnerships and respond to the following items.

1. Marriages are effective partnerships.

   A.   B.   C.   D.   E.
   seldom   frequently

2. I am involved in _____ partnerships.

   A.   B.   C.   D.   E.
   0–1   2–3   4   5   6 or more

3. I am involved in _____ relationships that could evolve into partnerships.

   A.   B.   C.   D.   E.
   0–1   2–3   4   5   6 or more

4. My parents/guardians had/have a working partnership.

   A.   B.   C.   D.   E.
   seldom   frequently

Respond to the following items with your current or most recent job or partnership in mind.

5. Active listening is stressed.

   A.   B.   C.   D.   E.
   seldom   frequently

6. Commitment to goals is clear and shared.

   A.   B.   C.   D.   E.
   seldom   frequently

7. Communication is part of the culture.

   A.   B.   C.   D.   E.
   seldom   frequently

8. Conflict resolution is part of the structure.

   A.   B.   C.   D.   E.
   seldom   frequently

9. Trust is high in the jobs in which I have worked.

   A.   B.   C.   D.   E.
   seldom   frequently

10. Teamwork is part of my job.

   A.   B.   C.   D.   E.
   seldom   frequently

11. We have regular evaluations of job progress.

   A.   B.   C.   D.   E.
   seldom   frequently

12. Understanding information is important on this job.

   A.   B.   C.   D.   E.
   seldom   frequently

13. Understanding feelings is important on this job.

   A.   B.   C.   D.   E.
   seldom   frequently

14. People are treated equally on this job.

   A.   B.   C.   D.   E.
   seldom   frequently

15. People making decisions consider as many views as possible on this job.

   A.   B.   C.   D.   E.
   seldom   frequently

16. Concern for self-esteem is important on this job.

   A.   B.   C.   D.   E.
   seldom   frequently

17. I feel good about this job.

   A.   B.   C.   D.   E.
   seldom   frequently

18. I would like to remain on or return to this job.

   A.   B.   C.   D.   E.
   not at all   definitely

19. I believe partnerships can work to meet goals.

   A.   B.   C.   D.   E.
   not at all   definitely

20. Partnerships waste time.

   A.   B.   C.   D.   E.
   seldom   frequently

Chapter Fifteen

Cross-Cultural Listening

In Chapter 2, we discussed culture and its role in the communication process: "Culture is a strongly held system of shared values, beliefs, traditions, legend and folklore, which is initiated and maintained by the group's leadership. Every country, every town, every family, and every organization has its own distinct culture." Whenever two or more people communicate regularly, a culture will develop; it might be simple or complex, casually understood over time or carefully written in bylaws, but for the group to exist, a culture will develop.

Listening and Culture

Our goal as listeners is to understand the traditions, expectations, and values—called *norms*—within a culture so that we assign accurate meaning to the symbols (behaviors, words, gestures, artifacts), which are embedded in the particular culture. Effective cross-cultural listening means that we form a partnership with the members of the culture, and operate within ". . . an agreed upon process to listen actively and work together to reach common goals."

To a great extent, then, culture determines how we listen and perceive the world. When we understand a culture, our perceptions are shared with members of that culture, a partnership is established, and listening accuracy is improved. With familiar cultures—families, friends, co-workers, classmates, or partners—little, if any research is needed to understand the cultural norms. We listen to understand symbols and values of those cultures: appropriate clothing; amount to spend on a meal; hug or handshake; formal or informal language; where to sit; gestures; discussion topics; when to leave; when to arrive; and so on. Within these known cultures, the stress is minimal and listening comprehension is relatively accurate. However, when the culture we are entering is new to us, misunderstandings increase. A word or nonverbal symbol from a familiar culture might carry a different or opposite meaning in the unfamiliar culture:

A General Motors auto ad with "Body by Fisher" became "Corpse by Fisher" in Flemish.

A Colgate-Palmolive toothpaste named "Cue" was advertised in France before anyone realized that *Cue* also happened to be the name of a widely circulated pornographic book about oral sex.

Pepsi Cola's "Come Alive With Pepsi" campaign, when it was translated for the Taiwanese market, conveyed the unsettling news that, "Pepsi brings your ancestors back from the grave."

Parker Pen could not advertise its famous "Jotter" ballpoint pen in some languages because the translation sounded like "jockstrap" pen.

One American airline operating in Brazil advertised that it had plush "rendezvous lounges" on its jets, unaware that in Portuguese (the language of Brazil) "rendezvous" implies a special room for having sex.[1]

To become competent cross-cultural listeners, we familiarize ourselves with the values and traditions of the new culture we are going to enter. We do this with cultural research. We have all performed this sort of research, even without giving it a name. For example, having been invited to a social event, perhaps a holiday gathering, we call a friend who attended last year to find out what to wear, if a gift is expected, the types of food and drinks served, how late the gathering lasts, and any additional information that might be helpful. The call takes five minutes or so, and afterward we have enough cultural information to be relatively comfortable. Of course, while attending the party, we gather more information and become more attuned to the culture.

Being culturally competent is fundamental to effective listening. To help us become culturally competent, we will first explore context cultures; second, cross-cultural listening in three common settings (simple groups, families, and complex organizations); third, cross-cultural communication and the variables discussed in Chapter 3 (semantics, vocalics, proxemics, kinesics, facial expressions and oculesics, haptics, olfactics, and chronemics); fourth, a research structure for listening in unfamiliar cultures; and fifth, adjusting to new cultures.

Context Cultures

"Context" refers to the nonverbal messages and relational variables that accompany communication events: context is the backdrop for the words. Like a set designed for a play or movie, context establishes the mood and gives insight into the characters' relationships.

Cultures range from low to high context. People communicating in a *low-context culture* ignore much of the nonverbal and relational information and focus on the words. When someone notices that a message was "taken out of context," they are describing an attribute of low-context culture. People communicating in a *high-context culture* give substantially more attention to the nonverbal and relational messages than to the words. Within the high-context culture, messages are put into an appropriate frame of reference.

Imagine the context in this scene: Ten-year-old Mike and his eight-year-old sister, Gracie, are going to a neighborhood shop where her bike had been repaired. Mike describes what happened when they arrived at the shop:

> My sister, Gracie, and I went to pick up her bicycle from Mr. Ritz at the bike shop. When we got there, Mr. Ritz gave us a quick, impatient glance, pointed to Gracie's bike over in the corner, told her to take it and, "Get out of here." Gracie thanked him and asked how much she owed him. Mr. Ritz's back still to us, he kept working: "Look you brats, I'm busy," and dismissed us with, "Are you going to hang out here all day and pester me? Beat it!"

In what appears to be a low-context culture, Mike and Gracie could reasonably conclude from his words that Mr. Ritz viewed his sister and him as a nuisance; in fact, disliked them, had no time for them, and wanted them out of his shop.

However, Mike, Gracie, and Mr. Ritz are operating in a high-context culture: the three of them have a long-term relationship, since their families have been friends for years. Ritz has known the kids since they were born—he is considered their adopted uncle. Also, Mr. Ritz is well known and respected in the neighborhood, and those that know him realize that inside his grumpy exterior is a kind, fair, and caring soul.

So, given this high context culture, we can understand that when Mike and Gracie left the shop, they smiled at each other, and knew, in spite of the literal meanings of his words, that Mr. Ritz was saying, "I love you guys. The repair work is a gift. It's a great day, so go out and enjoy it."

Low-Context Cultures

Low-context cultures exist in heterogeneous groups or countries where there is a diverse ethnic population and a history of personal independence. Where there is great diversity, and little pertinent interpersonal knowledge between group members, the shared language—words—becomes the center of the communication.

Chapter 9, "Listening Comprehensively," and Chapter 11, "Listening Critically," discuss many of the listening behaviors found in low-context cultures. In fact, the premise of Chapter 10 emphasizes many of the elements of low context: minimize the holistic, nonverbal variables and maximize attention on the words and logic: data, warrant, claim, backing, qualifier, rebuttal. Low-context cultures value getting to the point, not beating around the bush, saying what you mean, and documenting assertions.

Picture a group of mechanical engineers trying to solve a problem that has shut down a major production line. These men and women are not primarily concerned with the nonverbal or relational aspects of the group members. Rather, their listening attention is on the words that target possible causes and solutions for the problem. They are focused on facts, data, and linear logic that address the task. Any personal interest in the group members is limited to each individual's area of engineering expertise.

High-Context Cultures

In contrast, high-context cultures occur in groups or countries that are homogeneous: they are unified, ethnically similar. Since many of the core cultural values in these groups are held in common, there is shared understanding. Consequently, much of the listening relies on the context, that is, the nonverbal meanings that accompany the words: voice, pitch, rate, gestures, facial expression, eye contact, movement, and intensity. (Refer to Chapters 3, "Listening Holistically," 5, "Listening to Communication Movement," and 10, "Listening Therapeutically.")

Imagine a close-knit family: a mom, a dad, and three kids. They frequently share meals and go to various entertainments together; they are a homogenous group. Theirs is a high-context culture. As they sit at the dinner table discussing an event, the words are descriptive and carry some meaning, but more listening attention is given to the holistic, nonverbal meanings: sincerity, enthusiasm, vividness of the language, eye contact, gestures, tone of voice, energy, and more.

With an understanding of cultural context, we can adjust our listening expectations appropriately. In a low-context culture we would attend to words and logical structure. In a high-context culture, we would be sensitive to nonverbal and relational symbols.

Context cultures have been carefully researched, and some professional and national cultures have been ranked from high to low. Knowing these rankings is helpful when adapting to

the various cultures. The professions and cultures listed below are ranked from high context to low context: the highest context profession is "Human Resources;" the lowest is "Finance." The highest context culture is "Japanese;" the lowest is "German-Swiss."

Professional and National Context Culture Rankings[2]

Professions

Below is a ranking of professions listed from high- to low-context.

Human resources
Marketing and sales
Manufacturing products
Research and development
Technical
Information systems
Engineering
Finance

National Cultures

Below is a ranking of cultures listed from high- to low-context.

Japanese
Chinese
Arabic
Greek
Mexican
Spanish
Italian
French
French Canadian
English
English Canadian
American
Scandinavian
German
German Swiss

Listening in Common Cross-Cultural Settings

Simple Groups

Garrett Kinsley leaves his house before sunrise to meet with his "Fox Den" colleagues—an informal group of friends who are committed to keeping Northland swamp from being land filled and bulldozed into a parking lot for a proposed shopping mall. The goal is clear—save the swamp. The group was started by Janie Redfox, a retired lawyer who had been a state prosecutor for nearly forty years.

Even though the meetings were casual, the members wanted to keep moving toward their goal, so they did not mind that from the very start, Janie ran these early morning meetings like a courtroom. She sat judge-like at the head of the table, legal pads neatly aligned, agenda written out in front of her. It would not have been surprising to see a gavel at her right hand. She relied on *Robert's Rules of Order* to take votes, record motions, and limit discussion. In spite of the stiff and regimented appearances of the culture, the meetings were friendly and satisfying.

As founder of the group and self-assigned leader, after the first couple meetings, Janie had established the culture (a balance of low and high context) of the Fox Den group, and everyone knew what to expect. The cultural values and traditions were in place: We start on time, we keep the goal in sight, we document our assertions, we persuade with some emotion (but overly reactive comments are not tolerated), we use logic to arrive at claims, we limit our comments and keep discussion on the topic, and we adjourn at 7:15. In addition, members were assigned to bring coffee and rolls.

When Mark Williams, who was also concerned about the swamp, found out about Fox Den, he contacted Garrett to get some information. Once Garrett confirmed that the goal of the group was to save the swamp, Mark asked if he could join. Naturally, he was welcome.

Mark realized that to be an effective participant, he needed to be brought up to date, so he asked Garrett about the culture of the group. Garrett told him about the members and informed him of the values and traditions that Janie had established. Mark listened carefully and imaged the meetings until they were reasonably familiar. As an outcome of his cultural preparation, even at the first meeting Mark was prepared, felt relatively comfortable, and was able to contribute significantly to the discussion.

Ralph Plingston is also opposed to the swamp draining; in fact, he is very upset about it. He contacts Garrett, finds out about Fox Den, and shows up at the next meeting about twenty minutes late.

He flops down in a chair, and at the first opportunity begins to rail on the city council for considering the swamp drainage, and starts assassinating the character of the developer who is proposing the entire mall project. He believes the Fox group should promote a special election "to get rid of the money-grubbing city council members." "Moreover," he asserts, "the mayor is just a tool of the big money interests who has taken bribes to move forward with the project." After he rambles on for about five minutes, Janie calmly mentions that she appreciates his concerns, but "we need to stay with the agenda," and she points out that copies of the agenda are available near the door.

Ralph is puzzled. He wonders, "Who is this woman curtailing my speech?" and "What has an agenda got to do with this swamp situation?"

When Ralph finally quiets down, he listens holistically, and begins to notice the culture of the group, and he recognizes that this is not a group that values complaining and blaming, but is, rather, a goal-oriented problem-solving group. When he was ready to rejoin the discussion, it was 7:15, and the meeting was adjourned.

Families

Peter Reugan grew up in Chicago, finished law school at DePaul University and went into practice with a firm in Omaha. His new job found him on the road in small Nebraska and Iowa towns, handling various legal issues.

Throughout his rural experiences, Peter hung on to his Chicago family values and traditions. He and his two brothers and two sisters all attended Chicago schools—grade school through college.

The father, a dentist, and the mother, a talent agent, were recognized for their charitable work and active participation in the Democratic party. In addition, they received some notoriety for their renovation of a large home in Old Town. They loved fine restaurants, art museums, the Shed Aquarium, the Museum of Science and Industry, theaters, department stores, the White Sox, and the Bulls. Chicago was in their blood.

Holidays found the Reugan family at the theater or a sporting event. Christmas was a restaurant dinner and concert or theater production. Birthdays brought them together at a favorite neighborhood restaurant in the party room.

Back to Peter: Legal business brought him to North Platte, Nebraska, where he met an attractive woman, Ginny Hoffman, at a small, local restaurant. He was reviewing notes from a case, she was grading her students' English essays. They both sipped their coffee and enjoyed the quiet, sunny dining room booths they were in.

Their meeting came from a mix-up: she got his bill; he got hers. There was only a dollar difference, but she noticed it first, and mentioned it to the server. The exchange of bills brought them together.

Ginny smiled, mentioning she didn't want someone she didn't know paying her higher bill. He said he didn't notice but was glad someone was watching out for his fortune. They laughed and ordered another coffee, sat down together, and visited.

Their cultures overlapped in a number of areas. They were both professionals—she, a high school teacher. Ginny, like Peter, also had four siblings (three brothers, one sister), enjoyed family get-togethers, loved to read, enjoyed theater, concerts, museums, and sports. In addition, their senses of humor were on the same wavelength: both enjoyed puns and subtle sarcasm.

Ginny's parents were originally from Spalding, Nebraska, a small town of about nine hundred. The economy base was agricultural—soy beans, corn, and cattle. Through hard work and careful negotiating, her parents had acquired a number of large, productive farms.

Ginny's father managed Hoffman Farms, and after the five children were out of the house (three of them graduating from college), he put his oldest son in charge of the operation. Mrs. Hoffman became active in politics and was elected Republican state representative.

Family traditions were routine, with little variation. Thanksgivings were at the parents' home in North Platte. The menu was, for the most part, fixed. Mom and Dad prepared the turkey; one family brought the vegetable tray and dip; another, the dessert; and others brought their expected foods. Afterward, football and naps by the fireplace. Early evening, turkey sandwiches. The grandkids who weren't in front of the TV, would play in the recreation room—videogames, ping pong, table hockey. Christmas was about the same, although it might be celebrated at one of the kid's houses, and the gift exchange came after dinner around the tree. Ginny's family culture was warm and family oriented, with few surprises.

As Peter and Ginny's relationship tightened, family cultures became more of an issue. Their cultures were both high context and shared many values and traditions, but the rural and urban differences were somewhat challenging. As they dated, they realized that these cultural differences would need to be faced and compromises would have to be reached if they were to have a future together.

Complex Organizations
....

In simple groups, like Fox Den, people come together to address a problem of mutual interest, and a culture evolves to ensure a process that will solve the problem. The group exists to address one problem, and when it is resolved, the group disbands.

However, in complex organizations, the culture is constantly generating new goals, challenges, and innovations. Consequently, these groups take on a more permanent life. This cycle of perpetuation is needed for the survival of many organizations. For example, the computer and cell phone industries must constantly reach forward to the next generation of computers or cell phones. Consequently, they become complex, multilayered organizations with divisions for innovation, engineering, production, sales, and marketing.

In the efforts to ensure continued success, the leaders develop charters, or other declarations of the goals or purposes of the organization, which clearly state the values, expectations, and limits of what now is a formalized, complex organization. These charters attempt clearly to set the cultural tone of the organization.

Understandably, complex organizations often have subgoals within the various divisions that exist to meet the overall goal. For example, if we were to enlarge the Fox Den's goal to "improve water quality in the county," one subgoal could be "to keep the swamp from being destroyed" (which was originally the main goal); another subgoal might be "to keep polluted water run-off from entering the local river," and another subgoal could be, "to keep chemicals from polluting any water." Clearly, then, as an organization adds more divisions, the probability of subcultures becomes greater, and even though these subcultures may not be *formally* recognized within the organization, they do exist and can be helpful or detrimental to the success of the organization.

A big part of becoming culturally competent listeners is to listen holistically to subcultures, realizing that subculture traditions and values may vary greatly from department to department within the organization. As an example, we will follow Jasmine Docker on a visit to a company she is considering for a job.

The company is a large tire-manufacturing plant in Ohio. Jasmine grew up in a household where production was a daily topic, her mother being a manager with Hewlett-Packard and her father a supervisor with Toyota. Jasmine, with a degree in business and communication, is interested in the human resource management position. She has finished her interview with the general manager, the newly transferred human resource manager whom Jasmine would be replacing, and the production manager. She is now touring the plant with the production manager, Jeff Bolger.

Jasmine is pleased with the visit so far: She is comfortable with the values and traditions that the management team has presented, and she asks Mr. Bolger if he could lead her to the various departments and then let her visit privately with personnel. He agrees, and they are on their way. With freedom to visit and observe, Jasmine can get information and listen to the values and traditions of the subcultures in the various departments. She is aware that not everyone will be willing to share confidentially with her, but with attentive holistic listening, she will gain information and a *feel* for the various subcultures. After all, she reasons, these are the people she will be working with directly.

Jasmine has some cultural criteria she listens for: worker morale, openness, sense of commitment to the corporation, respect for management and coworkers, clarity of job assignments, satisfaction, trust, frustration, honesty, effectiveness of communication, freedom to innovate, availability of resources, pride, and comfort. Bringing her holistic listening skills into action, she gains insight and knowledge to evaluate these subculture variables.

Communication Variables and Cross-Cultural Meanings

In Chapter 3, "Listening Holistically," we discussed semantics, vocalics, proxemics, kinesics, physical appearance/artifacts, facial expressions, oculesics, touch, smell, and time. Here, we will review these multisense categories in a cross-cultural context. As we listen across cultures, we

find that symbols from one culture might carry different meanings in another culture, and obviously, if we are not aware of these differences, accuracy of meaning will deteriorate. Here are some brief examples of cultural differences for each of the communication categories:

- *Semantics:* The study of word meanings.
- *Vocalics:* The vocal meaning embedded in the words. Categories include volume, pitch, rate, pausing, and quality.
  - *Volume:* People from Thailand speak quietly. Calling attention to oneself is viewed as crude and insensitive.
  - *Pitch:* Native Americans prefer a narrow, quiet pitch range, especially when non-Native Americans or elders are present.
  - *Rate:* North Americans judge slow speakers as having lower credibility, whereas rapid speech indicates nervousness.[3]
  - *Pausing:* The Japanese frequently use silence when negotiating, which Americans find annoying and artificial.
  - *Quality:* Voice quality is unique to each individual. In any culture, it may also carry social information, as in a sarcastic, superior, or submissive manner of speaking.[4]
- *Proxemics:* Assigning meaning to space. This includes territory and personal space.
  - *Territory:* In a comparison of North American and French children at a beach, the French children tended to stay in a relatively small territory near their parents, while U.S. children played in a wide area of the beach.[5]
  - *Personal space:* In Saudi Arabia, a comfortable conversational distance is about two feet, a distance that would be considered uncomfortably intimate in North American culture.[6]
- *Kinesics:* Meaning is drawn from movements and gestures.
  - In the United States, creating a dramatic scene by pointing at people or things and using large animated hand gestures might be effective in getting the desired attention; however, in Thailand this behavior is not acceptable.
- *Physical appearance and artifacts:* Meanings are derived from physical appearance and clothing.
  - If a man were to board an airplane in Detroit wearing a Jalabiya-Bisht, a loose fitting Middle-East Muslim garment, the clothing might convey concern for some of the passengers.
- *Facial expressions and oculesics:* Messages are derived from the face and eyes.
  - *Facial expressions:* In Asian cultures including Indonesia, smiling is used to cover emotional pain or embarrassment.[7]
  - *Oculesics:* To look away is a sign of respect when visiting with people from India; however, in the United States, respect is shown by looking directly at the speaker. The French use direct and intense eye contract, which to Americans conveys aggressiveness and stubbornness.

- *Haptics:* Meaning is derived from touch.
  - Mexicans use touch to show confidence: a hand on the upper arm. Americans who avoid the *abrazo* (Latin American embrace) are judged to be aloof and cold.
- *Olfactics:* This is what odors communicate.
  - North Americans find certain body odors offensive because they have been conditioned to wash off natural odors and replace them with neutral, or substitute smells. Consequently, Americans view people with natural body odors and smells as being dirty; this is especially noticed with the French, who are comfortable with their natural body odors.
- *Chronemics:* Messages are derived from time.
  - Unlike Americans, the Chinese and Spanish are usually not pressured by time. However, being late for a business meeting would cause a Chinese host to lose respect and trust for the tardy person.[8]

So far we have looked at how listening is affected by cultural differences in terms of context and cross-cultural settings. We have also discussed a range of cultures from simple to complex; national to international. When entering another culture our listening effectiveness can be increased by gaining as much information as possible about the new culture, so next we will explore some ways to research these cultures.

Structuring Cross-Cultural Research

Cultural competency and effective cross-cultural listening begin with getting information from all available sources. For simple cultures, usually phone calls, e-mails, or talks with group members provide enough information to function in the culture. However, for complex and national cultures these sources of information should be supplemented with more structured research drawing information from libraries, websites, interviews, and authoritative briefings.

Before exploring specific cultural research categories, we need to keep in mind that culture is not born into human nature. Rather, it is based on symbols that evolve to meet the basic human needs that were discussed in Chapter 6: survival, love and belonging, power, freedom, and fun. For example, as a culture evolved in a geographical setting surrounded by water, it would likely develop symbols for rituals, laws, and even religious beliefs that relate to the water environment: fishing, water games, and perhaps the phases of the moon that affect the tides.

To improve cross-cultural listening, we do not need to know which specific symbols address any of the five human needs, but we do need to be sensitive to the fact that the symbols represent the core traditions and values of the culture, and therefore should be thoroughly respected. In addition, when dealing with members from other cultures, we should honor and appreciate their cultural norms and avoid judgments about symbols and rituals that seem strange or bizarre, realizing that as we grow more familiar with a culture, the connection between human needs and symbols will often become apparent.

With a positive, curious outlook we are now ready to begin a four-step structured program of research: Step 1, become familiar with appropriate cross-cultural categories; Step 2, determine the culture to be researched (Japan's culture is used for this example); Step 3, prioritize the categories; and Step 4, perform the research.

Cross-Cultural Categories
....

Whether getting information from the library, the Internet, personal interviews, or first-hand observation, it is helpful to structure your research using cultural topics. Here are some possibilities:

Age	Attitudes toward animals
Approaches to completing tasks	Attitudes toward conflict
Art	Attitudes toward disclosure
Artifacts	Behaviors

Beliefs

Chronemics

Clothing

Context

Currency

Customs

Daily life

Decision-making styles

Diet

Drama (theater)

Dress

Economy

Education

Entertainment

Eye movements

Facial expressions

Foods

Gender treatment

Geography

Gestures

Government

Haptics

History

Holidays

Language

Laws

Libraries

Literature

Location

Make-up

Music

Myths

Physical appearance

Popular culture

Proxemics

Races

Racial/ethnic groups

Religion

Rituals

    Funerals

    Graduations

    Weddings

    Religious

Semantics

Sexuality/sexual identity

Smell

Stability

Star constellations meanings

Sub-cultures

    Casts

    Classes

    Royalty

    Worker

Symbols

Technology

Time

Traditions

Transportation

Use of space

Values

Vocalics

Choosing a Culture to Research

So far, we have discussed three of the possible hundreds or even thousands of subcultures within the North American culture—simple group, family, and complex organization. With some research and active holistic listening, from the examples earlier in this chapter, we discussed how Garrett, Mark, Peter, Ginny, and Jasmine gained enough information to make a personal evaluation as to whether to remain in the culture or get out. The main criterion for the decisions is their comfort with the other culture's values and traditions.

Listening to national cultures involves an additional step, since now cultural competency requires us first to understand values and traditions of a new major culture, rather than a subculture. Recall that Peter and Ginny experienced some differences in subcultural values and traditions that came from geography—her rural versus his urban background. However, over a relatively short time, they were able to understand these differences and evaluate the impact they would have on their relationship.

Now imagine preparing to travel to Osaka, Japan, to meet the family of your fiancé, whom you met while working in Seattle. Of course, you know your fiancé and you are in love. You also realize that you are marrying into another culture, and for long-term happiness and fulfillment with your partner, you want to share in that other culture. Naturally, over this three-year relationship you have learned some details about your fiancé's family members—they speak English, they are well educated, mother is a social worker, father is a teacher, the older brother is married to an American—and you have gained some knowledge of the high-context Japanese culture. However, as you prepare to meet the family in their homeland, this listening assignment is much more daunting than if your fiancé were from Chicago or North Platte, Nebraska.

Prioritizing Categories

At this point in your cultural preparation you need information, so you go to the list of cultural categories and choose three interests. Of course, you can select as many as you want, and can add new categories, as well. In this case, you have chosen *context*—for an overview of the culture; *attitude toward animals*—you love animals and you want some insight about pets; and *diet*—to minimize surprises over what is served for various occasions. Now you begin your research.

Performing the Research

Try to utilize all available means of getting information: Internet, library, interviews, lectures, classes, briefings, or workshops. This example used the Internet—the Google search engine—which provided many sources of information for each of the categories.

For the first category, *context*, the key words "cultural context Japan," located *The Society for Intercultural Education, Training and Research—Houston, Articles of Intercultural Interest, Page 4* (http://www.sietarhouston.org/articles/articles4.htm).

Here, many of the anecdotes and articles gave valuable insights into Japan's high-context culture. One, for example, told of a man who was stationed in Japan, who with his

> . . . Japanese friend were going from one city to another and they got lost. They stopped the car and his Japanese friend went to ask for directions. He spent about ten to fifteen minutes talking to a man at the side of the street. Finally he came back and said that the person did not know how to get there. The American asked the obvious question, "Then what were you talking about all that time?" The Japanese replied, "First I asked him how he was doing. Then I asked him about his family and he inquired about mine. We chatted for a while and then he asked me if we were lost and was I looking for directions. I told him yes. Then he mentioned that one time his uncle went that way but he personally has not made that journey and was not sure how to get there."

Attitude toward animals was the category for the next Google search. The key words, "animal pets treatment Japan," produced a number of interesting results. One, *WHAT'S COOL IN JAPAN April–June 2000 Small Pet Animals (Hamsters, Ferrets, and More)* (http://web-japan.org/kidsweb/cool/00-04-06/smallpets.html), discussed the current pets of interest to Japan's youngsters:

> Recently, more and more people are adopting small animals, which are relatively easy to care for, as pets. Particularly popular with kids are hamsters and ferrets.
>
> Hamsters first gained broad public attention in Japan ten years ago, when a comic book featuring one as the main character became a hit. Then in 1996—the year of the rat in the Chinese zodiac—hamsters became a favorite topic on television and in magazine features because they are closely related to the zodiac animal. Since then, more hamster comic books have come out.

The last search with the key words "Japanese diet," produced a source, *The Japanese diet,* (http://www.accesseonline.com/travel/travel_art.php?id=3), that focused on the traditional Japanese diet and added some vivid evaluative comments:

> The amount of fish consumed in the traditional diet is a key factor in the low levels of heart disease in Japan. According to Clive Barnett, in Nutrition News (Number 85), the Japanese

on average eat twice as much fish as meat, compared with Westerners who eat on average a startling 47 times more meat than fish. Yuck!

The Japanese eat an incredible variety of fish in an equally incredible variety of ways. Japan's fish cuisine ranges from the marvelously subtle to the rancid: the delicately sliced and succulent *maguro* (raw tuna) that is eaten in sushi and sashimi; the squirm-inducing *shiokara* (squid guts and bits pickled in salt) that is served as a side-dish with alcohol; and the strictly-for-locals *kusaya*, a dried-fish product whose vile stench is so strong it is rumored to linger in your house for up to three months after *kusaya* is fried there.

Cross-Cultural Adjustment

Becoming comfortable in a new culture can be challenging, and requires diligent intrapersonal listening, so you can prepare to manage the four psychological stages that occur with cross-cultural adjustment at four stages; 1) excitement, 2) anger, 3) humor, and 4) feeling at home.

Stage 1: Excitement

You are going on an adventure to a new world—to work or study in a different country. You are anticipating the journey and looking forward to interacting with and pleasing new acquaintances. However, this excitement over your desire to befriend and please may lead to frustration, because in spite of your efforts, you are misunderstood, and cultural differences are greater than you expected. Now you enter Stage 2.

Stage 2: The Angry Stage

At this point, you feel anger, anxiety, and possibly depression. You are tired of speaking and listening to a foreign language, and even though you thoroughly studied the language and the cultural values and traditions of your new country, you feel frustrated because no one really seems to understand you. On top of all this, you may not feel well because of erratic sleeping and eating patterns.

With all this building up, you might want to just go home. Even though you may want to withdraw, it is important to interact with those to whom you feel closest, since you know this is a natural cross-cultural adjustment stage. You trust that Stage 3, The Humor Stage, will probably arrive shortly.

Stage 3: The Humor Stage

At last you can begin to laugh and joke about the mistakes and misunderstandings that were major concerns in the angry stage, and you have some friends you can relax and share with.

Stage 4: The Feel at Home Stage

Your new country is your "home away from home." You function well in your new culture, feeling secure, sociable, productive, and at peace with your life. Your primary allegiance is still your country of origin, but your new country has part of your loyalty as well.[9]

Summary

All cultures have unique symbols that represent the values, traditions, expectations, behaviors, and context of that specific culture. Moreover, they have a context that determines which symbols are emphasized. A high-context culture focuses on nonverbal and relational messages; a low-context culture focuses on words.

Since each culture is unique, listening effectiveness is directly tied to understanding the culture of choice, which may be common like a simple group or family, or a complex organization, or a national culture. All cultures have unique differences. The common cultures have somewhat subtle differences; the national have more significant differences.

Symbolic meanings from semantics, vocalics, proxemics, kinesics, facial expressions, oculesics, haptics, olfactics, and chronemics differ across cultures. A symbol in one culture might have a different or opposite meaning in another.

Cross-cultural listening competency depends on knowledge of the culture, so structured research is necessary. All available means of information gathering should be used—libraries, Internet, interviews, briefings—and the investigation should target cultural categories of value. Also important to a successful cross-cultural experience is intrapersonal listening to help us cope with the four stages of cultural adjustment.

Notes

1. http://www.diplomacy.edu/Language/Communication/main.htm

2. Mary O'Hara-Devereaux and Robert Johansen, *GLOBALWORK: Bridging Distance, Culture, and Time*, Chapter 2, "A Multicultural Perspective Transcending the Barriers of Behavior and Language" (San Francisco: Jossey-Bass Publishers, 1994), pp. 54–56. http://sll.stanford.edu/projects/tomprof/newtomprof/postings/255.html

3. (http://mt.middlebury.edu/middblogs/kpoehlin/poehling/2005/05/)

4. http://members.aol.com/nonverbal2/tone.htm

5. Barbara F. Okun, Jane Fried, and Marcia L. Okun, *Understanding Diversity: A Learning as Practice Primer* (Pacific Grove, Calif.: Brooks/Cole Publishing, 1999), p. 67.

6. http://www.totse.com/en/ego/literary_genius/nonverbl.html

7. Non-Verbal Communication: The "Silent" Cross-Cultural Contact With Indonesians Muhammad Handi Gunawan, S.Pd Lembaga Bahasa LIA BuahBatu Bandung. MuhamadHandigunawan.doc

8. http://www.chinateachingnet.com/non-verbal.shtml

9. Gregory Trifonovitch, Illinois Study Abroad office, http://www.ips.uiuc.edu/sao/parents/culture.html

Chapter Fifteen
Awareness Exercises

Name_____ ID#_____

1. We all belong to a number of cultures. List two of yours in these categories:

    A. Simple

       1.

       2.

    B. Family

       1.

       2.

    C. Complex

       1.

       2.

2. Compare one of these cultures in terms of:

    A. Formality

    B. Language

    C. Values

    D. Traditions

    E. Behaviors

3. Discuss context cultures with which you are familiar (knowledge of these cultures might come from first-hand experience or from reading, drama, movies, etc.).

    A. High context

    B. Low context

4. Discuss the similarities and differences in these two cultures in:

    A. Haptics

    B. Chronemics

5. Report and analyze a situation where listening was degraded because of cultural differences.

    A. The cultural setting

    B. The listening problem

    C. Analysis

6. Report and analyze a situation where listening was effective.

    A. The cultural setting

    B. The effective listening

    C. Analysis

7. Pick a national culture and search "recreational activities" or a related topic.

    A. The culture

    B. The source and identity of the information (example, book, web address, magazine, newspaper, interview)

    C. Summary of what you found

8. Describe someone in a new culture (this can be you, an acquaintance, a friend, or a character from a book, movie, or play) experiencing:

    A. The Excitement Stage

    B. The Angry Stage

    C. The Humor Stage

    D. The At Home Stage

Chapter Fifteen
Awareness Database

Name_____ ID#_____

1. I belong to _____ simple cultures.

   A.   B.   C.   D.   E.
   0–1   2–3   4   5   6 or more

2. I belong to _____ family cultures.

   A.   B.   C.   D.   E.
   0–1   2–3   4   5   6 or more

3. I belong to _____ complex cultures.

   A.   B.   C.   D.   E.
   0–1   2–3   4   5   6 or more

4. I am familiar with _____ national cultures.

   A.   B.   C.   D.   E.
   0–1   2–3   4   5   6 or more

5. I am comfortable in my family cultures.

   A.   B.   C.   D.   E.
   not at all   definitely

6. I am comfortable in my complex cultures.

   A.   B.   C.   D.   E.
   not at all   definitely

7. I interact with _____ national cultures per month.

   A.   B.   C.   D.   E.
   0–1   2–3   4   5   6 or more

Chapter Sixteen

Listening Improvement

Awareness of the variables that contribute to active listening is the first step in becoming an effective listener, and the goal of each chapter in *Sensible Listening* is to bring about this awareness. With this goal in mind, the eight chapters in the first half of the book are organized to do the following: (1) examine the importance of listening in face-to-face settings, (2) develop a model to understand and analyze the listening process, (3) expand the model to include nonverbal, holistic listening, (4) compare and contrast face-to-face and media listening, (5) show how communication movement affects listening, (6) examine the importance of listening to ourselves, (7) discuss the connection between personality types and listening, and (8) examine the effects of stress on listening. These first eight chapters give the background for practicing active listening. Chapters 9 through 13 focus on specific listening roles: comprehensive, therapeutic, critical, consumer, and appreciative. Chapters 14 and 15 address listening in partnerships and cross-cultural relationships. This final chapter, *Listening Improvement*, overviews the entire text.

Listening Analysis and Preparation

Any task—whether performing in a play, a concert, an athletic competition, or driving or flying—takes analysis and preparation. Listening is no exception. The goal is to become effective active listeners by reducing noise and stress. Listening analysis and preparation are conducted *before, during,* and *after* we listen, and our analysis should examine sender, listener, message, culture, climate, and movement.

Analysis *before* Listening

Sender

Before the listening interaction, we should acquire as much information as possible about the sender. This information can come from a variety of sources: people who know the sender as well as the sender. We should organize our research to gain information in these six categories:

1. How the sender spends his/her occupational time (Is the sender a parent, manager, coworker, student, new employee, physician, salesperson, attorney, or police officer?)

2. The cultural, social, and educational background of the sender

3. The reason for the interaction

4. The political orientation of the sender (Knowing this ahead of time will signal possible differing viewpoints.)

5. The age and sex of the sender

6. The economic level of the sender

By knowing the sender and the reasons for the interaction, we can prepare for the listening role. If the interaction is primarily informative, we would ready ourselves for the comprehensive role; if the sender indicates personal problems, the therapeutic role; if the sender's goal is to persuade or sell, the critical or consumer role; and if the goal is enjoyment, the appreciative role. If the setting includes a partnership agreement and/or cross-cultural interaction, we prepare for those contingencies.

Listener

Before we listen to others, we need to monitor and regulate our own internal noise. Chapter 6, "Listening to Ourselves," discusses the idea that effective *interpersonal* communication—listening to others—begins with intrapersonal communication—listening to ourselves. Preparing ourselves to listen involves regulating our level of self-esteem, our feelings of worthwhileness and confidence, and deciding to accept or reject these perceptions and feelings about ourselves. Also, we can review our personality type (discussed in Chapter 7) to remind ourselves of certain traits that affect our listening behavior. When intrapersonal listening reveals stressors (Chapter 8) such as fears, anxieties, or traits that could interfere with effective listening, we take steps to minimize these stressors so we can focus on *what we want* from the interaction: "I want to understand completely the information the sender is going to give," "I want to help the sender come to his or her own decisions about these important personal problems," "I want to listen carefully so the best decision can be made," or "I want to enjoy this."

Once we have monitored and dealt with our own internal concerns and stressors, we can continue our intrapersonal preparation by using our imaginations to picture the people and the setting where we will be listening.[1] In preparation for a listening role, we can imagine the size and location of the meeting place, decorations, lighting, temperature, colors, furniture, noises, and smells. Next, we can imagine the people. We picture where they are sitting or standing, the sound of their voices, their faces, eye movements, gestures, and clothing. Once we have listened intrapersonally to our feelings and have imagined the setting and the people in the listening scene, we are ready to prepare for the message.

Message

Whenever possible, we should determine the general nature of the upcoming message. Perhaps the sender sent a memorandum indicating the goal of the meeting. For example, the memo might read: "Jen, I would like to discuss the Bolger contract at 9:00 on Monday," indicating a comprehensive listening role to share information. If the memo read: "We need to look at some changes in the routing slips," we could expect some decision making in the critical listening role. A salesperson's appointment would indicate consumer listening. Someone requesting time to visit about a problem would predict a therapeutic message. A smiling friend stopping us to share an event from the last weekend would be appreciative.

If the listening is with a group, an agenda may be available that shows the topics to be discussed, and the content would alert us to the type of message to expect. A public speech, lecture, or workshop might have a title or explanation of the content or intent of the message. In each case, if we are alert to the general ideas to be discussed, we can prepare for the listening role by adjusting for the nature of the expected message.

Culture

It is important to know ahead of time if we are going to be listening in a cross-cultural situation. As discussed in Chapters 2 and 15, every organizational unit has its own culture: its own set of values, traditions, rules, rewards and punishments. If the sender is from another culture, we need to remind ourselves of the cultural differences, and allow extra time to become comfortable with each other's cultures. For example, when a union steward has made an appointment with a supervisor to discuss a production problem, the steward and the supervisor need to be aware that two different cultural systems are functioning. The union culture values clear and precise technical and production information. The management culture values increased production while maintaining high quality.

The *setting* where the listening takes place is also a reflection of cultural values. If we are to be listening to another cultural setting, we should try to imagine it or visit it ahead of time. We might be listening in a noisy, busy production unit, a quiet, tastefully decorated private office, a seminar room with ten or twenty other people, or an auditorium with three hundred people.

The setting will reflect cultural values. In the example with the union steward and the supervisor, cultural values are an integral part of both workplaces. In fact, most workplaces offer valuable cultural information. A physician's office and examination room reflect cultural values through pictures, degrees, instruments, and diagrams explaining various aspects of health and health care. A restaurant's decorations, server's clothing, pictures, type of menu, silverware, and tablecloths will tell the listener what that restaurant values. In private or public places, if the culture values listening, the setting will reflect this value: comfortable chairs and spacing of furniture, a place to hang coats, a quiet, relaxed atmosphere, a closed door for privacy. Cultural values will also be reflected in the meeting time, formality, and preparation:

1. *The time of day.* Will the meeting occur at the beginning of the day, when minds are more likely to be active? Or will we be listening at the end of the day when we could be tired and more easily distracted?

2. *The formality of the setting.* Is the occasion a formal interview to assess the quality of work or offer a promotion? Or is it an informal, routine visit?

3. *Time constraints.* Is the time limited? Do we need to get down to business quickly? Is there plenty of time? Is there time to get a cup of coffee and relax with the sender?

4. *Interruptions.* Are phone calls put on hold? Are other interruptions controlled?

Cross-cultural listening on an international level carries our preparation further. Now, we need to analyze and prepare for language and symbol differences and substantial differences in values and traditions. The best help here is research—find out all you can about the culture using the Internet, library, and interviews.

Climate

Culture can be analyzed over a period of time before the interaction, since culture is a fixed part of the communication setting. The communication *climate*, however, is more difficult to analyze ahead of time, since it can change quickly, without warning. As listeners, we should be in touch with the prevailing climate, whether it is joy, frustration, optimism, anger, or despair, and should adapt accordingly. For example, you are on your way to an appointment with a co-worker when you find out that he has just been promoted. With this information, you mentally prepare to listen in the happy climate that awaits. In fact, because of the climate, part of the discussion might be about the promotion and not the originally planned agenda.

However, the climate might affect listening without advance warning. You may walk into a room, listen to the nonverbal messages and realize that the atmosphere is not what you expected. At this point, you adjust your listening to get a sense of the climate and adapt to it.

Movement

As discussed in Chapter 5, all communication is accompanied by movement: place, push, pause, please, or pull. By understanding the personality type of the sender, the nature of the message, and the culture and climate, we can anticipate and prepare for the kinds of movement we might find in the communication setting. For example, perhaps we know the sender to be a calm and controlled person who has asked for a meeting to clarify a procedure. His cultural values are objectivity and fairness, and nothing has happened to change the climate. In preparing to listen in this setting, we can reasonably predict place moves, where facts, figures, and ideas are placed in a nonthreatening atmosphere.

By contrast, we might know a sender who is upset about some delays in production. He has called for a meeting to "streamline this operation," and we know the climate is highly energized. His cultural values center on "getting things done," and so we prepare to listen to a series of push moves in the meeting.

Analysis *While* Listening

Communication is a dynamic process; it involves the interaction of a number of elements and interdependent variables which change as the communication progresses. We analyzed before listening, and we analyze *while* we listen to adjust to any changes and to reduce noise coming from sender/message, listener, culture, climate, and movement.

Sender/Message

While listening, we want to stay alert to spoken as well as nonverbal messages. As discussed in Chapter 3, this holistic listening helps us access the range of messages being sent through sight, sound, touch, smell, and taste.

As we listen to the sender's words, we also listen to vocalics—the pitch, rate, and pauses. We listen for vocalizations that might indicate the sender's underlying attitude about a topic or acknowledgments of receiver feedback.

We listen with our eyes to the sender's use of space. Does he prefer to be close or distant? We listen to kinesics. Does she seem relaxed, comfortable, and confident, or nervous, disinterested, and uninvolved? We listen for oculesics and facial expressions. Is the eye contact direct and natural? Does the eye movement reflect interest and vitality? Does the sender look away in thought or disinterest? Does the facial expression indicate sincerity, confidence, enjoyment, intensity, confusion, or indifference, or are you getting a blank look that tells you the sender is mentally somewhere else?

We listen to haptics. Is the handshake firm and sincere? Is the touch on the back or arm friendly, a genuine expression of warmth and concern? Is the touch appropriate for the situation?

We listen to olfactics. Does the sender smell of smoke or alcohol? Are there smells that might add to the noise in the listening situation? Perhaps the meeting is right before lunch, and the smell of popcorn enters the office, or the smell of something burning distracts us.

We listen to chronemics. Does the sender seem in a hurry, under time pressure? Or relaxed, having all the time in the world? One of the most obvious clues concerning time can be sensed by how often the sender glances at a watch or a clock.

We listen for immediacy, power, and responsiveness. Immediacy tells us how much the sender wants to communicate with us. The sender's smiles, frowns, distance, touches, words, and attention give an overall indication of how much she wants to be in this situation.

We listen for how much power the sender is using. Does the sender lean over us and physically dominate? Does he ignore the accepted norms of space and push into our personal space? Does he ignore questions and feedback?

Very importantly, while we are communicating we constantly evaluate the overall responsiveness of the participants. Are we, as senders and listeners, sensitive to feedback, and nonverbal cues? Are we alert, aware, and focused?

Listener

The nature of the message that the sender transmits determines our listening role. As listeners, it is crucial that we be aware of what role we are taking. Being sensitive to different messages alerts us to subtle listening role changes that may take place *while* we are interacting. For example, we might begin an interaction in a comprehensive listening role, only to have the message shift to a critical listening role. Being aware of this shift is necessary because it takes the listener from being an *information gatherer* to a *decision maker,* and the listener will need to change the perspective from one of understanding information to one of critical analysis for a decision. The steps to help us remain effective *during* an interaction are to: (1) monitor the message to determine the current listening role, and (2) activate listening behaviors appropriate to that listening role.

To monitor the message we are always alert to the listening role we are taking: comprehensive, therapeutic, critical, consumer, or appreciative. Next, we need to behave appropriately for the role by keeping the goals of each role in mind: comprehensive, understand and retain information; therapeutic, allow the sender to unburden; critical/consumer, understand and evaluate; appreciative, enjoy. Following are some guidelines for each of these listening roles.

Comprehensive Listening Guidelines

1. We can take accurate notes. This gives us a written record to review later. We can record key words, outline the message, or write periodic summaries. Any note-taking system devised should record enough information to reconstruct the message.

2. It is helpful to remember items in sequence (first, second, third, and so on). "First she said this, then this. . . ."

3. Asking relevant questions is an important part of *active* listening. As listeners, we have an *obligation* to ask questions to clarify a message.

Sometimes when we are in a group, important questions are not asked because of fear of being looked upon as "inattentive" or "slow thinking." This is usually not the case. Granted, an interrupting question, or one that has just been answered, may be out of place at that time, but as listeners, we must realize that the responsibility of accurately receiving a message is our own. Consequently, we work to be comfortable about asking reasonable questions. Questions should be placed before the speaker genuinely and appropriately.

4. Observe intensely and remain objective.

5. Put the pieces together.

6. Be energized and relentless in your search for information.

7. Imagine what this information might mean.

Therapeutic Listening Guidelines

When in the therapeutic listening role, we can follow guidelines that will help adapt our listening to the sender. These guidelines might find application in other listening roles, but they are more appropriate in the therapeutic setting.

1. *Establish an appropriate setting.* Provide a quiet atmosphere that minimizes distractions and interruptions, so the entire focus can be on the speaker.

2. *Develop active, attending behaviors.* In the therapeutic role we need to shift the focus to the sender. Attending involves looking at the sender in a relaxed, non-threatening way; having direct body orientation that faces the sender; leaning forward; and having close (but not uncomfortably close) interactional distances. In

addition, while attending to the sender, the therapeutic listener should not initiate new topics, but should make comments or ask questions about some aspect of the sender's message.[2]

3. *Establish a supportive communication climate.* This means that a safe and comfortable climate is provided for the sender to disclose and talk out problems. Support is shown by being considerate. For example, by offering the sender a chair, a drink of water, or a tissue, we show concern and support. Being supportive tells the sender, "I care about you. I accept you for who you are. I am interested in your feelings and thoughts. I respect you."

4. *Offer supportive responses.* Supportive responses are usually place moves that are *descriptive* ("I sense that you're troubled about the new accounting procedure"), *problem-oriented* ("If possible, I'd like to help you deal with the procedure"), *spontaneous* ("The options give you a good deal to consider, don't they?"), *empathic* ("I understand the concern and worry you're feeling as a result of the change"), and *equal* ("I respect your concerns about this and am willing to listen as you work out your options").[3]

Our responses can help keep continuity in the communication by minimizing interruption or sending unrelated messages. Moreover, appropriate responses give the sender an opportunity to focus on his or her own concerns because we are responding in a supportive manner that encourages the speaker to unburden problems.

Critical/Consumer Listening Guidelines

We must be aware of the critical listening role. Gradually or abruptly, the sender might switch to a persuasive message by asking us to loan something, approve a policy, buy something, or do something. Listener awareness is vital here, and we can engage our left brain and apply our listening knowledge to make the best decision. We need to be aware of the following:

1. *Speaker credibility.* Is the sender trustworthy and knowledgeable? Does s/he have my best interest in mind?

2. *Logic.* Is the message structured in a straightforward pattern? Are the claims drawn from valid data? Are the warrants clear?

3. *Reasoning.* Is the message responsibly constructed? Does it stay on the topic? Does emotion dominate the persuasive appeal?

4. *Persuasive techniques.* What techniques are being used—band wagon, good ole days, plain folks, testimonials, emotional appeal, transfer, new and improved, card stacking, or that's incredible?

Appreciative Listening Guidelines

We usually know when we are in the appreciative listening role. Someone comes into our office with a smile on her face and says, "Hey, I just heard a good one," and starts to tell the story or joke. Other examples are when we turn on our favorite TV show, put our feet up, and relax. Maybe we walk into the theater, concert hall, or auditorium to spend an evening away from usual activities. Or we take a walk or a jog and enjoy the scenes and sounds around us.

While listening appreciatively, we activate the right hemisphere of the brain. We take in the whole scene and relax, letting our listening carry us into the plot of the play or movie, or the environment around us.

By trying not to evaluate, we can experience involvement in the activity. The goals of appreciative listening are to have fun and learn something. While listening, we occasionally try to remind ourselves of these goals. If we find ourselves drifting into a critical role, we need to bring ourselves back to the reasons for the diversion: fun, learning, or both.

Culture

While listening, we need to be sensitive to cultural cues—messages that indicate traditions or values. We can compare expressed values with previous impressions of the culture before the listening took place. Was the cultural perception accurate? Are there some differences in values, rewards, or punishments that need to be incorporated into a new cultural picture? For example, perhaps cultural analysis prior to the interaction led us to believe that *people* in the organization were the highest concern, but as the interaction continues, we get message cues that the *stated* culture values people, but the real value is based on numbers and profit. In short, the organization said people were valued when, in fact, production and profit were the actual cultural values. Gaining this insight into actual cultural values can help us adapt to more subtle ideas about the organization's culture.

While listening on the international level, we should humbly acknowledge that we understand only a fraction of the cultural world we are in. When appropriate, we ask questions with a sincere willingness to learn and share with the participants.

Climate

The sender and/or the setting can alter the climate. The sender may begin the interaction in a high state of energy, and as the message unfolds, the sender becomes more calm and at ease, changing the climate from tense to relaxed. The setting can also impact the climate. For example, two people are communicating in a quiet office with comfortable chairs, while soft music plays in the background. The message is on a thoughtful topic, progressing smoothly and productively. A knock on the door from a technician working on the ventilation system interrupts the interaction and distracts the sender. The technician asks a few questions about the temperature and comfort of the room and proceeds to adjust some of the controls. This five-minute interruption significantly changes the climate from productive to nonproductive.

After experiencing this change in climate, we might try to bring the conversation back to the earlier climate by summarizing the message, or we might say to the sender, "Let's see. Where were we?" Through careful listening and responding, we can help bring the climate back to one that is productive.

Movement

While listening, we are sensitive to communication movement. We listen for the sender's placing, pushing, pausing, pleasing, and pulling. If uncomfortable, we can analyze the source of the discomfort. Is the sender pausing some important issues? Constantly pushing? Trying to pull us into an inappropriate topic? By monitoring and analyzing the movement in the interaction, we can give the sender feedback that we are uncomfortable. The feedback should usually take the form of place moves: "It seems that you keep ignoring the part the weather played in the accident." "I think that's an interesting topic, but I'd like to stay with our original agenda." "I realize that you want me to do something, but first I need to know exactly what happened." While listening, we need to be sensitive to the moves being used to communicate. The moves indicate the kinds of force in the message.

Analysis *after* Listening

It is over. The meeting, lecture, seminar, production report, conversation, presentation, interview, movie—whatever we have been listening to—is finished. A natural temptation is to move on to the next responsibility. Before we move on, we should ask ourselves, "What have I learned from this about listening? What behaviors would I repeat? What would I change?"

Future listening can be improved if we take some time to analyze the listening we just finished. To correct problems and reinforce positive aspects, successful people take the time to analyze the details of an event: parents review interactions with their kids; family members discuss

••• **Figure 16.1**   Listening Checklist

1. Sender
_____ Comfortable?
_____ Given the opportunity to talk?
_____ Given the opportunity to listen?
_____ Internal/external noise reduced?

2. Listener
_____ Comfortable?
_____ Attentive?
_____ Gave feedback?
_____ Internal/external noise reduced?
_____ Appropriate listening role(s) taken?
        _____ comprehensive
        _____ therapeutic
        _____ critical
        _____ consumer
        _____ appreciative

3. Message
_____ Clear?
_____ Questions answered?
_____ Adequate feedback?

4. Culture
_____ Thoroughly researched?
_____ Conducive to listening?
_____ Visible to the sender?

_____ Understood by the sender?

5. Climate
_____ Conducive to listening?
_____ Noninterfering?

6. Movement
_____ Sender
        _____ place
        _____ push
        _____ pause
        _____ please
        _____ pull
        _____ varied
_____ Listener
        _____ place
        _____ push
        _____ pause
        _____ please
        _____ pull

7. Result
_____ Information understood?
        Remembered?
_____ Sender unburdened?
_____ Decision considered?
_____ Purchase considered?
_____ Enjoyable time?

how the reunion or holiday gathering went; doctors talk with colleagues after a surgical procedure; attorneys meet with peers after a court presentation; pilots discuss the unusual weather conditions with other pilots after an unusual flight. Likewise, we should take the time to debrief after a listening experience. Every time we listen, there is something to be learned about increasing listening effectiveness and reducing noise. To organize our analysis after we have listened, we can use a checklist, shown in Figure 16.1.

Summary

This chapter emphasizes the importance of analyzing listening interactions, before, during, and after they happen. The analysis centers on topics discussed in the preceding chapters, focusing specifically on the elements in the communication model: sender, listener, message, climate, culture, and movement. The purpose is to increase listening effectiveness by reducing noise in the listening interaction.

Before the communication happens, the listener should find out as much as possible about the sender and the setting. Moreover, the listener should intrapersonally explore self-esteem, motivations, personalities, and stress. With this information, the listener can prepare for listening behavior by imagining the details of the meeting. *While* listening, the listener is flexible to changes in the message and the setting. S/he keeps constantly aware of shifts to the critical or consumer listening role. *After* the listening is finished, the listener analyzes what went well and what should be changed. The listener uses a checklist to help in this analysis.

When these guides to effective listening are functioning, the listener will experience strengthened relationships; improved morale and productivity; responsible decisions and purchases; efficient use of time; clarified information, directions, and procedure; increased economic and personal rewards; and the satisfaction of being a responsible person contributing to a productive culture.

Notes

1. Doug Harms, "Mental Rehearsal Effects on Business Communication," unpublished master's thesis, Iowa State University, Ames, Iowa, 1988.

2. Allen E. Ivey, *Microcounseling: Innovations in Interviewing Training* (Springfield, Ill.: Charles C. Thomas, 1971), p. 36.

3. Jack R. Gibb, "Defensive Communication," *Journal of Communication*, vol. 11 (September 1961).

Chapter Sixteen
Awareness Exercises

Name_____   ID#_____

You are ready to plan for your next listening interaction.

1. What will be your listening role?

2. What preparations will you make *prior* to the interaction? Respond in these categories.
    A. Sender

    B. Listener

    C. Message

    D. Climate

    E. Culture

    F. Noise

    G. Movement

3. What reactions do you have *after* the listening interaction? Respond in these categories.

    A. Sender

    B. Listener

    C. Message

    D. Climate

    E. Culture

    F. Noise

    G. Movement

Chapter Sixteen

Awareness Database

Name_____ ID#_____

You can use this database to evaluate and prepare for any specific listening experience.

This is to be completed after a listening interaction. Please check the type of interaction:

____ comprehensive   ____ therapeutic   ____ critical   ____ consumer   ____ appreciative.

Preparation

Listener Preparation

Cultural Research
Response levels:

| A. | B. | C. | D. | E. |
| ready to listen | | | | not ready to listen |

Physical Preparation
Response levels:

| A. | B. | C. | D. | E. |
| ready to listen | | | | not ready to listen |

1. Rest

| A. | B. | C. | D. | E. |

2. Food

| A. | B. | C. | D. | E. |

3. Health

| A. | B. | C. | D. | E. |

4. Relaxed

| A. | B. | C. | D. | E. |

5. Comfortable

| A. | B. | C. | D. | E. |

6. Overall physical preparation

| A. | B. | C. | D. | E. |

Psychological Preparation
Response Levels:

A.	B.	C.	D.	E.
ready to listen				not ready to listen

7. Personal problems

A.	B.	C.	D.	E.

8. Distractions

A.	B.	C.	D.	E.

9. Clear mind

A.	B.	C.	D.	E.

10. At ease

A.	B.	C.	D.	E.

11. Overall psychological preparation

A.	B.	C.	D.	E.

Physical Setting Preparation
Response levels:

A.	B.	C.	D.	E.
comfortable				uncomfortable

12. Temperature

A.	B.	C.	D.	E.

13. Lighting

A.	B.	C.	D.	E.

14. Noise level

A.	B.	C.	D.	E.

15. Personalization

A.	B.	C.	D.	E.

16. Type of furniture

A.	B.	C.	D.	E.

17. Arrangement of furniture

A.	B.	C.	D.	E.

18. Colors

A.	B.	C.	D.	E.

19. Mood of the environment

A.	B.	C.	D.	E.

20. Overall physical setting

| A. | B. | C. | D. | E. |

Overall Listening Preparation
Response levels:

| A. | B. | C. | D. | E. |
| poor | | average | | excellent |

Beginning
Response levels:

| A. | B. | C. | D. | E. |
| comfortable | | | | uncomfortable |

21. Greeting

| A. | B. | C. | D. | E. |

22. Small talk

| A. | B. | C. | D. | E. |

23. Appropriate build-up

| A. | B. | C. | D. | E. |

24. Appropriate climate for listening

| A. | B. | C. | D. | E. |

25. Time limits acknowledged

| A. | B. | C. | D. | E. |

26. Supportive

| A. | B. | C. | D. | E. |

27. Cultural recognition

| A. | B. | C. | D. | E. |

28. Overall beginning

| A. | B. | C. | D. | E. |

Nonverbal Listening Messages
Response levels:

| A. | B. | C. | D. | E. |
| appropriate | | | | inappropriate |

29. Focused on the sender

| A. | B. | C. | D. | E. |

30. Eye contact

| A. | B. | C. | D. | E. |

31. Physically oriented to the sender

    A.   B.   C.   D.   E.

32. Overall nonverbal messages

    A.   B.   C.   D.   E.

Verbal Listening Messages
Response levels:

    A.   B.   C.   D.   E.
    appropriate   inappropriate

33. Paraphrasing

    A.   B.   C.   D.   E.

34. Placing facts/feelings

    A.   B.   C.   D.   E.

35. Pushing

    A.   B.   C.   D.   E.

36. Pausing

    A.   B.   C.   D.   E.

37. Pleasing

    A.   B.   C.   D.   E.

38. Pulling

    A.   B.   C.   D.   E.

39. Giving advice

    A.   B.   C.   D.   E.

40. Empathic

    A.   B.   C.   D.   E.

41. Topic jumping

    A.   B.   C.   D.   E.

42. Judgmental

    A.   B.   C.   D.   E.

43. Open questions

    A.   B.   C.   D.   E.

44. Yes/no questions

    A.   B.   C.   D.   E.

45. Silence

   A.   B.   C.   D.   E.

46. Amount of talking I did as a listener

   A.   B.   C.   D.   E.

Overall evaluation of the listening interaction

   A.   B.   C.   D.   E.
   poor   average   excellent

Index

Note: An *f* following the page number indicates that the material is located within a figure.

CPSIA information can be obtained at www.ICGtesting.com
Printed in the USA
LVOW01s1653130515

438235LV00003B/3/P